LSAT®

ANALYTICAL REASONING

by
David Lynch
& the Examkrackers Staff

ISBN-10: 1-893858-51-0
ISBN-13: 978-1-893858-51-0

1st Edition

To purchase additional copies of this book or any other book in the Examkrackers LSAT 3-volume set,
call 1-888-572-2536 or fax orders to 1-859-255-0109.

examkrackers.com
osote.com
audioosmosis.com

Printed and bound in China

Acknowledgements

This book is dedicated to my wife, Sophie. You are my best friend and my inspiration, and none of this could have been possible without your unwavering support.

The efforts of many others also made this book possible. Thanks to Steven Horowitz, Joshua Searcy, and Andrew Marx for their written contributions. Thanks to my editor, Cullen Thomas. Thanks to my parents and family for their support and editing contributions. Thanks to Chris Thomas for a skilled production job and thanks, of course, to Jonathan and Silvia Orsay for creating, building, and fostering the Examkrackers organization.

CONTENTS

CHAPTER 2: RULE TESTERS

LECTURE ② CHAPTER 3: BINARY GAMES

CHAPTER 4: TRUTH QUESTIONS

Chapter 12: Minimum/Maximum Questions

LECTURE 7 Chapter 13: Advanced Techniques

Chapter 14: Complete Configuration Questions

LECTURE 8 Chapter 15: Analytical Reasoning Review

IN-CLASS EXAMINATIONS

EXPLANATIONS TO THE IN-CLASS EXAMINATIONS

INTRODUCTION

INTRODUCTION

i.1 THE LSAT

If you're reading this book, you're probably getting ready to take the LSAT. Although taking the LSAT is probably less fun than getting a root canal, it's a necessary step in getting into law school.

The LSAT is a hard test. Even though people who take the LSAT are a very intelligent group, 99% of them answer at least **ten** questions incorrectly, and most people miss many more than that.

The good news is that the LSAT is also a very predictable test. Certain patterns of reasoning appear over and over. These patterns of reasoning often trick people the first time—or even the tenth time. But this book will give you everything you need to be able to spot, understand, and master those patterns. If you're willing to put in a lot of hard work and many hours of practice, you *can* raise your LSAT score substantially.

i.1.1 THE STRUCTURE OF THE TEST

The LSAT has six sections:

> 2 Logical Reasoning sections (These are often called the "Arguments" sections.)
>
> 1 Analytical Reasoning section (This is often called the "Games" section.)
>
> 1 Reading Comprehension section
>
> 1 Unscored section
>
> 1 Writing Sample section

You are given 35 minutes to complete each section, and (except for the Writing Sample), each one contains 22–28 questions. The Writing Sample is always the final section of the test, but the other five sections may appear in any order.

LSAC uses the unscored section to analyze the questions they plan to use in future versions of the LSAT. You get to pay for the privilege of being their guinea pig! The unscored section is always one of the first three sections of the test.

The unscored section may consist of Logical Reasoning, Analytical Reasoning, or Reading Comprehension. Thus, your test may contain a total of three Logical Reasoning Sections, two Analytical Reasoning sections, or two Reading Comprehension sections. The person sitting next to you will have a different unscored section from yours, and will see a different order of sections.

Your performance on the unscored section does not count toward your score. However, there is **absolutely no way** to tell which section is the unscored section, so you must treat each one as if it does count toward your score. While standing in line to take the LSAT, I overheard a person saying that, the last time he had taken the test, he "figured out" which section was unscored—so he *skipped* that section. He put his head down and rested his brain. I'll leave it to you to figure out why he was standing in line to take the test again.

Like the unscored section, the Writing Sample does not count toward your score. However, your essay is scanned and sent to the schools to which you apply. Some schools read them, while others don't.

The entire test-taking experience will last at least four hours, and could take much longer if there are a lot of people in your testing center.

i.1.2 Scoring

The four scored sections will contain 100 or 101 questions, and the number you answer correctly is called your Raw Score. Using a conversion chart, the Raw Score is then converted to a Scaled Score, which can range from 120–180. This is the score that gets reported to law schools.

Never, ever leave a question blank on the LSAT. Even if you don't have time to finish a section, pick a Guess Letter and fill in that bubble for all the remaining questions.

The LSAT does not differentiate between wrong answers and questions left blank, so you should never leave a question blank. Even if you don't have time to read a question at all, you still have a 20% chance of getting the question right by guessing randomly.

The LSAT also does not differentiate between hard questions and easy questions. No question is worth more than any other, so spending five minutes on a difficult question is a bad use of your time if you could use that same five minutes to answer three or more easier questions.

Different LSATs vary slightly in difficulty, so the same Raw Score does not always result in the same Scaled Score. For example, answering 70 questions correctly may yield a Scaled Score of 159 on some tests but only 157 on other tests. However, the scoring scale is adjusted to compensate for any variations in difficulty, so there is no advantage to be gained by taking the test at one time of the year as opposed to another.

The LSAT is designed to produce a range of scores in the shape of a bell curve—lots of people score in the middle, while few people score very high or very low. Nearly 70% of LSAT test-takers score between 140 and 160, but only about 4% of people score below 130 or above 170.

i.1.3 Test Administration

The LSAT is administered four times every year by the Law School Admission Council (LSAC). The four administrations usually occur in early February, early June, early October, and early December. Many law schools require that the LSAT be taken by December for admission the following fall. However, taking the test earlier—in June or October—is often advised.

The registration fee for the LSAT is currently $123. If you meet certain criteria, you may qualify for an LSAC fee waiver. Late registrants must pay an additional $62.

If you haven't already registered for the test, we suggest that you do so as soon as possible. If you wait, the most convenient test center for you may fill up, forcing you to take the LSAT in a less convenient location. In addition, most people find that having a firm deadline for perfecting their LSAT skills helps to focus their studying and improve their motivation.

Go to **www.lsac.org** to find details about testing dates and locations and to register.

i.1.4 LSDAS

Almost all ABA-approved law schools require that you register for the Law School Data Assembly Service (LSDAS). The LSDAS prepares a report for each law school to which you apply. The report contains information that is important in the law school admission process, including an undergraduate academic summary, copies of all undergraduate, graduate, and law/professional school transcripts, LSAT scores and writing sample copies, and copies of letters of recommendation processed by LSAC.

The registration fee for the LSDAS is currently $113. To register for the LSDAS and learn more, visit **www.lsac.org**.

> You need to register well ahead of time for the test. Regular registration ends about a month before the test; there are only a few days after that deadline in which you can register late, and late registration comes with an additional fee.

i.2 THE ANALYTICAL REASONING SECTION

The Analytical Reasoning section of the LSAT consists of 22 to 24 multiple choice questions, which you have 35 minutes to complete. Each question will be associated with a "game," and the section will contain a total of four games.

The games are presented in a rough order of difficulty, so they tend to be more difficult as the section progresses. Likewise, the questions following a particular game tend to increase in difficulty. However, games and questions of all difficulty levels are sprinkled throughout the section. So you should expect to see more challenging games as you move through the section, but you should not be surprised by difficult games early on or easy games toward the end. Furthermore, you should not be surprised by questions of varying degrees of difficulty following a particular game.

i.2.1 WHAT IT TESTS

The Analytical Reasoning section of the LSAT tests three skills:

1. Reading

Although this section of the test contains far less text than the other sections, careful reading may be even more important here than in other sections. Missing or misunderstanding a single word in the rules of a game can lead to incorrect answers on half a dozen questions or more. The Analytical Reasoning section uses certain words to mean very particular (and sometimes counterintuitive) things, so learning this specialized language is vital.

2. Reasoning

Each game will give you a set of rules, and most of the points you earn on this section come from using reasoning and logic to deduce more information about the game using these rules. Many questions give you additional information that you must use within the game, and your job is to draw logical conclusions about the structure of the game. Your reasoning will always be carried out in the form of a diagram that you will draw for each game.

3. Time Management

To complete an Analytical Reasoning section, you need to spend an average of 8 minutes, 45 seconds on each game. That means you need to read the rules, draw a diagram, make deductions, understand 5–8 questions, make more deductions, go through every answer choice, and bubble in your answers—all in less than nine minutes!

Of course, you shouldn't budget a specific amount of time per game, since not every one is equally difficult. The 8:45 figure is just to show you how tight the time constraints are if you are to answer every question. Not everyone can accurately get through all four games in the section, but this book can show you how to score well even if you don't finish.

i.2.2 Importance to Your Score

The Analytical Reasoning section contains 22–24 of the 100–101 questions on the test. Thus, your performance on this section determines a little less than a quarter of your score. It's less important than the two Logical Reasoning sections, but most students find that the Analytical Reasoning section is the one in which they can achieve the most improvement through practice and preparation.

i.3 GAMES

i.3.1 THE PIECES OF A GAME

When you open your test booklet to the Analytical Reasoning section, this is what you'll see:

Questions 1-6

A mechanic will service each of six cars—P, R, S, T, U, and X—in a single day, one at a time. He will service the first three of them in the morning and the remaining three in the afternoon. The following conditions apply:

S is the first or the last car of the day to be serviced.
T is serviced directly before R.
If T is serviced in the morning, then X is serviced in the afternoon.
U is either the last car of the morning or the last car of the afternoon to be serviced.

1. Which one of the following could be a correctly ordered list of the cars serviced in the morning?

   (A) P, T, R
   (B) P, X, U
   (C) S, R, P
   (D) S, U, R
   (E) S, X, T

2. If X is serviced first, then which one of the following must be serviced second?

   (A) P
   (B) R
   (C) S
   (D) T
   (E) U

3. If P is serviced immediately after R, then which one of the following must be true?

   (A) P is serviced immediately before U.
   (B) S is serviced immediately before T.
   (C) U is serviced immediately before T.
   (D) X is serviced immediately before U.
   (E) X is serviced immediately before R.

4. If T is serviced third, then which one of the following could be true?

   (A) P is serviced second.
   (B) R is serviced first.
   (C) S is serviced sixth.
   (D) U is serviced fifth.
   (E) X is serviced fourth.

5. If X is serviced immediately after P, then which one of the following CANNOT be true?

   (A) R is serviced third.
   (B) R is serviced fourth.
   (C) T is serviced first.
   (D) T is serviced second.
   (E) T is serviced fourth.

6. Which one of the following could be a continuous ordered part of the sequence?

   (A) R, P, U
   (B) R, X, S
   (C) S, T, P
   (D) U, P, S
   (E) X, U, T

SITUATION

RULES

QUESTION STEM

ANSWER CHOICES

1. The Situation

The **situation** introduces you to the context in which the game takes place. For example, a typical situation might tell you that six scientists must be seated in a straight line. The situation gives you the overall picture of how the game works, and it also gives you the **elements** of the game—the things you have to manipulate. In the previous example, the elements would be the six scientists.

2. The Rules

Every situation is accompanied by a set of **rules** that you must follow as you manipulate the elements. You earn points by using these rules to make further deductions about how the game works.

3. The Diagram

The diagram is *not* something you see when you open your test booklet. That's because you have to draw it yourself. The diagram is the place where the convoluted text of a particular situation and its accompanying rules becomes simple, intuitive visual symbols. It's also the place where you do most of the work for each question. You will not be given any scrap paper to use for your diagram, but there is usually enough blank space at the bottom of pages. When there isn't, you have to get creative and use your microscopic writing skills.

Deciding on the right diagram is incredibly important. A bad diagram can turn a simple game into a nightmare. Fortunately, there are four simple, closely related diagrams to choose from, one of which will work perfectly for any given game. This book will tell you how to choose the right diagram every time.

4. The Question Stem

The question stem gives you a task to complete. Some question stems are **Universal**: they ask you about the overall structure of the game as defined by the situation and the original set of rules. Other questions are **Local**: they confine themselves to particular situations as defined by an additional rule that applies only on that question.

There are a small number of common tasks that question stems can ask you to perform, and each one can have several variations. Question stems may ask you to

- Find a configuration of elements that follows the rules of the game
- Determine where a certain element must be placed
- Determine which element must occupy a certain spot
- Or perform one of several other related tasks

This book discusses each variation on these tasks in detail, but it's important to recognize that the different tasks are largely rearrangements of the same basic set of skills. We will point out the similarities between question stems throughout the book.

5. The Answer Choices

Every Analytical Reasoning question is accompanied by five answer choices, labeled (A) through (E). Your job is to find the *right* answer.

This is different from the other sections of the test. On the other sections, your job is to find the *best* answer. It may not be perfect, but it's better than the rest. Not so in the Analytical Reasoning section. Here, one answer is 100% correct, and all the rest are 100% wrong. That means you *don't* have to read every answer choice. As soon as you find the right answer, you can confidently move on to the next question.

Here's how the various pieces of a typical game might work together:

The situation may tell you that seven colored teapots (the elements) must be placed on three shelves. The rules could dictate that the second shelf holds exactly two teapots, the orange teapot may not be on the same shelf as the green, and the blue and red teapots must be on the same shelf. Your diagram would be a simple representation of the shelves. A typical question stem may ask, If the purple teapot is on the first shelf, which teapot must be on the third shelf? The answer choices would give you a list of teapots to choose from.

Some people have protested that the skillful arranging of teapots has nothing to do with being a lawyer. What do you think?

i.3.2 More Than One Configuration

Imagine that you were asked to arrange eight people in a line. "What are the guidelines?" you may ask. There could be several different answers.

If the guidelines say that you must put the people in alphabetical order by last name, then there is only one possible way you could do it: arrange them alphabetically.

If the guidelines say that you can arrange the people however you like, then there would be thousands of possible ways to do it (40,320 to be exact).

Finally, the guidelines may be somewhere in between. Perhaps they say you can have no more than three consecutive women, and that each person must be within 10 years of age of the next person in line. Then there would be more than one way to arrange them, but far fewer than 40,320.

LSAT games are like the last situation. The rules are chosen so that there could be anywhere from four to a few dozen possible arrangements, but certainly not thousands. But it's not as if the elements are arranged into one secret configuration that you are trying to uncover. There could be several valid ways to arrange them, and different questions will ask you about different valid arrangements.

i.3.3 Questions Are Independent

Each question operates independently from the other questions. If a question gives you a new rule or new piece of information, you should not apply that rule to other questions. The only rules that apply for all questions are the ones given in the original situation and set of rules.

Remember that different questions may ask about different valid configurations of the elements. So if you find out that Sandeep is third in line in Question #3, that doesn't mean that Sandeep will also be third in line in Question #4.

There are, however, some situations in which you can use your work from previous questions to answer later questions. For example, if a question asks you to name a place in line where Sandeep could possibly be, you could look back to Question #3 and see that you proved Sandeep could be third. If "third" was one of the answer choices, then you could choose it with confidence without doing any additional work.

i.4 GENERAL STRATEGY

i.4.1 The Six-Step Approach

The Examkrackers approach allows you to solve every single Analytical Reasoning question using the same six-step approach.

The first three steps are concerned with the situation and the rules:

1. Identify the Game

First, *identify the game* type by reading the situation and the rules. Almost every game fits into one of four major categories. Before you put your pencil on the page, you should know what type of game you are about to work on.

2. Set Up

Second, *set up* a diagram to use for the game. This step includes drawing the diagram, taking stock of the elements, and converting the complex language of the rules into simple, intuitive symbols. Once you have done this step, there will be no need to look back at the text of the situation and rules. All the information you need will be represented graphically in your diagram, and you will have a compact place to store all your work.

3. Deduce

Third, *deduce* as much as you can about how the game works. Almost every game contains relationships that are *implied* but not *stated* by the rules. For example, if you are told that Yasmine is older than Zeke, then you can deduce that Zeke is not the oldest person in the group.

Making good deductions is the best way to earn points on the Analytical Reasoning section. Many people spend little or no time doing this because they feel like it is a waste of time—after all, you're not answering any questions during this step. However, nothing could be further from the truth. Making deductions actually *saves* you time in the long run because you'll have to do far less work when it comes to answering the questions. You'll be able to answer many questions without doing any additional work if you make good deductions. Don't neglect this step!

The next three steps are repeated for each question within a game:

> The two most important Analytical Reasoning skills that you should work hard to build are the ability to quickly and accurately choose the best diagram, and the ability to make insightful and useful deductions.

4. Identify the Question

For each question, first *identify the question type*. The most important thing to notice here is whether the question is **Universal** (with no new rules given) or **Local** (with a new rule given). This will dramatically affect how you approach the question.

Also take note of the question task. This book will provide techniques that will help you approach each task.

> You will learn how to recognize and deal with Universal and Local questions in Chapter 2.

5. Work the Diagram

Some questions, especially Local questions, call for most of your work to be done on the diagram. When a new rule is given, put it directly on the diagram and *make new deductions*. Just as your overall deductions for the game are the source of many of your points, the subsequent deductions you make for each Local question allow you to earn points quickly. You will often be able to definitively answer the question at this point, allowing you to skip the final step.

6. Attack

Finally *attack* the answer choices. When you have already determined the answer by working the diagram, this simply means circling the answer you arrived at.

However, some questions, especially Universal questions and harder Local questions, call for you to examine each answer choice and do something with it in order to determine whether it's right or wrong. This books provides many techniques for attacking answer choices.

i.4.2 Pacing

Time is tight on the LSAT, so you need to have a pacing plan. There are some general pacing principles that you should follow:

1. **Work as quickly as you *without sacrificing accuracy.*** You have limited time, so you need to work quickly, but it makes no sense to blaze through the section carelessly. You should find a pace at which you can work quickly but comfortably enough to remain accurate. Understand that you may not finish the entire section.

2. **Work the games that will give you the most points in the shortest time first.** While there is no simple formula for what makes a game difficult, you will develop a sense of what makes a game take a long time. In general, if the diagram is complicated or there are lots of elements, then the game might take a long time. If a time-consuming game is accompanied by only a few questions, *skip it* and return to it if you have time later. There's no reason to spend twelve minutes answering five questions when you could spend that same amount of time answering eight questions.

3. **Work each game as a unit.** Skipping around between different games is a bad idea. Each time you change games, you have to refamiliarize yourself with the rules and how the game works. This can be a significant waste of time. When you begin a game, keep working on it until you have finished all the questions associated with it. Only if a question has you completely stumped should you guess and move on to the next game. Return to it if you have extra time remaining after answering everything else.

i.5 HOW THIS BOOK IS STRUCTURED

i.5.1 Lectures

This book is divided into eight lectures. The lectures are the fundamental units of the text—you should study each lecture in order, one at a time. After you finish each lecture, you should complete the corresponding exam in the back of the book.

i.5.2 Chapters

Each lecture contains two chapters. The first discusses a certain *game type* in detail. The second discusses one or more *question type*s in detail.

Any question type can be associated with any game type, so don't assume that a certain question type will show up only on the game type presented in the same lecture. However, we have constructed the lectures to contain game and question types that fit well together as a discussion.

Every lecture has the same structure, which is organized around the six-step approach. In the first chapter, there are four sections:

1. Identify the Game

In the first section, you learn how to identify the chapter's game type by looking at the situation and rules.

2. Set Up

Next, you learn how to construct a diagram for that game type. You also learn some symbols that are used to represent rules that commonly appear with that game type.

3. Deduce

Here, you learn how to make deductions. Mastering this important step will increase the number of points you can earn in the Analytical Reasoning section.

4. Putting It All Together

After going through the first three steps in detail, you get to put all of the steps together in this section. This section includes a complete situation and accompanying rules, just like on the LSAT, and you will practice identifying, setting up, and making deductions. Each practice game is accompanied by complete explanations. You will use the diagram you develop here as you go on to study a question type in the next chapter.

In the second chapter of every lecture, there are three sections to accompany each question type:

1. Identify the Question

In this section, you learn how to identify the chapter's question type, and you see examples of that type in both Universal and Local versions.

2. Work the Diagram

Next, you see how to use the diagram to answer that question type. The examples will use the diagram that you developed in the "Putting It All Together" section earlier in the same lecture.

3. Attack

In this section, you learn how to deal with the answer choices when working the diagram is not enough to find the correct answer. Again, the questions require the use of the diagram that you developed earlier in the lecture.

Within each of these sections, there are short drills to test your understanding of the specific topics covered. These drills isolate each of the skills necessary for success on the lecture's game and question types. By working through the drills and their explanations, you are better prepared to put the entire technique together.

i.5.3 EXAMS

Every lecture has a corresponding exam in the back of the book. Each exam is like a miniature LSAT. It covers all the game and question types discussed within the lecture, and it allows you to test your skills while being exposed to many different questions. Each exam is followed by full explanations.

i.5.4 EXTRA PRACTICE SUGGESTIONS

This book contains hundreds of sample problems, but serious students will want to get as much practice as they can, including taking full-length, timed exams. LSAC has published over 5,000 official questions from past tests, which we did not include in this book in order to keep it under $200! You can purchase as many of these past tests as you wish from **www.lsac.org**, and we provide a list of extra practice drills and ideas for ways to use this official material.

i.5.5 THE USE OF COLOR

This book uses color to help make important concepts stand out. Of course, we don't expect you to take the LSAT with a fist full of colored pencils. In fact, everything in this book would still be valid and complete if converted into black and white. However, accentuating important concepts and categories with different colors helps you understand them, keep them straight in your mind, and train yourself to pay attention to them as you work through the games.

You can find practice and homework regimens specifically tailored to a variety of schedules and intensity levels at www.examkrackers.com.

Colorblind students need not worry. You can still get one hundred percent of the useful information from this book without the colors.

We use different colors to mean the following:

Green: Things that are definite and fixed. For example, if you know **M** must definitely be placed second in line, then **M** would appear in green in the second spot on the diagram.

Blue: Things that might be true or could vary. For example, if **K** must precede **L** by an undetermined number of spots, then the symbol would be written in blue.

Red: Things that are wrong or forbidden. For example, if **N** is forbidden to be next to **O**, then the symbol would be written in red.

Orange: Used for the names of important techniques (Tools) and for the list of steps that constitute the Tool.

Teal: Used for Conditionals, a special kind of logic used extensively in the Analytical Reasoning section.

Tan: Used for Scenarios, which are a way to split a game into several major possibilities and explore each one.

LECTURE ① CHAPTER ①

ORDERING GAMES

1.1 IDENTIFY THE GAME

1.1.1 WHAT IS AN ORDERING GAME?

An **Ordering game** requires you to put the elements into an order.

Ordering games usually ask you to place one element first, another element second, another third, and so on. "First" could signify the earliest, the most popular, the farthest to the left, the tallest, or any other attribute that can be ordered.

Other Ordering games ask you place the elements into spots that already have a naturally occurring order, such as Monday, Tuesday, Wednesday, and so on.

While the elements and the situation vary from game to game, the nature of all Ordering games and your approach to them is always the same.

Ordering games are very common. Almost every test features at least one Ordering game.

1.1.2 HOW TO RECOGNIZE ORDERING GAMES

You can identify an Ordering game by looking at the situation and the rules.

If a situation asks you to order, place, position, or arrange a single set of elements, it is an Ordering game. For example:

> Six flags—French, German, Haitian, Icelandic, Jamaican, and Kyrgyzstani—must be placed on six consecutive flag poles outside the United Nations.

> The order in which the contestants in the National Spelling Bee will compete is determined according to the following rules.

Sometimes, however, an Ordering game will not make itself so easy to spot. Look at this example:

A salesman will travel to six towns—L, N, O, P, R, and V—over a six-day period from Monday to Saturday. He will arrive at the first town on Monday morning. On each following morning, he will leave the town he traveled to the previous day and travel to the next town. He will visit each town exactly once.

Here, the situation makes no explicit mention of ordering, placing, positioning, or arranging. However, it does mention something with a natural order—the days of the week. It also makes it clear that the salesman's itinerary will be a sequence of six towns, one on each day. Any game that requires you to put a set of elements into a natural or imposed order is an Ordering game.

You can also identify an Ordering game by looking at the rules. Ordering games always contain at least one of the following types of rules, and often both:

> **Always read the situation and rules completely before deciding what kind of game you're dealing with.**

1. A rule indicating that one element must come **before** or **after** another element in the order. For example:

    Town R must be visited after town O.

    The red dress is on a lower-numbered hanger than the blue dress.

2. A rule indicating that two elements must be (or are forbidden to be) **adjacent** or **consecutive**. For example:

    Gretchen sits immediately next to Sophie.

    The muenster and the brie may not be evaluated in consecutive sessions.

Although every Ordering game contains rules like these, just seeing these rules is not enough to guarantee that you are looking at an Ordering game. Some more complex types of games also contain these types of rules. **The one characteristic that sets Ordering games apart from all other types of games is that all the elements fit into a single order**—there are no elements left out of the order, there is no ordering within two separate groups, and there is no more than one order to be determined.

1.1.3 Drill: Identifying Ordering Games

Determine whether each of the following situations or rules could be part of an Ordering game.

1. Six soloists must perform, one at a time, at a high school recital.

   Part of an Ordering game? ☑ Yes ☐ No

2. Five of eight books must be selected for a display in a bookstore window.

   Part of an Ordering game? ☐ Yes ☑ No

3. Mrs. Jones must decide on the order in which to feed her pet mice and what food to give to each one.

   Part of an Ordering game? ☐ Yes ☑ No

4. The professor must occupy a room numbered exactly one higher than that of the skipper.

   Part of an Ordering game? ☑ Yes ☐ No

5. If M is selected then both P and Q must be selected.

   Part of an Ordering game? ☐ Yes ☑ No

6. Sally must be either first or last.

   Part of an Ordering game? ☑ Yes ☐ No

7. Pop music is played only if jazz is also played.

   Part of an Ordering game? ☐ Yes ☑ No

8. The cruise ship must dock in Aruba some time after docking in Barbados.

   Part of an Ordering game? ☑ Yes ☐ No

Answers & Explanations

1. **Yes.** The statement includes a set of elements and implies that they need to be ordered so that they perform one at a time.

2. **No.** The statement offers a set of elements but indicates not that they are to be put into an order, but rather selected or not selected.

3. **No.** The statement explicitly mentions that there is an order, but there are *two* sets of elements—the mice and the foods—and thus two separate orders to be determined.

4. **Yes.** The rule indicates that two elements must be adjacent.

5. **No.** The rule does not mention order or occupying adjacent spots.

6. **Yes.** The rule indicates that an element must be in a specific spot in an order.

7. **No.** The rule does not mention order or occupying adjacent spots.

8. **Yes.** The rule specifies that an item must come after another item.

1.2   SET UP

The Set Up step for every game is composed of three parts:

1. Draw the diagram

2. Symbolize the stock of elements

3. Symbolize the rules

1.2.1   HOW TO DRAW AN ORDERING GAME DIAGRAM

The diagram for an Ordering game starts with a **backbone**, which is simply the names of each of the spots in the order. This will usually be 1, 2, 3…, or it may be the days of the week or the hours of a day. Write this backbone near the top of your working space.

The backbone is like an empty framework or skeleton onto which you put the rules, elements, and other important components of the game.

Below the backbone, leave room for a collection of rows. Each row will contain a possible order of the elements. Since the different questions refer to different valid orders, your collection of rows will contain lots of different orders. As you encounter each question, you will add a new row or rows to the diagram, depending on how much work you need to do to find the answer to the question.

To the left of the diagram, write your stock of elements and symbolize the rules.

Your stock of elements is simply the first initial of each element, written as a list next to your diagram. It will help you remember which elements you must place into the sequence without needing to refer back or write out long names. In more complicated games, the stock will also contain additional information about the elements. The LSAT writers will never give you two elements with the same first initial. This is one of the few instances in which they make your life easier!

Here's an example:

> An orchestra will play a piece by each of seven composers—
> Handel, Mozart, Neefe, Puccini, Schubert, Vivaldi, and
> Wagner—during an evening performance, one at a time. The
> order in which the pieces are performed must conform to the
> following restrictions:

In this situation, the **backbone** is simply the chronological order of the classical pieces: first, second, third, up to seventh. On your diagram, just use the numbers 1 through 7.

When you draw your diagram, use as many or as few lines as you need to keep yourself well-organized. The style you choose may depend on the neatness of your handwriting.

Some people like this kind of diagram...

1	2	3	4	5	6	7
N	M	H	W	P	S	V
W	P	N	H	S	V	M
S	H	W	P	V	N	M

...while others prefer this...

1	2	3	4	5	6	7
N	M	H	W	P	S	V
W	P	N	H	S	V	M
S	H	W	P	V	N	M

...or even this.

1	2	3	4	5	6	7
N	M	H	W	P	S	V
W	P	N	H	S	V	M
S	H	W	P	V	N	M

The stock in this situation is simply

H M N P S V W

Put it to the left of the diagram, near the top of your working space.

1.2.2   USING THE SPACE ON THE PAGE

> It's better to have all your work in one place, rather than scattered around the page next to individual questions.

Most games give you plenty of space to work with. When you have space, arrange your work as shown on page 15. By using a standard layout, you will always know where to look for a particular bit of information, so you won't waste time searching for something. Even better, you won't lose time and points by misinterpreting the meaning of the diagrams you create. Its location on the page and in your diagram determines the meaning of a particular piece of information and when it should be used.

Unfortunately, a few games leave you almost no room at all in which to work! In those cases, you have to get creative, plan ahead, and find a place to squeeze in your diagram. Still, you should try to keep the standard layout in mind and stick to it the best you can.

Questions 1-6

A mechanic will service each of six cars—P, R, S, T, U, and X—in a single day, one at a time. He will service the first three of them in the morning and the remaining three in the afternoon. The following conditions apply:

S is the first or the last car of the day to be serviced.

T is serviced directly before R.

If T is serviced in the morning, then X is serviced in the afternoon.

U is either the last car of the morning or the last car of the afternoon to be serviced.

1. Which one of the following could be a correctly ordered list of the cars serviced in the morning?

(A) P, T, R
(B) P, X, U
(C) S, R, P
(D) S, U, R
(E) S, X, T

2. If X is serviced first, then which one of the following must be serviced second?

(A) P
(B) R
(C) S
(D) T
(E) U

3. If P is serviced immediately after R, then which one of the following must be true?

(A) P is serviced immediately before U.
(B) S is serviced immediately before T.
(C) U is serviced immediately before T.
(D) X is serviced immediately before U.
(E) X is serviced immediately before R.

4. If T is serviced third, then which one of the following could be true?

(A) P is serviced second.
(B) R is serviced first.
(C) S is serviced sixth.
(D) U is serviced fifth.
(E) X is serviced fourth.

5. If X is serviced immediately after P, then which one of the following CANNOT be true?

(A) R is serviced third.
(B) R is serviced fourth.
(C) T is serviced first.
(D) T is serviced second.
(E) T is serviced fourth.

6. Which one of the following could be a continuous ordered part of the sequence?

(A) R, P, U
(B) R, X, S
(C) S, T, P
(D) U, P, S
(E) X, U, T

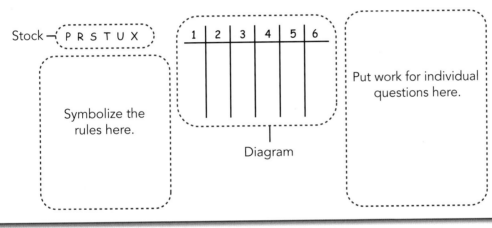

Stock ⌐ P R S T U X

| 1 | 2 | 3 | 4 | 5 | 6 |

Symbolize the rules here.

Diagram

Put work for individual questions here.

1.2.3 SYMBOLIZING THE RULES

Symbolize every rule to the left of your diagram or in the first empty row of the diagram, depending on the rule.

Each game will be accompanied by a set of rules that limits the number of valid orders. Don't try to keep the rules in your head or constantly look back at the long, confusing sentences in which they are expressed. Instead, spend a few minutes turning them into easy-to-read symbols that work directly with your diagram. In the end, symbolizing the rules will save you a lot of time and a lot of frustration.

Your symbols should be

1. **Complete.** Each symbol should contain exactly the same information as the rule. The more complicated a rule, the more careful you have to be to make sure the symbol captures the full meaning of that rule.

2. **Compact.** Don't waste space and time cluttering up the page with an elaborate symbol.

3. **Standardized.** Although the rules can be worded in many different ways, there is a small set of symbols that can express nearly every rule you are likely to encounter. Boiling these esoteric rules down into standard symbols makes strange games feel more familiar and prevents misinterpretation.

Here are some rules that appear frequently in Ordering games and the symbols you should use to represent them.

Relative Order

Relative order rules tell you that one element must come either before or after another element in the order, but they don't give any information about how far apart the elements must be. The elements could be right next to each other or on opposite sides of the diagram. For example,

V starts before T.

To symbolize a relative order rule, write the two elements separated by a straight line. Place this symbol to the left of your diagram.

 V—T

The line between the elements is like a rubber band. It can stretch to allow the elements to be far apart, or it can contract to let them be close together. However, the relative order of the two elements can never be reversed.

It's important to keep the orientation of the symbol consistent with that of the diagram. For example, if your diagram has the tallest player on the left and the shortest player on the right, then the rule

Spud is not as tall as Julius.

should be symbolized

 J—S

If your symbol is backwards relative to the diagram, you *will* make mistakes and lose points.

Block

Block rules tell you that two elements must be immediately adjacent or consecutive. For example,

French is taught immediately before Japanese.

To symbolize a block rule, write the two elements next to each other in the correct order. Then draw a box around them. Draw this symbol to the left of the diagram:

 FJ

The box around the elements means that they must act as a single unit. They can't be separated or appear in a different order.

Again, it is important to write your block in the same orientation as your diagram.

Antiblock

Antiblock rules are the exact opposite of block rules. Instead of telling you that two elements must be immediately adjacent or consecutive, they tell you that two elements are forbidden to be next to another. For example,

Jeffrey cannot sit immediately to the left of Maya.

To symbolize antiblock rules, write the two elements next to each other in the order that is forbidden by the rule. Draw a box around them and then draw a diagonal line through the box:

 JM

As in a block rule, the box refers to the elements in the exact orientation that they are written. The diagonal line indicates that the orientation of the elements in the box is NOT allowed.

LSAC uses a variety of different wordings to indicate these common rules. As you practice, try to notice the different ways in which they say the same thing.

Exact Spot

Exact spot rules do exactly what their name implies: they tell you the exact spot an element must occupy. For example,

Xavier competes third.

Unlike relative order and block rules, this kind of rule does not need to be written to the left of the diagram. There's no need to write something like **X** = 3 (eww, math!) when you can simply place **X** directly into the third spot.

1	2	3	4	5	6	7
		X				

By putting a rule that applies to the entire game into the first row of your diagram, you begin to create the **master diagram**. The first row is different from the other rows because it does not simply contain one possible order—it contains rules that will be followed in every valid order. Thus, you should differentiate the first row of the diagram from the rest of the diagram by drawing a box around it when you have finished filling in all the rules and deductions that apply to the entire game. This reminds you that the first row is the master diagram and applies to every question.

Since, in this example, every valid order will feature **X** in the third spot, it can be helpful to fill in the first few rows of your diagram with **X** in the third spot. This ensures that you won't accidentally put a different element there.

> Your master diagram is a template on which every valid configuration of the elements is based. Refer back to it often, especially as you create new rows in your diagram to hold the work for individual questions.

Forbidden Spot

Forbidden spot rules tell you which spot an element is forbidden to occupy. For example,

Wilbur cannot compete fifth.

Again, symbolize this directly on your diagram in the first row (as part of the master diagram). Write **W** in the fifth column with a "~" in front to make it clear that the element CANNOT be placed there. (Throughout the test, you will use "~" in many contexts to mean *not* or *forbidden*).

1	2	3	4	5	6	7
				~W		

Barbell

A **barbell** rule is similar to an exact spot rule, except you are told that an element must go in either of *two* spots.

Valerie must be visited on either Monday or Friday.

Like an exact spot rule, this information can be added directly to your diagram. Write the element in the top row in one of the possible spots and circle it. Then draw a line through your diagram to the other possible spot and draw an empty circle there.

Sun	Mon	Tues	Wed	Thurs	Fri	Sat
	(V)				O	

The line is like a track that **V** slides along and the circles are like the stops. **V** must always end up in one of the circles—if it is pushed out of one, then it slides along the track to land in the other.

1.2.4 Drill: Symbolizing the Rules

Draw the symbol for each of the following rules in the space provided. Decide whether the symbol should be drawn to the left of the diagram or directly on the diagram.

1. Terry cannot perform immediately after Velma.

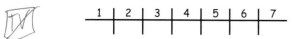

2. If O is not repaired fourth, then it is repaired seventh.

3. K is not the fastest.

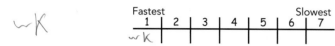

4. The plane to Winnipeg must take off after the plane to Toronto.

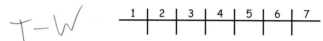

5. Shaila cannot be directly preceded by Niya.

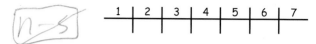

6. U is west of R.

7. The Picasso is hung immediately to the right of the Monet.

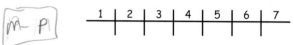

8. Y must leave after Z, but before Q.

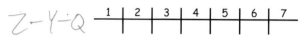

Answers & Explanations

1. 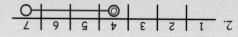 This is an antiblock rule that says that T cannot be directly after V.

2. 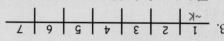 The rule means that O is either fourth or seventh. This is a barbell rule, so it is symbolized with one circle in the fourth spot and the other in the seventh.

3. This is a forbidden spot rule that tells you that K cannot be the fastest. Since "fastest" is on the left-side of the diagram, place the symbol in the left-most spot.

4. T—W This is a relative order rule that states that W must come after T.

5. This is an antiblock rule that tells you N cannot be directly before S.

6. U—R This is a relative order rule. U must be to the left of R because the left side of the diagram represents west.

7. This is block rule that says that P must be immediately after M.

8. Z—Y—Q This is a relative order rule with three elements. You are told that Y must leave at sometime after Z, so Y is to the right of Z. Q must come after Y, so it is written to the right of Y.

1.3 DEDUCE

Making good deductions is critical to your success on the Analytical Reasoning section. The rules for nearly every game are structured to allow you to discover further, unwritten rules that govern how the elements can fit into the diagram. These unwritten rules are called deductions. Many questions will directly ask you about these deductions. Even the questions that don't are made vastly easier when you have a better understanding of how the game works, an understanding that you attain when you spend time at the beginning of a game making deductions.

As you prepare for the LSAT, spend as much time as you can looking for deductions on every practice game. When you take the real test, you will have only a limited amount of time for deductions, but the more time you spend looking for deductions in practice, the better prepared you will be to find them quickly and accurately on the real thing.

> As you work on untimed homework games, spend lots of extra time looking for deductions. Then when you work on timed practice tests, you'll be more skilled at knowing which avenues of thought lead to useful deductions, and you can work on making them more quickly.

Here are a few types of deductions that can commonly be made on Ordering games. This is not an exhaustive list of all the possible deductions you can make for any Ordering game. Many games will have unique nuances that lead to unique deductions.

1.3.1 COMBINING THE SYMBOLS

When two symbols contain the same element, they can often be combined into one larger symbol that conveys more information than the two separate symbols individually. This is especially true with block and relative order symbols.

> A great place to start looking for deductions is to search for two rules that involve the same element.

- When two block symbols contain a common element, you can create one large block.

  For example, $\boxed{QS}$ and $\boxed{SR}$ can be combined to form the $\boxed{QSR}$ symbol.

- When two relative order symbols contain a common element, you can create one large symbol:

  For example L—M and O—L can be combined to form O—L—M.

- Relative order symbols can also be combined to form branching symbols.

  For example, the two symbols P—R and P—K tell you that P must precede *both* R and K, but you don't know the relationship between R and K. Represent that situation like this:

  A single rule directly stating that P must precede both R and K would be symbolized the same way.

- Branching relative order symbols can be further combined with other relative order symbols.

  For example, the symbols R—T and P (with branches to R and K) can be combined to form:

- Finally, block symbols can be combined with relative order symbols.

  For example, the symbol X—Y means that X must precede Y, and the symbol $\boxed{XZ}$ means that X and Z act as a single consecutive unit. Together, this means that the unit of $\boxed{XZ}$ must precede Y. You can combine the symbols like this: $\boxed{XZ}$—Y

1.3.2 Finding Forbidden Spots

You can often deduce where elements *cannot* be placed because doing so would break a rule.

- Blocks and relative order rules always lead to **forbidden spots** at the ends of your diagram.

  If you have the rule G—F, you can deduce that G cannot be last in the order since F must come *after* G. Likewise, F cannot be first since G must come *before* it. These deductions lead you to add the following symbols to your master diagram:

1	2	3	4	5	6
~F					~G

  The block GF would lead to precisely the same deductions for the same reasons.

  A more complicated relative order rule, for example O—L—M, can lead to even more deductions. In this case, O cannot be last or second-to-last because **two** elements must follow O. Likewise, L cannot be last or first, and M cannot be first or second. Your additional deductions would look like this:

1	2	3	4	5	6
~M ~L	~M			~O	~L ~O

- You can often make deductions using forbidden spots and blocks.

  For example, if one rule tells you that W cannot be fourth, and another rule tells you that R must immediately follow W, then you know R cannot be fifth. Trying to put R fifth would force you to break one of the rules:

 and WR leads to

1.3.3 Finding Either/Or Spots

Sometimes, your deductions allow you to figure out that a particular spot must always be occupied by one certain element. When that happens, treat the deduction like an exact spot rule and put that element in your master diagram.

More often, your deductions allow you to figure out that there are only two elements that could possibly occupy a particular spot. When that happens, put those two elements in that spot on your master diagram, separated by a "/" to mean "or."

For example, take a look at the following situation:

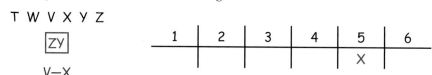

Think about which elements could possibly be sixth. Neither Y nor Z can be sixth because there is no room on either side for the other half of the block. V cannot be sixth because it must precede X. Finally, X cannot be sixth because it is already fixed in the fifth spot. That leaves only two possible choices for the sixth spot: T or W. Thus, you should add the following deduction to your master diagram:

These so-called endpoint deductions are common, predictable, and often quite useful, so it pays to get skilled at making them effortlessly.

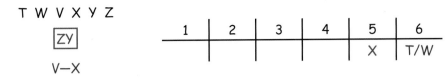

T W V X Y Z

A rule directly telling you that either **T** or **W** must be sixth would be symbolized in precisely the same way.

Although it is possible to create an either/or/or spot (e.g. "**K/L/M**") if you deduce that there are only three elements that could possibly occupy a particular spot, this usually adds too much clutter and not enough useful information to your diagram, and thus is usually better left off.

1.4 PUTTING IT ALL TOGETHER

1.4.1 Drill: Ordering Games

Below is a situation with rules. Identify the type of game and set it up by drawing an appropriate diagram and symbolizing the stock and rules. Then make as many deductions as you can.

Exactly seven comedians—Garrett, Hassan, Lucille, Myrna, Pearl, Tavares, and Valencia—will perform in an evening show, one at a time. The sequence in which the comedians perform must conform to the following restrictions:

Garrett performs second or sixth.
Valencia does not perform immediately after Tavares.
Hassan performs directly before Pearl.
Tavares does not perform last.
Lucille performs after both Hassan and Myrna.

1.4.2   Answers & Explanations

Identify

Several features identify this as an Ordering game. The situation asks you to put the seven comedians in a certain *order*. Furthermore, there are rules that talk about certain people performing *before* or *after* others, and the rules discuss certain comedians performing *consecutively*. Finally, there are no elements left out of the order, there is no ordering within two separate groups, and there is no more than one order to be determined. This is an Ordering game.

Set Up

The diagram for this game is a collection of rows, starting with the numbers 1–7 as the backbone. The numbers represent the first comedian, the second, and so on.

The stock in this game is composed of the initials of the seven comedians: G H L M P T V. This is written to the upper left of the diagram:

G H L M P T V

1	2	3	4	5	6	7

To complete the Set Up step, symbolize each of the rules.

Rule 1 is a barbell rule, so add it directly to the diagram. It stretches between the second and sixth spots in the top row as Ⓖ————————◯

Rule 2 is an antiblock rule. Symbolize it as 🔲TV (crossed out)

Rule 3 is a block rule. Symbolize it as HP

Rule 4 is a forbidden spot rule. Add it directly to the diagram in the seventh spot in the top row as ~T.

Rule 5 is a relative order rule. There are two elements that must be before L. Symbolize this as H , M → L to show that L must come after both M and H.

At this point, your page should look like this:

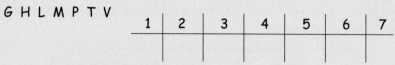

Deduce

Finally, make as many deductions as you can.

Rule 3 and rule 5 both contain H. They can be combined to form this large symbol:

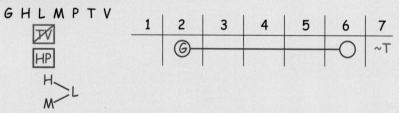

Now you can make a number of deductions at the ends of the diagram. L cannot be first, second, or third because there are three elements that must come before it. H cannot be sixth or seventh because there are two elements that must follow it. P cannot be first because H must precede it. And neither P nor M can be seventh because L must follow them.

Add these deductions to your diagram.

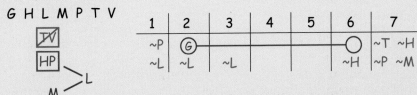

Now look at the seventh spot. You've written four elements that are forbidden there. You also know that G cannot go there because it is restricted to second or sixth. That leaves only two elements that could fill the last spot: L or V. Erase all the forbidden letters and symbolize this as an either/or spot.

That's about all the deductions you can make. Your diagram should look like this:

MASTER DIAGRAM

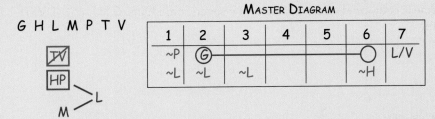

Since this diagram contains every single piece of information stated in the original situation and rules, and every single unwritten rule (deduction) that you discovered for the game, it's called the **master diagram**. Once you have created the master diagram, there is no need to look back at the text of the situation and rules.

Since the information in the master diagram applies to every question, you should put a box around it and not modify it unless you make new deductions as you work the questions. As you work on each question, add new rows below the master diagram to contain your work. On any question, you can easily refer back to the top row to see the rules that must apply throughout the game.

NOW MOVE ON TO THE SECOND CHAPTER OF LECTURE 1. WHEN YOU HAVE COMPLETED IT, YOU CAN GET FURTHER PRACTICE WITH ORDERING GAMES IN THE CORRESPONDING EXAM AT THE END OF THE BOOK.

RULE TESTERS

1. Which one of the following lists an acceptable order in which the comedians may perform?

(A) Valencia, Hassan, Pearl, Tavares, Myrna, Garrett, Lucille
(B) Hassan, Pearl, Myrna, Lucille, Garrett, Tavares, Valencia
(C) Myrna, Garrett, Tavares, Valencia, Hassan, Pearl, Lucille
(D) Tavares, Garrett, Hassan, Pearl, Lucille, Myrna, Valencia
(E) Myrna, Valencia, Hassan, Pearl, Lucille, Garrett, Tavares

2.1 APPROACHING THE QUESTIONS

About half of the questions in the Analytical Reasoning section provide you with a new rule that you must apply as you are answering *that question only*. Such questions are called **Local** questions because they deal with a more restricted set of valid configurations of the elements. They usually begin with the word "if," such as in, "If Lewis competes third, then which one of the following…"

Since every Local question gives you a new rule, you should deal with that rule just as you do with the original rules of the game: **symbolize the new rule, either directly on the diagram if you can, or to the *right* of the diagram.** Remember, the overall rules of the game are symbolized to the *left* of the diagram. The new rule given in a Local question applies only to that question, so you don't want to get it confused with the overall rules of the game. Set aside a new row below your master diagram to work on the question at hand, and symbolize the new rule in or to the right of that row.

Next, **make as many deductions as you can from the new rule**. You will *always* be able to make deductions from a new rule, and the correct answer will *always* be concerned with these new deductions. If you neglect to make new deductions before looking at the answer choices, you are guaranteed to lose time and points. Never forget to make new deductions on a Local question.

The other half of Analytical Reasoning questions do not provide you with a new rule. These questions are called **Universal** questions because they deal with all the configurations that are valid under the overall rules of the game. They usually begin with the word "which," such as in, "Which one of the following could be true?"

Since the Universal question stems give you no new information to work with, the only things you have at your disposal are your master diagram and the answer choices.

Looking for the words *if* and *which* at the beginning of question stems is an easy way to tell whether almost any question is Local or Universal.

In general, you want to complete the questions for a particular game in order. Sometimes, however, you will come across a question—usually a Universal question—that is best answered by looking back at the work you did on previous questions. In those cases, the more work you have to look back on, the easier the question becomes. Thus, if you run across a question like this, you should put off answering it until later in the game, when you will have a more extensive set of work to refer back to.

Your approach to each question looks like this:

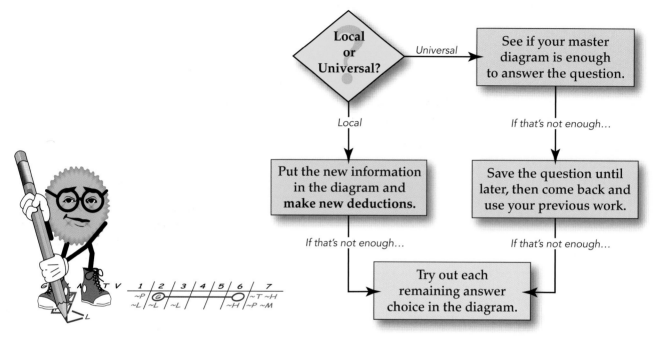

There are about half a dozen different question types, and each of those question types could appear as a Local question or as a Universal question. In this chapter, we discuss one question type: Rule Testers.

2.2 RULE TESTERS

Rule Tester questions commonly occur in games of all types, not just Ordering games.

Rule Testers are questions that ask you to find a configuration of the elements that doesn't break any of the rules. They are among the easiest questions on the Analytical Reasoning section.

2.2.1 IDENTIFY THE QUESTION

Rule Testers all share the following characteristics:

1. The question stem asks you to pick the answer choice that *could be* a valid configuration, often using the phrase *complete and accurate* or *acceptable*.

2. Each answer choice contains a full configuration of the elements. For example, if you are working on an Ordering game with eight spots, each answer choice would contain all eight elements.

3. Rule Testers, when they appear, are almost always the first question for a particular game.

Here are some examples of Rule Tester question stems:

> Which one of the following could be the order in which the inventors present their devices, from Monday through Saturday?

> Which one of the following could be a complete and accurate matching of children to toys?

> Which one of the following could be a complete and accurate list of the engineers who are selected to serve on the board?

2.2.2 WORK THE DIAGRAM

One of the reasons that Rule Testers are easy is that they require absolutely no work on the diagram. In fact, you don't even need to *have* a diagram in order to get a Rule Tester correct. All of your work comes when you attack the answers.

2.2.3 ATTACK

Attacking the answers on Rule Testers is very straightforward:

1. Look at a rule.
2. Eliminate the answer choices in which it is broken.

That's it. Just repeat this for each rule until there is only one answer choice left.

Take a look at these examples.

Avoid doing Rule Tester questions backwards—an inefficient method that involves staring at choice (A) until you see which rule it breaks, then doing the same for choice (B), and so on.

Rule Tester, Universal Version

This question comes from the Comedians game you worked on at the end of chapter 1.

1. Which one of the following lists an acceptable order in which the comedians may perform?
   - (A) Valencia, Hassan, Pearl, Tavares, Myrna, Garrett, Lucille
   - (B) Hassan, Pearl, Myrna, Lucille, Garrett, Tavares, Valencia
   - (C) Myrna, Garrett, Tavares, Valencia, Hassan, Pearl, Lucille
   - (D) Tavares, Garrett, Hassan, Pearl, Lucille, Myrna, Valencia
   - (E) Myrna, Valencia, Hassan, Pearl, Lucille, Garrett, Tavares

Look at rule 1, which says that G is second or sixth. Where is it broken? Choice (B) has G fifth, so eliminate choice (B).

Rule 2 says that V cannot be immediately after T. This is broken in choice (C).

Rule 3 says that H is directly before P. This rule is not broken in any answer choice, so move on to the next rule.

Rule 4 is broken in choice (E), which features T last.

Finally, rule 5 is broken in choice (D), since L is before M.

Only one answer choice is left, so you know **choice (A) is the correct answer.**

The Rules

Garrett performs second or sixth.
Valencia does not perform immediately after Tavares.
Hassan performs directly before Pearl.
Tavares does not perform last.
Lucille performs after both Hassan and Myrna.

Once you have found the correct answer to a Rule Tester question, you can put that permissible configuration on a new line in your diagram. This allows you to start building a collection of work that can be useful on later questions.

A summary of the material in this and every other lecture can be found in the review on page 159.

Rule Tester, Local Version

This question comes also from the Comedians game:

2. If Pearl performs before Myrna, which one of the following could be a complete and accurate list of the comedians' performances, from first to last?

(A) Hassan, Garrett, Pearl, Myrna, Tavares, Lucille, Valencia

(B) Hassan, Pearl, Valencia, Myrna, Lucille, Garrett, Tavares

(C) Valencia, Tavares, Garrett, Hassan, Pearl, Myrna, Lucille

(D) Tavares, Garrett, Valencia, Myrna, Hassan, Pearl, Lucille

(E) Tavares, Garrett, Hassan, Pearl, Myrna, Lucille, Valencia

This is a Local version of a Rule Tester. The only difference between this one and the last one is that it gives you in the question stem just one more rule to follow. That's no problem at all. Simply treat the new rule just like the other rules and look for the answer choice in which it is broken.

Start with the new rule from the question stem. Where is it broken? Choice (D) has P after M, so eliminate choice (D).

Now just continue on by looking at the rest of the rules for the game. Rule 1 is broken in choice (C), which does not have G second or sixth.

Rule 2 is not broken in any of the answer choices.

Rule 3 is broken in choice (A), since H is not directly before P.

Rule 4 is broken in choice (B), which features T last.

At this point only one answer choice is left, so you don't even have to bother with Rule 5. You can say for sure that **choice (E) is the correct answer.**

STOP. THIS IS THE END OF LECTURE 1. DO NOT PROCEED TO THE CORRESPONDING EXAM UNTIL INSTRUCTED TO DO SO IN CLASS.

BINARY GAMES

3.1 IDENTIFY THE GAME

3.1.1 WHAT IS A BINARY GAME?

A **Binary game** requires you to sort elements into two groups.

Binary games give you a single set of elements and ask you to place each element into one of two groups, such as "Teachers" and "Administrators," according to various rules. Some Binary games explicitly identify two groups and require you to divide all of the elements between those two groups.

Other Binary games don't explicitly identify two groups, but ask you to select *some* of the elements and use them to create a smaller group. Working such a game requires you to determine which of the elements should be placed into the *selected* group and which should remain in the *not selected* group.

While these games may look somewhat different, they are both Binary games and should be approached in the same manner.

Binary games are slightly less common than Ordering games, but most tests feature one.

3.1.2 HOW TO RECOGNIZE BINARY GAMES

You can identify a Binary game by looking at the situation and the rules.

If a situation asks you to separate the elements into two groups, it is a Binary game. For example:

> Each of exactly six lawmakers— Faber, Gibson, Knoll,
> LaValle, Scarnati, and Waugh—will serve on exactly one of
> two committees—appropriations and oversight.

Another type of Binary game does not identify both groups for you, but it can be inferred that two groups must be created. Consider the following example:

A dance troupe must select at least four dancers from a group of seven— Kayra, Leylak, Maia, Najah, Ori, Rafi, and Segel —to perform at an exposition.

While the situation makes no explicit mention of a second group, it does indicate that only some of the dancers will be performing at the exposition. Those dancers who are not selected for the exposition can be said to occupy a second (*excluded*) group. Any game that requires you to divide the elements into two groups is a Binary game.

Binary games *do not* contain any feature that puts the elements in an order, nor do they refer to elements being adjacent to each other or mention any element being *before* or *after* another element. Simply put, **in Binary games, order is irrelevant**.

You can also look at the rules to help you determine whether a game is a Binary game. Binary games always contain at least one of the following types of rules, and often both:

> The most important difference between Binary games and Ordering games is that **order is irrelevant** in Binary games.

1. A rule indicating that one element must be (or cannot be) in the **same group** as another element. For example,

   > Faber must serve on the same committee as Gibson.

   > The apples and the bananas cannot be sold at the same stand.

2. A rule that makes the placement of one element into a group **dependent on which group another element is in**. For example,

   > Maia cannot be selected unless Ori is also selected.

   > If Knoll serves on the appropriations committee, Waugh serves on the oversight committee.

Rules like these can appear in other types of games, so their existence will not guarantee that you are looking at a Binary game. They can serve as a valuable tip-off, but you still need to look at the situation to determine whether it involves dividing the elements into two groups. That's the one characteristic that sets Binary games apart from every other game type.

3.1.3 Drill: Identifying Binary Games

Determine whether each of the following phrases or rules could be part of a Binary game.

1. Five of eight books must be selected for a display in a bookstore window.

   Part of a Binary game?   ☑ Yes   ☐ No

2. Six soloists must perform, one at a time, at a high school recital.

   Part of a Binary game?   ☐ Yes   ☑ No

3. Six people will each give exactly one presentation at a two-day meeting. Each person will present on either Monday or Tuesday.

   Part of a Binary game?   ☑ Yes   ☐ No

4. From a group of nine company employees, six will be assigned to teams for a project. Three will be assigned to Team 1, and the other three will be assigned to Team 2.

   Part of a Binary game?   ☑ Yes   ☐ No

5. Twelve basketball players will be divided into two teams.

   Part of a Binary game?   ☑ Yes   ☐ No

6. A publisher must distribute advance copies of exactly eight books among three critics.

   Part of a Binary game?   ☑ Yes   ☐ No

7. If M is selected, both P and Q must also be selected.

   Part of a Binary game?   ☑ Yes   ☑ No

8. Sally must be either first or last.

   Part of a Binary game?   ☐ Yes   ☑ No

9. Pop music is played only if jazz is also played.

   Part of a Binary game?   ☑ Yes   ☐ No

Answers & Explanations

1. **Yes.** The statement says that some of the elements will be selected and some will not be selected.

2. **No.** The statement indicates that the elements will be placed in a specific order, not that they will be divided between two groups.

3. **Yes.** While the statement may initially look like an Ordering game because it mentions days of the week, closer examination shows that all elements will be placed into one of only two groups (Monday or Tuesday).

4. **No.** Although the statement says that the elements must be divided into smaller groups, there are actually three groups here—Team 1, Team 2, and not on a team.

5. **Yes.** The statement indicates that the elements will be divided into two groups.

6. **No.** The books must be sorted into three groups, not just two.

7. **Yes.** The rule states that the selection of one element necessitates the selection of other elements.

8. **No.** The rule references an order.

9. **Yes.** The rule makes the selection of one element contingent upon the selection of another element.

3.2   SET UP

As you saw before, the Set Up step for every game is composed of three parts:

1. Draw the diagram

2. Symbolize the stock of elements

3. Symbolize the rules

> Use these three Set Up steps for *every* game, no matter what type.

3.2.1   How to Draw a Binary Game Diagram

Start your diagram for a Binary game by writing the names of the two groups near the top of your working space. Draw a vertical line to separate the groups. Below this backbone, leave room for a collection of rows. As you work, each row will contain a different possible way to sort the elements into the two groups.

Binary games often have an additional layer of uncertainty not found in Ordering games: many of them do not tell you how many elements must be placed into each group. Many Binary games allow the two groups to vary in size while still following the rules. However, you should use any knowledge you have about the size of the groups by placing an underlined spot under a group heading for each element you know must be there. For example, if you know that one of the groups must have at least two elements, you would draw two blank underlined spots under the heading for that group.

After you draw your diagram, list the stock of elements next to it. Remember, this is simply the first initial of each element.

Here's an example:

> A circus must select at least four clowns from a group of seven—Floppy, Grover, Hano, Jingles, Krusty, Lucky, and Noodles—to perform in a traveling show.

This situation doesn't name two groups, but it does talk about creating a smaller group by selecting elements from a larger one. That means there are two groups: the *Selected* group and the *Not Selected* group. These two groups form the backbone of your diagram.

The situation doesn't tell you exactly how many of the elements will fit into each group, but you do know that the Selected group will contain at least four. Symbolize this on your diagram by drawing four blank underlined spots in the Selected group.

Finally, symbolize the stock next to your diagram:

F G H J K L N _____ Selected _____ | _____ Not Selected

___ ___ ___ ___ |

3.2.2 Symbolizing the Rules: Conditional Statements

Conditional statements represent a special kind of logical structure that appears frequently throughout all sections of the LSAT. Binary games, in particular, are often heavily dependent on conditional statements.

3.2.2.1 The Basic Conditional Statement

The basic conditional statement is a sentence with the words *if* and *then*. Any time you see a sentence with *if* and *then*, you should always symbolize it using an arrow. Write the *if* part of the sentence on the left side of the arrow, and the *then* part of the sentence on the right side of the arrow. Feel free to use abbreviations to save time.

For example,

If you are in California, then you are in the United States.

is correctly symbolized like this:

$$CA \rightarrow US$$

In English, sentences can be rearranged—or even have words left out—without changing their meaning. You can see that these three sentences all mean precisely the same thing:

If you are in California, then you are in the United States.

If you are in California, you are in the United States.

You are in the United States if you are in California.

Since all three sentences mean the same thing, they should all be symbolized precisely the same way: with the *if* part of the sentence on the left, and the *then* part on the right (even when the word *then* is missing). It doesn't matter whether the *if* part appears at the beginning or the end of the sentence.

Conditional symbols should always be read left to right. Never go backwards or against the arrow.

Notice that the two sides of the symbol tell you nothing about time. It is **not** true that the left side always occurs earlier in time than the right side. A sentence that says, "If you are in law school, then you must have taken the LSAT" would be symbolized

$$Law \ school \rightarrow LSAT$$

Law school is on the left side of the conditional, but it occurred *after* the person took the LSAT. Conditional symbols have nothing to do with before and after.

3.2.2.2 The Contrapositive

For every conditional statement, you can create a **contrapositive**—a way to write precisely the same information in another form. This might seem like a waste of time, but it is often useful on the LSAT. In fact, contrapositives are so useful that not understanding them could easily lower your LSAT score by **ten points**! Writing the contrapositive should be your automatic, knee-jerk, instantaneous reflex response every time you write a conditional. Every *if-then* sentence should produce a pair of symbols: the original conditional symbol and its contrapositive.

The rule is:

To make the contrapositive,
Switch and Negate

That is, reverse the order of the two parts, and negate **both** of them using the "~" symbol, which means *not*.

To continue with the California example, the original conditional symbol was

$$CA \longrightarrow US$$

Thus, switching and negating will produce

$$\sim US \longrightarrow \sim CA$$

If you turn this symbol back into an English sentence, it reads

> If you are not in the United States, then you are not in California.

This makes a lot of sense. If you are outside the U.S., there is clearly no way you could be in California.

When making contrapositives, be sure not to make these common mistakes:

This mistake	Produces this symbol	Which means	Which is wrong because
Going backwards	$CA \longleftarrow US$	If you are in the United States, you are in California.	You could be in Florida.
Switching without negating	$US \longrightarrow CA$	If you are in the United States, you are in California.	You could be in Ohio.
Negating without switching	$\sim CA \longrightarrow \sim US$	If you are not in California, you are not in the United States.	You could be in New York.

So, never go backwards (against the arrow), and stick to Switch and Negate. This way, you'll never go wrong.

3.2.2.3 Only If

The LSAT writers often dress up the basic conditional statement in complicated language. Learning to understand each of these syntactic variations inside and out is one of the most important things you can do to increase your LSAT score.

One common trick used by the LSAT writers is the phrase *only if*.

> The car will start only if you put gas in it.

You may be tempted to write "Gas $\longrightarrow$ Start," but that is not a correct representation of the statement. That symbol means "If you put gas in the car, then it will start," which is not necessarily true. Yes, gas is needed, but there are many other things required to make the car start, such as spark plugs, a battery, and a key. Without those, gas won't do much good.

The easiest way to deal with *only if* is to simply cross out the phrase and write an arrow in its place. Whatever immediately follows the arrow always goes on the right hand side of the conditional symbol. The correct way to write the conditional is:

$$\longrightarrow$$

> The car will start ~~only if~~ you put gas in it.
> $$Start \longrightarrow Gas$$
> $$\sim Gas \longrightarrow \sim Start$$

This says that if you see that the car has started, you're guaranteed to find gas in the tank. Also, if you don't put gas in the tank, you're guaranteed to have a car that won't start.

The phrase *only if* works completely differently than the word *if*, so ignore the fact that they contain the same word. Cross out the entire phrase *only if* and replace it with an arrow. Whatever the arrow points to goes on the right-hand side of the conditional symbol.

3.2.2.4 Unless

The word *unless* is also commonly found in conditional statements, and it is a little tricky:

> You cannot be a professional musician unless you practice.

Test-takers often make a lot of mistakes with *unless*, but you don't have to. **The easiest way to deal with *unless* is to cross it out and write *if not* in its place.** This may produce some funky grammar, but don't worry. As always, whatever immediately follows the *if* should be written on the left side of the conditional symbol.

> *if not*
> You cannot be a professional musician ~~unless~~ you practice.
> ~Practice ⟶ ~PM
> PM ⟶ Practice

This makes sense: If you don't practice, then you're guaranteed not to be a professional musician. If you are a professional musician, you must have practiced.

3.2.2.5 All, Every, Always, Whenever

These words can also be included in conditional statements. For example

> All fish can swim.
>
> Every fish can swim.
>
> Fish can always swim.
>
> Whenever you see a fish, you know it can swim.

This one is pretty simple to symbolize. **Whatever follows *all* goes on the left side of the conditional symbol.**

> Fish ⟶ Swim
> ~Swim ⟶ ~Fish

You shouldn't write "Swim ⟶ Fish" because there are some things that can swim but that are not fish, such as whales and people and penguins.

3.2.2.6 No, None, Never

No, *none*, and *never* are only slightly trickier.

> No dogs have six legs.
>
> None of the dogs has six legs.
>
> Dogs never have six legs.

To symbolize a conditional with *no*, *none*, or *never* make sure the "~" is always to the right of the arrow.

> Dog ⟶ ~6 Legs
> 6 Legs ⟶ ~Dog

If you see a dog, you know it won't have six legs, and if you see a six-legged creature, you know it's not a dog (and you should probably go get the bug spray). Be careful not to say "~Dog ⟶ 6 Legs" because there are some animals that are not dogs but that don't have six legs—cats, for example.

3.2.2.7 And and Or

Some conditional statements include the word AND or OR, which you can simply write as part of the conditional symbol. For example,

> If you make a cake, you must use flour and sugar.

> Cake ⟶ Flour AND Sugar
> ~Flour OR ~Sugar ⟶ ~Cake

The original conditional symbol is straightforward enough, but something interesting happened in the contrapositive: When negated, the AND became an OR. Upon examination, this makes sense. If you leave out flour, OR if you leave out sugar, your result will not be a cake. You don't need to leave out both; simply omitting one of them will guarantee a non-cake result.

Here's another example:

If you unplug the TV or pour water into it, it will not work.

Unplug OR Water ⟶ ~Work
Work ⟶ ~Unplug AND ~Water

It happened again. This time, the negated OR became an AND. It makes sense to say that if you see a working TV, you can be sure that it is both plugged in AND water free.

Another example:

If you play pro football without a helmet, you will get hurt.

Football AND ~Helmet ⟶ Hurt
~Hurt ⟶ ~Football OR Helmet

The contrapositive says that if you didn't get hurt, then you either didn't play pro football or you wore a helmet.

To summarize:

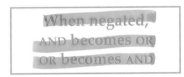

When negated,
AND becomes OR
OR becomes AND

Recall that dealing with the word *unless* entails changing it to *if not*. The word *not* introduces a negation, so pay close attention to conditionals that contain both *unless* and AND or OR.

if not
You cannot go to Hawaii ~~unless~~ you take a plane or a boat.

~Plane AND ~Boat ⟶ ~Hawaii
Hawaii ⟶ Plane OR Boat

Another related situation is the word *nor*. It means the same thing as "not or." Since it involves negating an OR, the result will be an AND.

If you are afraid of animals, you will visit neither the zoo nor the circus.

Afraid ⟶ ~Zoo AND ~Circus
Zoo OR Circus ⟶ ~Afraid

"Neither A nor B" means "Not A AND Not B."

3.2.2.8 When A Conditional Rule Applies
Recall the football example:

Football AND ~Helmet ⟶ Hurt
~Hurt ⟶ ~Football OR Helmet

If you see someone who *is* hurt, what can this rule tell you?

The answer is: nothing at all. If the left-hand side of a conditional statement doesn't apply, then don't even bother looking at the right-hand side. You can't go backwards against the arrow and start making statements about football. Maybe the person fell down the stairs. Or had a car accident. Or maybe he *did* play football but wore a helmet and hurt his knee. The scenario of someone who is hurt is simply not addressed within the realm of this conditional. All conditional rules apply only under certain conditions, and if those conditions aren't met, then the rule doesn't matter.

Simply put, don't go backwards against the arrow. If the left side isn't true, ignore the conditional statement.

3.2.2.9 Drill: Symbolizing Conditional Statements

Using abbreviations, draw the appropriate symbols (including contrapositives) for each of the following rules in the space provided.

1. If the pool is not cleaned, then the lobby is cleaned.

   ~P → L

   ~L → P

2. Blue is used to paint the high school only if green is not used.

   B → ~G

   G → ~B

3. The computers are not repaired unless the desks are repaired.

   C → D

   ~D → ~C

4. Only if sushi is served will wasabi be served.

   Unless

   W → S

   ~S → ~W

5. Whenever raincoats are on sale, umbrellas are not.

   R → ~U

   U → ~R

6. Only if the giraffes or the hippos are exhibited will the kangaroos be exhibited.

   G or H → K

   ~K → ~G & ~H

7. No literature tests are multiple choice tests.

   L → ~MC

   MC → ~L

8. If the Dalí is displayed, then the Cezanne and the Goya are also displayed.

   D → C & G

   ~C or ~G → ~D

9. Baltimore is one of the stops on the tour if Atlanta is not.

   B → A

   A → ~B

10. All coral reefs are endangered.

    C → E

    ~E → ~C

11. Henry cannot serve on the committee unless both Jack and Ingrid also serve on the committee.

    H → J & I

    ~J or ~I → ~H

Answers & Explanations

1. ~P → L
   ~L → P

2. B → ~G
   G → ~B
   Remember that the *only if* should be replaced by an arrow. This also tells you that if green is used to paint the high school, then blue is not used.

3. ~D → ~C
   C → D
   Replace the word *unless* with *if not*.

4. S → W
   ~S → ~W
   Replace the *only if* with an arrow and put what follows the arrow on the right side.

5. R → ~U
   U → ~R
   Whenever functions like the word *if*.

6. K → G or H
   ~G and ~H → ~K
   Remember, when negated, the OR becomes AND.

7. L → ~MC
   MC → ~L
   Remember that "No...." statements are always symbolized with the "~" to the left of the arrow. If you know a test was based on literature, you know it was not multiple choice. If it was a multiple choice test, it was not based on literature.

8. D → C and G
   ~C or ~G → ~D

9. ~A → B
   ~B → A

10. CR → E
    ~E → ~CR

11. ~J → H
    ~H → ~J or ~I
    When you see *unless*, cross it out and write *if not*. In this case, the *not* also modifies the AND, which means you have to change it to OR.

3.3 DEDUCE

Here are a few types of deductions that can commonly be made on Binary games. This is not an exhaustive list of all the possible deductions you can make for any Binary game. Many games will have unique nuances that lead to unique deductions.

3.3.1 COMBINING CONDITIONAL SYMBOLS

3.3.1.1 Conditional Chains

If you are presented with more than one conditional statement, there is a good chance that you will be able to link them. In order to be able to link conditional symbols, you must find something *identical* on the left side of one symbol and on the right side of another symbol. It's important to note that **A** and **~A** do not count as identical, since one is negated but the other isn't.

When you find identical elements on the left and the right, you can put them together to create a conditional **chain**.

Conditional 1: A ⟶ F
                ~F ⟶ ~A

$A \to F \to \sim M$

Conditional 2: F ⟶ ~M
                M ⟶ ~F

$M \to \sim F \to \sim A$

You'll notice that **F** is on the right side of conditional 1, and an identical **F** is on the left side of conditional 2. That means you can put **F** in the middle of the chain:

Chain 1: A ⟶ F ⟶ ~M

You'll also notice that **~F** is on the left side of conditional 1, and an identical **~F** is on the right side of conditional 2. That means you could also put **~F** in the middle of a chain.

Chain 2: M ⟶ ~F ⟶ ~A

Sharp-eyed readers will have noticed that the second chain looks a lot like the first chain, only backwards and with everything negated. That's because the second chain is the **contrapositive** of the first chain. No matter how long a chain is, you can always make the contrapositive of it if you **switch** the entire order backwards **and negate** everything.

Thus, every chain should be written as two symbols: the original chain and its contrapositive. If you want to search through your original conditional symbols to find the identical elements that make up the contrapositive chain, that's perfectly valid. However, it's usually faster and simpler to just complete one chain and then **switch and negate** it to create the contrapositive.

3.3.1.2 Chains With *And* and *Or*

Sometimes you can create a chain using conditionals that contain AND and OR. Consider the following:

Conditional 1: B ⟶ G AND R
                ~R OR ~G ⟶ ~B

$B \to G \ \partial \ R$
$\searrow \sim n$

Conditional 2: G ⟶ ~N
                N ⟶ ~G

If you know **B** is true, that guarantees both **G** AND **R**. Furthermore, **G** alone is enough to guarantee **~N**. So these two conditionals can be linked together to make a branching chain:

Chain: B ⟶ G AND R
                ↘
                ~N

$\sim R \ \partial \sim G \to \sim B$
$\nearrow$
$N \to \sim G$

What about the contrapositive? Well, think about the original conditional symbols. If **N** is true, that guarantees **~G**. And either **~G** or **~R** is enough to guarantee **~B**. So it is possible to link the contrapositives as well, and this also shows you how to make the contrapositive of a branched chain.

Contrapositive: ~R OR ~G → ~B
                              ↗
                          N

However, you can't *always* link conditionals that contain AND and OR. Think about this situation:

Conditional 1: X → L
                ~L → ~X

Conditional 2: C AND L → H
                ~H → ~C OR ~L

There is an **L** on the right-hand side of conditional 1 and an identical **L** on the left-hand side of conditional 2. If **X** is true, that guarantees that **L** is true, but **L** alone is **NOT** enough to guarantee that **H** is true—you would also need **C**. Thus, you can't make a chain.

Similarly, if you know you have **~H**, then you are guaranteed to have either **~C** or **~L**, but *you don't know which one*. That means you can't say for sure whether you will get **~X**. Therefore, you can't link the contrapositives here either.

This is the rule when the identical element in two conditionals is part of an AND or an OR:

> **You can make a chain only when:**
> AND **is on the right side**
> OR **is on the left side**

3.3.1.3 How To Use Chains

Chains can be tremendously useful tools because they can consolidate a lot of complex information into a single compact symbol, but it's important to understand how they work. Imagine you have constructed the following chain:

Chain: L → M → N → O → P
        ~P → ~O → ~N → ~M → ~L

Whenever you know that one part of the chain is true, then you know that everything to the <u>right</u> of it is also true. For example, if **M** is true, then **N**, **O**, and **P** are also true.

Don't make the mistake of going backwards against the arrow. Many questions will try to trick you by tempting you to go backwards along the chain. For example, a question may tell you that **~L** is true and ask you what you can say about the other parts of the chain. The answer is: nothing. You have no information about the other parts of the chain because you can't go backwards.

3.3.1.4 When To Make Chains

No matter what it is, you should only do something on the LSAT if it's a good use of your time. That is, it should be leading to your getting points faster and answering questions with a higher degree of success than anything else you could be doing at that time.

When you see a game that contains a lot of conditional language and repeated elements that can be linked together in a chain, it's almost always a good use of your time to create a conditional chain. The LSAT writers love to test your ability to make contrapositives and link conditionals.

You can still complete any game even if you choose not to make chains. But if you don't, instead of seeing in one symbol every result of placing an element somewhere, you'll have to keep returning to your list of conditional symbols to see if the result of one conditional triggers any additional rules. It becomes an iterative process.

However, sometimes in the Analytical Reasoning section, it's not a good use of your time to make chains. Such occasions would be when:

- Making a chain is likely to confuse you, lead to mistakes, or take an extraordinarily long time. This can be true when there are a large number of ANDs and ORs.

- Getting points does not depend on making a chain. This can be hard to predict, but sometimes a glance at the questions and answer choices tells you that the game is focused elsewhere.

That being said, it pays to get as fast and accurate as you can at making chains. In the end, this skill is likely to bring you more points.

3.3.2 Conditional Symbols Within Binary Games

You can probably see how this method of symbolizing rules can be applied to Binary games in which some elements are *selected* and some are *not selected*. It may be less obvious, but this approach can also be very effective in Binary games that don't revolve around *yes* and *no*—for example, games in which the groups have names.

Binary games are, by definition, concerned only with two groups. There is no need to alter your approach to these games merely because the two groups are given names. Instead, reorient how you look at the groups and simply designate one group as the *yes* group and the other as the *no* group.

For example, if a situation tells you that elements will be assigned to either a red team or a green team, you should think of all assignments in terms of *one* of the teams. Thus, your diagram would look like this:

Red	Not Red (green)

This approach makes dealing with the rules much easier. If you saw the rule

> If Mike is on the red team, Nathan is on the green team.

you would not have to get involved in something ugly like

> Mike red → Nathan green
> Nathan not green → Mike not red

Having to sort out the difference between red, green, not red, and not green can get very confusing very fast. Instead, it's better to think of the rule in terms of just one of the groups, like this:

> Mike red → Nathan not red
> Nathan red → Mike not red

Or more simply:

> M → ~N
> N → ~M

Now these symbols look a lot more familiar. This lets you know that if Mike is on the red team, Nathan is *not* on the red team (i.e. he's on the green team). In addition, if Nathan is on the red team, Mike is *not* on the red team (i.e. he's on the green team).

Symbolizing rules in this manner will allow you to approach every Binary game the same way. You won't have to reorganize all your symbols simply because the groups have names. When you create your diagram, make sure to always put the *yes* group on the left side of your diagram and the *no* group on the right side.

BINARY GAME = 2 GROUPS

> Using conditionals, you can often make deductions by combining them into chains, but it is rare to be able to deduce exactly where an element must be placed. You usually have to wait until a question tells you where to put an element before you can figure out where any of them belong.

> For more conditional practice drills, visit www.examkrackers.com.

3.3.2.1 Drill: Binary Game Deductions

Draw a diagram and symbolize the rules in the space provided. For each question, make any deductions or chains that may be possible.

1. Each attendee will be seated at either table 1 or table 2.
   Lois is seated at table 1 unless Megan is seated at table 1.
   If Nora is seated at table 1, either Lois or Karen is seated at table 2.

   ~M → L
   ~L → M
   N → ~L or ~K
   L & K → ~N

3. Each student either packs a lunch or buys lunch at school. No student does both.
   If either Chris or Debbie packs a lunch, Brandon buys lunch at school.
   If Adam packs a lunch, Chris also packs a lunch.

   C or D → ~B
   B → ~C and ~D
   A → C
   ~C → ~A
   B → ~C and ~D → ~A
   D or C → ~B

2. Two shows—the whale show and the dolphin show—are playing at the same time. Each visitor watches exactly one of the two shows.
   George watches the whales only if Herman watches the dolphins.
   Frank watches the whales unless Herman watches the dolphins.

   G → ~H
   H → ~G
   H → F
   ~F → ~H

   G → ~H → F
   F → ~H → ~G

4. Each engineer will be assigned to exactly one of two panels—the research panel or the development panel.
   If Steve and Paul are on the research panel, Tim is on the development panel.
   Tim is on the development panel only if Russ is on the research panel.

   S & P → ~T
   T → ~S or ~P
   ~T → R
   ~R → T
   ~R → T → ~S or ~P
   S & P → ~T → R

These symbols can be linked because the identical element (T) appears on opposite sides of both symbols and is not involved in an AND or OR.

4. S AND P → ~T
   T → ~S OR ~P
   ~T → R
   ~R → T
   R → T
   S AND P → ~T → R
   ~R → T → ~S OR ~P

Research	Not Research (Development)

These symbols can be combined as shown.

3. D OR C → ~B
   B → ~C AND ~D
   A → C
   ~C → ~A
   D OR C → ~B
   B → ~C AND ~D → ~A

Packs	Does Not Pack (Buys)

Again, no combination is possible since the identical elements are not on opposite sides of the arrows.

2. G → ~H
   ~G → H
   H → F
   ~H → ~F

Whales	Not Whales (Dolphins)

3.3.2.2 DEALING WITH LONG LISTS OF CONDITIONALS

On many Binary games, symbolizing the rules results in a long list of conditional symbols. This can appear daunting, and although it takes some getting used to, dealing with these lists doesn't need to be difficult. Here are some principles to guide you:

- When checking for rules that apply, only look at the left-hand side of the list. Remember, if the left-hand side of a conditional statement is not true, you can ignore the entire rule.

- Make complete sweeps of the list. If you know **G** is selected, sweep your eyes down the left side of the entire list looking for **G**. If you encounter a rule in the middle of the list that is triggered when **G** is selected, then follow the rule, but don't forget to inspect the rest of the list after that.

- Re-examine the list after every new deduction you make. If **G** triggered a conditional that made **H** not selected, then you need to sweep down the list again looking for rules that are triggered when **H** is not selected. Keep repeating this process until no more rules are triggered.

This process can be somewhat tedious, but it's very methodical, and with practice, you can become quick and accurate at dealing with long lists of conditionals.

3.4 PUTTING IT ALL TOGETHER

3.4.1 Drill: Binary Games

Below is a situation with rules. Identify the type of game and set it up by drawing an appropriate diagram and symbolizing the stock and rules. Then make as many deductions as you can.

Each of exactly seven people—Flora, Greg, Howard, Kevin, Lois, Marcy, and Oscar—will serve on exactly one of two committees—planning and setup—to organize a party. The assignments to the committees must conform to the following conditions:

Flora serves on the setup committee only if Lois also serves on the setup committee.

Kevin serves on the planning committee unless Greg serves on the setup committee.

If Howard serves on the setup committee or Kevin serves on the planning committee, then Marcy serves on the planning committee.

If Flora serves on the planning committee, then either Greg or Marcy serves on the setup committee.

F G H K L M O

F → L ✓
~L → ~F
~K → ~G ✓
G → K
H or ~K → ~M
M → ~H ok
~F → G or M
~G or M → F

~L → ~F → ~G or M

~G or M → F → L

~F → G or M
      ↓K

~K → ~G
      or M → F

3.4.2 ANSWERS & EXPLANATIONS

Identify

Several features identify this as a Binary game. The situation asks you to sort the six people into *two groups*. Furthermore, there are rules that talk about some people being in the same or different groups, and some elements' group depends on which group others are in. Finally, there is no mention of any order, or of elements being adjacent to, before, or after other elements. This is a Binary game.

Set Up

The diagram for this game starts with columns for the two groups, separated by a vertical line. The two groups have names (Planning and Setup), but it's best to think of them as a *yes* group and a *no* group. Organize your thinking around one of the groups—for example, Planning and Not Planning.

The stock in this game is composed of the initials of the seven people: F G H K L M O. This is written to the upper left of the diagram.

| F G H K L M O | Planning | Not Planning | (Setup) |

To complete the Set Up step, symbolize each of the rules. In this case, they are all conditional rules, which is common in Binary games.

Rule 1 contains the phrase *only if*. Replace it with an arrow.

$$\sim F \longrightarrow \sim L$$
$$L \longrightarrow F$$

Rule 2 contains the word *unless*. Replace it with *if not*. If G is not in Setup, it is not in Planning.

$$G \longrightarrow K$$
$$\sim K \longrightarrow \sim G$$

Rule 3 contains OR, so remember to change it to AND when making the contrapositive.

$$\sim H \text{ OR } K \longrightarrow M$$
$$\sim M \longrightarrow H \text{ AND } \sim K$$

Rule 4 also has an OR phrase, this time to the right of the arrow:

$$F \longrightarrow \sim G \text{ OR } \sim M$$
$$M \text{ AND } G \longrightarrow \sim F$$

At this point, your page should look like this:

| F G H K L M O | Planning | Not Planning | (Setup) |

$$\sim F \longrightarrow \sim L$$
$$L \longrightarrow F$$
$$G \longrightarrow K$$
$$\sim K \longrightarrow \sim G$$
$$\sim H \text{ OR } K \longrightarrow M$$
$$\sim M \longrightarrow H \text{ AND } \sim K$$
$$F \longrightarrow \sim G \text{ OR } \sim M$$
$$M \text{ AND } G \longrightarrow \sim F$$

Deduce

Finally, make as many deductions as you can.

Rules 1 and 2 have the element F in common, so you can link them together in a chain. You don't have to worry about the OR being on the wrong side because the F isn't involved with the OR.

$$L \longrightarrow F \longrightarrow \sim G \text{ OR } \sim M$$

$$M \text{ AND } G \longrightarrow \sim F \longrightarrow \sim L$$

Rules 2 and 3 have the common element of K, and the OR is on the left-hand side, so they can also be linked:

$$\sim H \text{ OR } K \longrightarrow M$$
$$G \nearrow$$

$$\sim M \longrightarrow \sim K \text{ AND } H$$
$$\searrow \sim G$$

You can't link rule 4 to rule 2 or 3 because in those cases, the common element is involved with the OR, which is on the wrong side.

As you build the chains, you should think about using the space on your page wisely. For example, when you create the chain combining rules 1 and 4, you don't need to write both rules all over again. Just build off of rule 1 and extend it into a chain. After that, you can erase your original rule 4 to cut down on the clutter.

You can do the same thing when you combine rules 2 and 3. Just erase rule 2 and build the chain using rule 3 as it is already written.

The ultimate in efficiency is to build the chains as you symbolize the rules. Instead of writing a rule, then combining it, then erasing it, look for ways to build the chains right away.

You've probably noticed that the master diagram itself does not have *any* elements placed on it. This is often the case in games where all the rules are conditionals. You will not be able to figure out where any of the elements are until a question stem tells you to place one of the elements into one of the groups. After that, you will be able to use your symbolized rules to figure out where several other elements should be placed.

Your final master diagram should now look like this:

F G H K L M O	Planning	Not Planning (Setup)

$$L \longrightarrow F \longrightarrow \sim G \text{ OR } \sim M$$
$$M \text{ AND } G \longrightarrow \sim F \longrightarrow \sim L$$
$$G \searrow$$
$$\sim H \text{ OR } K \longrightarrow M$$
$$\sim M \longrightarrow \sim K \text{ AND } H$$
$$\searrow \sim G$$

NOW MOVE ON TO THE SECOND CHAPTER OF LECTURE 2. WHEN YOU HAVE COMPLETED IT, YOU CAN GET FURTHER PRACTICE WITH BINARY GAMES IN THE CORRESPONDING EXAM AT THE END OF THE BOOK.

TRUTH QUESTIONS

The majority of questions in the Analytical Reasoning section are **Truth** questions. The question stem of a Truth question does not ask *where* a particular element must be or *which* element must fill a certain spot. Instead, the stem is much vaguer. It asks what must, could, or cannot be true, and you must react to each answer choice.

4.1 IDENTIFY THE QUESTION

You can identify Truth questions by looking at the question stems. Every Truth question ends with one of the following phrases:

- must be true

- could be true

- cannot be true

- could be false

- must be false

4.1.1 OPPOSITES

The phrases above are related to each other in a very specific way: they form pairs made up of direct opposites.

For example, it's easy to see that the phrases *required* and *not required* are opposites. On the LSAT, the writers use the phrase *must be true* to mean *required*, and the phrase *could be false* to mean *not required*.

Opposites

Must Be True (required)	⟋⟍⟋⟍	**Could Be False** (not required)

Realizing that these two phrases form a pair of opposites makes it easier to deal with one of the confusing tricks the test writers like to use. When a Truth question stem uses the word *EXCEPT*, it is really just asking you about the opposite. For example, if you see a question stem that says

Each of the following could be false EXCEPT:

You can simplify it by crossing out "could be false EXCEPT" and writing "must be true."

which one   must be true?
Each of the following ~~could be false EXCEPT~~:

You can do the same thing in this case:

which one   could be false?
Each of the following ~~must be true EXCEPT~~:

The other phrases form a second pair of opposites. Again, it's easy to see that the words *possible* and *impossible* are opposites. On the LSAT, the writers use the phrase *could be true* to mean *possible*, and **two** phrases, *must be false* and *cannot be true*, to mean *impossible*.

Opposites

Could Be True (possible)	⟋⟍⟋⟍	**Must Be False** **Cannot Be True** (impossible)

Again, seeing this pair as opposites makes it easier to deal with the EXCEPT trick. If you see a phrase with EXCEPT, just cross it out and write the opposite:

which one   could be true?
Each of the following ~~must be false EXCEPT~~:

which one   must be false?
Each of the following ~~could be true EXCEPT~~:

In addition to allowing you to simplify questions stems, understanding these pairs of opposites is **critical** when it comes to attacking the answer choices.

4.2   WORK THE DIAGRAM

As with all Local questions, working the diagram is a vital step in Local Truth questions. Remember to deal with the new rule just as you do the original rules:

1. **Symbolize the new rule,** either directly on the diagram if you can or to the *right* of the diagram.

2. **Make as many deductions as you can with the new rule.**

As an example, take a look at the following question from the Committees game from the end of Chapter 3:

1.   If Greg serves on the planning committee, which of the following must be true?

   (A)   Flora serves on the setup committee.
   (B)   Howard serves on the planning committee.
   (C)   Kevin serves on the setup committee.
   (D)   Lois serves on the planning committee.
   (E)   Marcy serves on the setup committee.

First, symbolize the new rule in a new row on your diagram by putting **G** in Planning.

F G H K L M O	Planning	Not Planning (Setup)
L ⟶ F ⟶ ~G OR ~M	G	
M AND G ⟶ ~F ⟶ ~L		
G		
~H OR K ⟶ M		
~M ⟶ ~K AND H		
G		

Then, make all the deductions you can. A lot can be determined from just this one piece of information. The second chain puts **K** and **M** in Planning. Then you can use the first chain, because both **M** and **G** are now in planning. It tells you that **F** and **L** are not in Planning.

> As soon as you put something on the diagram, look for any conditionals that are triggered, and put those results on the diagram as well.

Your diagram should now look like this:

Planning	Not Planning (Setup)
G K M	F L

Most of the elements are definitively placed, but not all of them. You still don't know where **H** and **O** are, but you've probably done enough to answer the question. To check, look for the correct answer by examining each choice and comparing it to your diagram. Remember, the question stem asks you to find the choice that *must be true*. This means that one of the choices will be *required*, while the other four will be *not required*.

> (A)   Flora serves on the setup committee.

This is not required. In fact, it's not even allowed, since **F** is definitely in Not Planning. *Cut it.*

> (B)   Howard serves on the planning committee.

H could go in either group, so it's not required to be in Planning. *Cut it.*

> (C)   Kevin serves on the setup committee.

Again, this contradicts the diagram, so it's definitely not required. *Cut it.*

> (D)   Marcy serves on the planning committee.

Yes, the diagram shows that this is required, so you know it's the correct answer. You can pick this choice, and you don't have to bother with choice (E).

Choice (D) is the correct answer.

4.3 ATTACK

Universal Truth questions can present some interesting challenges. Some of them can be answered instantly using the overall deductions you made. Others take much longer. It pays to have a smart plan of attack for these questions so that you don't waste time. You have three major strategies, which you should use in this order:

1. **Check if your deductions are enough to answer the question.**

2. **Put the question off until you have answered all the other questions.** Then use the work you did for the previous questions to help you find the answer.

3. **Try out the answer choices in your diagram.**

> These three strategies apply to *all* Universal questions, not just Truth questions.

4.3.1 ARE YOUR DEDUCTIONS ENOUGH?

As you know, the more deductions you make before you start on the questions, the easier a game becomes. Take a look at the following question, which comes from the Comedians game at the end of Chapter 1:

> 2.   Which one of the following must be true?

This is a Truth question, and it doesn't give you any new rules, so it's also a Universal question. You can't do anything new with the diagram, so take a look at the answer choices and check your master diagram to see if you can find the right answer.

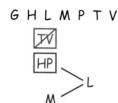

Master Diagram

1	2	3	4	5	6	7
~P	Ⓖ				◯	L/V
~L	~L	~L			~H	

(A)   Either Hassan or Myrna performs first.
(B)   Either Garrett or Pearl performs second.
(C)   Either Tavares or Valencia performs fourth.
(D)   Either Garrett or Lucille performs sixth.
(E)   Either Lucille or Valencia performs seventh.

As you looked at the first four answer choices, you should have noticed that nothing in the master diagram indicated that the choice was *required*. But your deductions show that choice (E) *is* required, and since the question stem asks for the choice that *must be true*, you know that **choice (E) is the correct answer.**

That was easy, right? For many Universal Truth questions, your deductions will be enough to answer the question, so always check there first.

4.3.2 USING YOUR PREVIOUS WORK

> Some of the best questions to delay until later are Universal Truth questions that can't be answered right away by looking at your deductions and master diagram.

When your deductions aren't enough to answer a Universal Truth question, put it off and come back to it after you have answered all the other questions. When you return, your diagram will contain a list of *some* of the valid configurations of the elements, and you can use that list to help you eliminate or select answer choices. This is an especially useful tactic when your master diagram does not contain many deductions, which is often true on Binary games.

Imagine you had answered a few questions in the Committees game and your diagram had a collection of previous work that looked like this:

Planning			Not Planning		(Setup)
G	K	M	F	L	O
L	F	H	M	K	G
M	O		H	L	
H	M		G		

Now take a look at this question:

3. Which one of the following could be true?

(A) Howard and Marcy serve together on the setup committee.

(B) Greg and Flora serve together on the planning committee.

(C) Kevin and Marcy serve together on the setup committee.

(D) Greg serves on planning committee and Marcy serves on the setup committee.

(E) Greg serves on planning committee and Kevin serves on the setup committee.

Since the question stem asks for something that is *possible* (could be true), you will be able to pick an answer choice if your previous work shows a permissible configuration in which that choice occurred. Examine each choice:

Choice (A): This did not occur in any of the previous work.

Choice (B): This also did not occur in any of the previous work.

Choice (C): This **did** occur in the second line in the diagram, so it could be true, which is what you're looking for.

Choice (C) is the correct answer.

In this case, the previous work was enough to get you the correct answer. Great! But there's a subtle yet very important point to this example. What should you have done with choices (A) and (B)? The answer is **not** to eliminate them right away.

When a question stem asks you to find the choice that *could be true*, then all the incorrect choices *must be false* (remember, those two phrases form a pair of opposites). However, just because you never saw something occur in any of your previous work does not guarantee that it must be false all the time, because your previous work does not contain every valid configuration. For example, look at this miniature question, using the same previous work:

4. Which one of the following could be true?

(A) Lois and Greg serve together on the planning committee.

(B) Flora serves on the planning committee and Lois serves on the setup committee.

In this case, neither answer choice was ever true in the previous work. But one choice is correct, while the other is incorrect! In this situation, the previous work is not enough to get you to the correct answer. Don't eliminate *either* of these choices based on the previous work—you'll have to find some other way to figure out the answer.

In the end, your previous work can show you what is *possible* and what is *not required*. But it **can't** show you what is *required* in all configurations or *impossible* in all configurations, since your previous work does not show all configurations.

> The exception to this is when, for some reason, your past work *does* show every single relevant possibility. In that case, something that was always true in your past work must be true.

This leads to the following:

	How To Use Your Previous Work			
	If the question stem asks you to find the choice that:			
	Must Be True	*Could Be False*	*Could Be True*	*Must Be False*
The **correct choice** is:	Required	Not required	Possible	Impossible
The four **incorrect choices** are:	Not required	Required	Impossible	Possible
If a choice was true in *all* your previous work:	Then it's possible, and you should **hold on to it.**	Then it's possible, and you should **hold on to it.**	Then it's possible, and you should **pick it.**	Then it's possible, and you should **eliminate it.**
If a choice was *sometimes* true and *sometimes* false in your previous work:	Then it's not required, and you should **eliminate it.**	Then it's not required, and you should **pick it.**	Then it's possible, and you should **pick it.**	Then it's possible, and you should **eliminate it.**
If the choice was false in *all* your previous work:	Then it's not required, and you should **eliminate it.**	Then it's not required, and you should **pick it.**	Then it's not required, and you should **hold on to it.**	Then it's not required, and you should **hold on to it.**

4.3.3 Trying Out the Answer Choices

Trying out the answer choices is your last resort because it is so time consuming. However, on every LSAT, you will encounter questions on which your deductions and your previous work are not enough to get you to the correct answer, so you should know what to do in those cases.

Remember, if using your previous work allowed you to eliminate *some* of the answer choices, you don't have to try those out. Just focus on the ones you have remaining.

Proving Something is Possible or Impossible

If you are faced with a question stem that asks you what *could be true* or what *must be false*, then your job is to discover which answer choices are possible and which are impossible. To do this, **put the answer choice, as it's written, into your diagram and see if any rules are broken.** This means trying to come up with a complete, legitimate configuration in which the answer choice is *true*.

If you can successfully come up with at least one complete legitimate configuration in which the answer choice is true, then you have proven it to be *possible*. If you can't, then you have proven the choice to be *impossible*.

Recall this example, which was unable to be answered using previous work:

    4.   Which one of the following could be true?

        (A)   Lois and Greg serve together on the planning committee.

        (B)   Flora serves on the planning committee and Lois serves on the setup committee.

Try putting choice (A) into your diagram:

F G H K L M O	Planning	Not Planning (Setup)
L → F → ~G or ~M	L G	
M and G → ~F → ~L		
G ↘ ~H or K → M		
~M → ~K and H ↘ G		

This looks OK so far, but remember, you have to create a *complete configuration* just to ensure that no problems arise anywhere. What else happens in this case? Since G is in Planning, then K and M must also be there. This means both G and M are in Planning, so the first chain tells you that F and L will have to be in Setup. But L is already is Planning. That's a problem. You can't put L in both places.

Planning				Not Planning	(Setup)
L	G	K	M	F	L

ILLEGAL

This answer choice is impossible, so you can eliminate it.

Now try choice (B):

Planning	Not Planning	(Setup)
F	L	

Again, this looks OK to start, but try to create a *complete configuration* to make sure. Since F is in Planning, you have to put G or M in Setup. Either one will do; try M:

Planning			Not Planning			(Setup)
F	H	O	L	M	K	G

Putting M in Planning then determines K, H, and G. Only O is left, and you could put it anywhere. Now every element is placed, and none of the rules have been broken. So there is at least one legal configuration that matches choice (B).

Any legal configuration can show that the choice is possible, and since the question stem asks you to find the choice that *could be true*, you know this is it.

Choice (B) is the correct answer.

Proving Something is Required or Not Required

If you are faced with a question stem that asks you what *must be true* or what *could be false*, then your job is to discover which answer choices are required and which are not required. This can be more difficult. If you simply tried putting the answer choice into your diagram to discover whether any rules were broken, you would not have completed the job—you would have proven that the choice is possible in at least one case, but that's not the same as proving it's required in all cases.

Instead, to prove something is required or not required, **use the diagram to try to disprove the answer choice.** This means trying to come up with a complete legal configuration in which the answer choice is *false*.

If you can successfully come up with at least one complete legal configuration in which the answer choice is false, then you have proven it to be *not required*. If you can't, then you have proven the choice to be *required*.

Consider the following miniature example. It's a Truth question from the Comedians game, and it's also a Local question. Trying out the answer choices is sometimes necessary on Local questions too, and the process works just the same as on Universal questions.

5. If Garrett performs second, which one of the following could be false?

   (A) Lucille performs no earlier than sixth.
   (B) Myrna performs no later than fifth.

First, put G in your diagram in the second spot. Unfortunately, no new deductions that allow you to answer the question are immediately obvious. You'll have to try out the answer choices.

To do so, first try to disprove choice (A). This means trying to come up with a complete legal configuration in which L *does* perform earlier than sixth. Try putting L fifth.

G H L M P T V

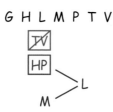

Master Diagram

1	2	3	4	5	6	7
~P	Ⓖ				◯	
~L	~L	~L			~H	L/V
	G			L		

You'll have to put M first and H and P third and fourth. You also know V must be seventh, but there's a problem here. The only element left for the sixth spot is T, but T isn't allowed to be right before V.

1	2	3	4	5	6	7
M	G	H	P	L		V

ILLEGAL

So you were unable to successfully disprove choice (A) by putting L fifth. But don't give up yet—are there any other ways you could try to put L earlier than sixth? Try putting it fourth.

1	2	3	4	5	6	7
	G		L			

ILLEGAL

This is no good either, since there is no room for the block of H and P. And now you're out of options, since your master diagram tells you that L can't be first, second, or third.

What happened here? You tried to disprove choice (A), but there was no legal way to disprove it. That means choice (A) *must be true*. Since the question stem asks for the choice that *could be false*, you can eliminate choice (A).

Now try to disprove choice (B). This means trying to come up with a complete legal configuration in which M *does* perform later than fifth. Try putting M sixth.

1	2	3	4	5	6	7
V	G	T	H	P	M	L

Several legal configurations are possible, and here's one. Since you could disprove it, you've shown that choice (B) is not required, and since this question stem asks for something that *could be false*, it's the correct answer choice.

Choice (B) is the correct answer.

This discussion can be summed up like this:

| | How To Try Out The Answer Choices | | | |
| | If the question stem asks you to find the choice that: | | | |
	Must Be True	*Could Be False*	*Could Be True*	*Must Be False*
The **correct choice** is:	Required	Not required	Possible	Impossible
The four **incorrect choices** are:	Not required	Required	Impossible	Possible
For each answer choice:	Try to come up with a complete configuration in which it's **false.**	Try to come up with a complete configuration in which it's **false.**	Try to come up with a complete configuration in which it's **true.**	Try to come up with a complete configuration in which it's **true.**
If you are **successful**:	Then it's not required, and you should **eliminate it.**	Then it's not required, and you should **pick it.**	Then it's possible, and you should **pick it.**	Then it's possible, and you should **eliminate it.**
If you are **unsuccessful**:	Then it's required, and you should **pick it.**	Then it's required, and you should **eliminate it.**	Then it's impossible, and you should **eliminate it.**	Then it's impossible, and you should **pick it.**

4.3.5   Drill: Using Your Previous Work

Below is a hypothetical collection of previous work. For each answer choice, examine the previous work and decide whether to pick it, hold on to it, or eliminate it.

Tacos				Not Tacos (Couscous)			
S	T	V	Y	U	W	X	
S	T	V	W	U	X	Y	Z
T	V	W	Z	S	U	X	Y
	T	U	X	S	V	Z	

Question Stem	Answer Choice	Pick it, Hold on to it, or Eliminate it?
Which must be true?	1. T orders tacos.	
	2. V orders tacos.	
	3. Both U and S order tacos.	
	4. U and X order the same dish.	
Which could be true?	5. U and V order the same dish.	
	6. Y orders tacos.	
	7. T orders couscous.	
	8. Either X or Z orders couscous.	
Which could be false?	9. U and X order different dishes.	
	10. U and V order different dishes.	
	11. At least 3 people order tacos.	
	12 Y orders couscous.	
Which must be false?	13. W and Y order different dishes.	
	14. At most 2 people order couscous.	
	15. T and Z order different dishes.	
	16. T orders couscous.	

Answers & Explanations

Questions 1–4: You're looking for something that's *required*.

1. **Hold on to it.** This was always true, so it's possible.

2. **Eliminate it.** This was sometimes false, so it's not required.

3. **Eliminate it.** This was always false, so it's not required.

4. **Hold on to it.** This was always true, so it's possible.

Questions 5–8: You're looking for something that's *possible*.

5. **Hold on to it.** This was always false, so it's not required.

6. **Pick it.** This was sometimes true, so it's possible.

7. **Hold on to it.** This was always false, so it's not required.

8. **Pick it.** This was always true, so it's possible.

Questions 9–12: You're looking for something that's *not required*.

9. **Pick it.** This was always false, so it's not required.

10. **Hold on to it.** This was always true, so it's possible.

Questions 13–16: You're looking for something that's *impossible*.

11. **Hold on to it.** This was always true, so it's possible.

12. **Pick it.** This was sometimes true, so it's possible.

13. **Eliminate it.** This was always true, so it's possible.

14. **Hold on to it.** This was always true, so it's possible.

15. **Eliminate it.** This was sometimes true, so it's possible.

16. **Hold on to it.** This was always false, so it's not required.

4.3.6   Drill: Trying Out the Answer Choices

For each answer choice, decide whether you should attack it by trying to prove it or by trying to disprove it, and how. Then decide whether you should pick the choice or eliminate it if you are successful. The first question is done for you as an example.

Question	Should you try to prove the choice or disprove it?	By doing what?	If you're successful, pick the choice or eliminate it?
1. Must it be true that X is third?	Disprove	Putting X not third	Eliminate it
2. Could it be false that Z is selected?			
3. Must it be false that G is fifth?			
4. Could it be true that M is not chosen?			
5. Must it be true that L is sixth?			
6. Must it be false that P is included?			
7. Must it be true that Q is in the same group as R?			
8. Could it be true that F is earlier than fourth?			
9. Could it be false that W is immediately before Y?			

Answers

Question	Should you try to prove the choice or disprove it?	By doing what?	If you're successful, pick the choice or eliminate it?
1. Must it be true that X is third?	Disprove	Putting X not third	Eliminate it
2. Could it be false that Z is selected?	Disprove	Making Z not selected	Pick it
3. Must it be false that G is fifth?	Prove	Putting G fifth	Eliminate it
4. Could it be true that M is not chosen?	Prove	Making M not chosen	Pick it
5. Must it be true that L is sixth?	Disprove	Putting L not sixth	Eliminate it
6. Must it be false that P is included?	Prove	Making P included	Eliminate it
7. Must it be true that Q is in the same group as R?	Disprove	Putting Q and R in different groups	Eliminate it
8. Could it be true that F is earlier than fourth?	Prove	Putting F earlier than fourth	Pick it
9. Could it be false that W is immediately before Y?	Disprove	Putting W not immediately before Y	Pick it

STOP. THIS IS THE END OF LECTURE 2. DO NOT PROCEED TO THE CORRESPONDING EXAM UNTIL INSTRUCTED TO DO SO IN CLASS.

LECTURE **3** CHAPTER **5**

GRID GAMES

5.1 IDENTIFY THE GAME

5.1.1 WHAT IS A GRID GAME?

A **Grid game** is any game in which the diagram needs more than one row to contain all the elements.

Grid games have a lot in common with Ordering games, since the spots are usually part of a natural order, and elements can be adjacent to, before, or after other elements.

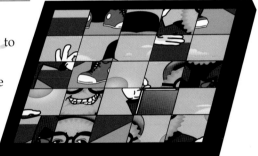

The difference is that all the elements in an Ordering game can fit into *one* row. In Grid games, *several* rows will be needed to contain all the elements. Thus, your diagram will be a **grid** with both rows and columns.

5.1.2 HOW TO RECOGNIZE GRID GAMES

A game that requires you to arrange elements into multiple rows and columns is a Grid game.

You can often tell that you need multiple rows by looking at the situation. Consider the following examples:

> Nine people are seated in a roller coaster car with three rows of seats. There are three seats in each row.

This situation indicates that the elements are arranged spatially. The diagram will have three rows and three columns.

> A gardener must plant eight trees in four adjacent parcels of land, numbered consecutively 1–4. Two trees will be planted in each parcel.

This situation identifies four sequential parcels and tells you that two trees are planted in each parcel. It looks a lot like an Ordering game, but since each numbered spot contains *two* trees, it is best to create two rows. For each numbered parcel of land, each row will hold one of the trees.

> Over a period of five consecutive days, Monday through Friday, a company will conduct an annual review of its five offices—J, K, L, M, and N. Each office will be reviewed once by the company's president and once by its vice president. Each executive will review one office each day.

This situation tells you that there is a sequence—Monday through Friday—for the reviews, and that there will be two reviews each day—one by the president and one by the vice president. In this diagram, one row would contain the order of the president's reviews, and the other row would contain the order of the vice president's reviews. Since they are both reviewing the same five offices, each element (office) would appear twice on the diagram—once in each row.

Although they may look different, each of these is an example of a Grid game. They all indicate that elements are arranged in multiple rows and columns.

Grid games are the most common type of game. Almost every test contains one or more Grid games.

These situations present pretty clear indications of Grid games, but sometimes you won't realize you are dealing with a Grid game until you read the rules. Consider the following example:

> An orchestra will perform musical compositions by three classical composers—Tchaikovsky, Verdi, and Wagner. Five compositions will be performed, each of which is a choral piece, an opera, or a symphony. The following conditions apply:
> > The composition performed third is an opera.
> > Neither the composition performed first nor the composition performed second was written by Wagner.

The situation in this game makes no explicit mention of sequencing, but the rules indicate that the compositions are performed in a sequential order. In this case, the backbone of the diagram would be the order of the compositions 1–5, and you would create one row to contain the *composer* of each composition and a second row to contain the *type* of each composition.

There are three common types of Grid games:

1. **Spatial arrangement**. For example, it is common to see Grid games in which the elements are sitting in several rows of seats. Elements can be next to each other *and* in front of or behind each other.

2. **Ordering with more than one element per ordered spot**. When you know each spot in the order will contain two or more elements, don't try to fit all the elements horizontally into the same row. Use several rows and arrange them vertically as well as horizontally.

3. **Games with more than two factors to figure out**. For example, in an Ordering game, you have only *two* factors to consider, such as 1) the person and 2) the place in the order. However, in a Grid game, you may have *three* factors to figure out: 1) the person, 2) the person's eye color, and 3) the place in the order.

This only applies when you have to *figure out* all three factors. If, in the previous example, the situation had told you every person's eye color before you started, then you wouldn't need to figure out the eye colors, and thus you wouldn't need a second row in the diagram. It would be a regular Ordering game.

5.1.3　Drill: Identifying Grid Games

Determine whether each of the following situations and rules indicates a Grid game.

1. Mrs. Jones must decide on the order in which to feed her six pet mice—Eek, Fuzzy, Gizmo, Hombre, Jumper, and Killer—and which food to give to each one. Mrs. Jones will give exactly one type of food—pellets, raisins, or sprouts—to each mouse. Her decision is subject to the following constraints:

    Pellets are given to the first mouse fed.
    If Eek is fed before Gizmo, then he is given sprouts.

    Indicates a Grid game?　□ Yes　□ No

2. In one day, a stock trader conducts transactions with exactly seven stocks, numbered 1 through 7. The trader either buys or sells each stock once in a manner consistent with the following conditions:

    If he buys stock 1, he sells stock 6.
    He does not sell stock 3 unless he also sells both stock 4 and stock 7.

    Indicates a Grid game?　□ Yes　□ No

3. A humane society houses exactly eight dogs—a husky, a Labrador, a Maltese, a pug, a rottweiler, a shepherd, a terrier, and a vizsla—in four kennels, numbered 1, 2, 3, and 4. The following conditions must apply:

    Each kennel houses exactly two dogs.
    The Maltese is housed in a lower numbered kennel than the vizsla.

    Indicates a Grid game?　□ Yes　□ No

4. Six paintings—a landscape, a montage, a portrait, a religious painting, a still life, and a tribal painting—are hung in two rows on a wall, with three paintings in each row. The arrangement of the paintings is consistent with the following conditions:

    The landscape is not hung directly below the still life.
    The tribal painting is hung to the left of the religious painting.

    Indicates a Grid game?　□ Yes　□ No

5. Seven trains—T, U, V, W, X, Y, and Z—arrive at a station, one train at a time. The order in which the trains arrive is consistent with the following conditions:

    T arrives at some time before W arrives.
    V arrives immediately after X arrives.

    Indicates a Grid game?　□ Yes　□ No

6. On each day of a certain week, a department store will have sales in exactly one of three departments—electronics, furnishings, or housewares. Each day, the department store will offer a discount of either 10%, 20%, or 30%. The following conditions must apply:

    Furnishings are never discounted more than 20%.
    Electronics are on sale on Friday.

    Indicates a Grid game?　□ Yes　□ No

7. At a company dinner, eight employees—a lawyer, a manager, an office assistant, a president, a recruiter, a secretary, a treasurer, and a vice president—are seated at three tables—numbered 1, 2, and 3. At least two people are seated at each table according to the following conditions:

    The president is seated at the same table as the vice president.
    The manager is not seated at table 1 unless the recruiter is seated at table 2.

    Indicates a Grid game?　□ Yes　□ No

Answers & Explanations

1. **Yes.** The situation indicates that an order will have to be determined and that there are two sets of elements (mice and food) that must be ordered.

2. **No.** The situation mentions numbers, but not order. Instead, the situation and rules indicate that the elements (the numbered stocks) must be divided into two groups (buy and sell). This is a Binary game.

3. **Yes.** The first rule states that two dogs will be placed in each kennel, and the second rule indicates that the order of the kennels is important.

4. **Yes.** The situation and rules indicate that the elements must be arranged in a manner in which both vertical and horizontal alignment are important.

5. **No.** The seven trains occupy a single order, with nothing else to be determined. This is an Ordering game.

6. **Yes.** The situation and rules mention an order (days of the week) and indicate that two elements (department and discount) must be placed in each ordinal position.

7. **No.** The tables do have numbers, but there is no spatial arrangement or ordering, as the rules do not mention adjacent or consecutive tables. The tables function merely as different groups that the elements have to be sorted into. This is a Grouping game.

5.2   SET UP

5.2.1   How to Draw a Grid Game Diagram

If a Grid game includes any feature with a natural order, use that order as your backbone (column headings).

The diagram for a Grid game, as you may have guessed, is a **grid** of rows and columns. Since most Grid games involve an ordering feature, the columns should be labeled with the names of the spots in the order. This will usually be 1, 2, 3…, or it may be the days of the week or hours of a day.

The rows usually need labels too. For example, in this situation,

> Over a period of five consecutive days, Monday through Friday, a company will conduct an annual review of its five offices—J, K, L, M, and N. Each office will be reviewed once by the company's president and once by its vice president. Each executive will review one office each day.

Each row is labeled to show which order it contains: the order of the president's reviews, or the order of the vice presidents reviews:

	Mon	Tue	Wed	Thu	Fri
President					
Vice president					

The Orchestra game presents a similar situation:

> An orchestra will perform musical compositions by three classical composers—Tchaikovsky, Verdi, and Wagner. Five compositions will be performed, each of which is a choral piece, an opera, or a symphony. The following conditions apply:
> The composition performed third is an opera.
> Neither the composition performed first nor the composition performed second was written by Wagner.

Here, one row contains the order of the composers, while the other row contains the order of the types of compositions:

	1	2	3	4	5
Composer					
Type					

Other times, however, the rows don't need labels. In this situation,

> A gardener must plant eight trees in four adjacent parcels of land, numbered consecutively 1–4. Two trees will be planted in each parcel.

There is no difference between the two trees on any one parcel of land—e.g., there is no front tree and back tree. The only thing that matters is which parcel a tree is in. Thus, the two rows are interchangeable. If you figured out that the spruce tree had to be in the third parcel, it wouldn't matter which row you put it in, as long as it was in the "3" column.

1	2	3	4

As with all types of games, set aside the first grid to contain your master diagram with all the overall rules for the game and any deductions you make. Leave room below the master diagram to draw new grids to contain the work for individual questions. On Grid games, this is slightly more complicated than on other games, since you will need several rows for each possible configuration. It's not a big problem though. Just draw as many lines as you need to keep your work organized and the different grids separated from each other.

5.2.2 THE STOCK

Symbolizing the **stock** on Grid games can be more complicated than on other types of games, since there are several different ways in which the elements could work with the diagram.

5.2.2.1 One Stock For the Whole Diagram

The simplest case is when any element in the stock could go anywhere on the diagram. In this case, just symbolize the stock off to the left of the diagram as you do for other types of games.

Take a look at this example:

> A gardener must plant eight trees in four adjacent parcels of land, numbered consecutively 1–4. Two trees will be planted in each parcel. The gardener must plant exactly one tree of each of the following types: fir, gingko, larch, maple, oak, pine, spruce, and walnut.

Here, any tree could go anywhere on the diagram, so the stock would be symbolized like this:

F G L M O P S W	1	2	3	4

5.2.2.2 One Stock, Repeated For Each Row

In other Grid games, the same stock is repeated, in a different order, in each row. In these games, you should write the stock to the left of each row that it will be used to fill.

For example:

> Over a period of five consecutive days, Monday through Friday, a company will conduct an annual review of its five offices—J, K, L, M, and N. Each office will be reviewed once by the company's president and once by its vice president. Each executive will review one office each day.

		Mon	Tue	Wed	Thu	Fri
J K L M N	President					
J K L M N	Vice president					

This signifies that you will have to place the entire stock in each row. The diagram will contain two of each element, but no element can appear twice in the same row.

5.2.2.3 Different Stock for Different Rows

There are also Grid games that contain different stocks for different rows. Write each stock to the left of the row that those elements will occupy.

Here's an example:

> An orchestra will perform musical compositions by three classical composers—Tchaikovsky, Verdi, and Wagner. Five compositions will be performed, each of which is a choral piece, an opera, or a symphony. The five compositions will be performed one at a time, in order.

		1	2	3	4	5
T V W	Composer					
C O S	Type					

Since there are only three composers for five different compositions, some of them will have to be repeated, but the elements T, V, and W can appear only in the top row. Similarly, C, O, and S will be repeated but can appear only in the bottom row.

5.2.2.4 Other Situations

Since every game comes with its own unique idiosyncrasies, you have to be ready for unique ways in which the stock may have to be symbolized. Your guiding principle, however, is that when a row has certain elements that must fill it, you should write the stock for that row next to the row.

Take a look at this example:

> An electronics store is open exactly five days every week: Monday through Friday. Its staff consists of exactly six people—Jared, Kevin, Nick, Olivia, Patrick, and Sandy. Exactly three of them—Jared, Nick, and Patrick—are technicians. Each day's staff consists of exactly two people, at least one of whom is a technician.

Since there must be two people working on each day, the diagram has two rows. To ensure that you remember to place at least one technician on each day, set aside one of the rows for technicians only. The stock for that row will contain only the technicians. The day's other employee could be anyone, so the stock for the second row will contain all the employees

		Mon	Tue	Wed	Thu	Fri
J N P	The required technician					
J K N O P S	The other employee					

5.2.3 SYMBOLIZING THE RULES

While Grid games contain the same order, block, barbell, and exact position rules that appear in Ordering games and the same conditionals that appear in Binary games, there are also some rules that apply especially to Grid games and have their own symbols.

Vertical Blocks

You are already familiar with block rules as they apply to Ordering games. They are typically used to symbolize elements that must be placed in *consecutive* spots in the order. Grid games can also contain rules that require elements to be placed in the *same* spot in the order. In such cases, use a **vertical block**.

Consider the following rule:

> The president reviews J on the same day on which the vice president reviews K.

> Your overall guiding principle for stocks is to put the elements that must fill a row or column next to that row or column.

This rule is correctly symbolized with a vertical block:

It's important to keep the vertical block in the same orientation as your diagram. In this example, the **J** is at the *top* of the vertical block because the president's order of reviews is the *top* row of the diagram.

Grid games in which you create a spatial arrangement can also feature vertical blocks.

Take a look at this rule:

Oscar sits directly behind Peter.

	Window	Middle	Aisle
Row J (front)			
Row K			
Row L (back)			

This rule is also symbolized with a vertical block because when a person sits directly behind another, the two people are vertically adjacent on the diagram. Thus, the symbol should match that vertical relationship.

Vertical Antiblocks

Use a **vertical antiblock** when a rule tells you that two elements may not be vertically adjacent on the diagram. For example,

No Tchaikovsky composition is an opera.

is symbolized

Similarly,

George may not sit directly in front of Harry.

is symbolized

to signify that George cannot be placed directly above Harry and Harry cannot be placed directly below George.

Soft Blocks

Many Grid games and Ordering games contain rules that tell you that two elements must be placed in consecutive spots, but they do not specify which element precedes the other. For these rules, you do not want to box the elements into a specific relative position because their order could vary. Instead, use a **soft block**—place an oval around the elements instead of a box to signify that they can move around within the oval but are still constrained by it. For example, a rule that reads

> Soft blocks are a very common feature in Ordering games.

The electricity is installed in U and V on consecutive days.

is symbolized

This tells you that U and V must remain adjacent, but their order may change. Either element could precede the other.

Vertical Soft Blocks

The same idea applies in Grid games to rules that tell you two elements must be vertically adjacent but that do not indicate which element is in which row. For example,

The magician performs at the same time as the puppeteer.

	2 PM	3 PM	4 PM
East Stage			
West Stage			

is symbolized

to signify that they must perform at the same time, but their respective stages could vary.

Soft Antiblocks

There are also rules that state that two elements cannot be horizontally or vertically adjacent, regardless of their positions relative to each other. For example,

The juggler and the sword swallower perform at different times.

	2 PM	3 PM	4 PM
East Stage			
West Stage			

should be symbolized like an antiblock, but with a oval instead of a box:

Similarly,

The electricity is not installed in T and Y on consecutive days.

is symbolized

These symbols show you that the two elements inside the soft antiblock are forbidden to be next to each other, regardless of their order.

Generic Rules

Many games contain rules that pertain to all of the elements. For example,

No consecutive songs are played with the same instrument.

Rather than writing a separate antiblock for every instrument, come up with a symbol that applies to all elements by using a generic letter to represent any instrument:

If you do this, make sure to use a letter that is not the first initial of one of the elements so as to avoid confusion.

Barbells Across Rows

A barbell symbol signifies that a single element must be placed on one of two spots in your diagram. Use this symbol regardless of whether those spots are in different rows and columns. So, a rule that states

Winterhaven either has carpet installed on Tuesday or is fumigated on Friday.

is symbolized

	Mon	Tue	Wed	Thu	Fri
Carpeting		Ⓦ			
Fumigation					◯

Barbells With Two Elements

Some barbell rules tell you that two elements must occupy two spots on the dia-gram, but they don't tell you which one goes where. In these cases, fill the two circles of the barbell with the two elements. This kind of rule could appear on any game type. For example,

The klezmer band and the rockabilly band are the first and the last bands to play, though not necessarily in that order.

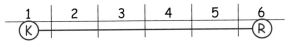

Just like the other barbells you have used before, the elements can slide along the line and stop in one of the circles. The difference here is that there are two elements sharing the same barbell, so if one of them moves, the other must switch places with it. You can say for sure that only **K** or **R** could be in the first spot, and only **K** or **R** could be in the last spot.

Exact Row or Column, Forbidden Row or Column

When an Ordering game tells you the exact spot an element must (or cannot) occupy, you symbolize it by placing it directly on the diagram in the appropriate spot. Some Grid games contain similar rules that tell you the exact row or column an element must (or cannot) occupy, but they don't narrow it down precisely to a single spot within that row or column.

You should still symbolize the rule directly on your diagram, but you won't be able to put the symbol in a particular spot. Instead, put it above the appropriate column or to the left of the appropriate row.

Take a look at this example:

Quincy sits in a middle seat.
Ralph may not sit in an aisle seat.
Shigeru sits in row J.
Tai may not sit in row L.

		Window	Q Middle	~R Aisle
S	Row J			
	Row K			
~T	Row L			

By putting **Q** above the column of middle seats, you create a miniature stock that says **Q** must be used in this column only. The **~R** symbol shows that **R** is forbidden in the column of aisle seats. The symbols for **S** and **T** show the same things for their respective rows.

Conditionals With Subscripts

So far, you have used conditionals only in Binary games, in which there are only two possible spots for each element, such as *yes* or *no*, *selected* or *not selected*. In many games, however, an element could occupy more than two different spots. When con-ditional rules appear in these games, the normal "~" symbol used for *yes* and *no* is not enough to denote all the different possible spots. In these cases, you have to add subscripts to your conditional symbols.

Consider the following rule:

If the pipes are unloaded fifth, then the tires are unloaded seventh.

This is clearly a conditional rule since it contains *if* and *then*. However, it is associated with an order that has at least seven spots. Symbolize it like this:

$$P_5 \longrightarrow T_7$$

In order to make the contrapositive, you have to Switch and Negate. How do you negate these symbols? The negation of "pipes fifth" is simply "pipes not fifth." Unfortunately, you can't get any more specific than that because there are lots of spots in the order that are not fifth. The symbol looks like this:

$$\sim T_7 \longrightarrow \sim P_5$$

5.2.4   Drill: Symbolizing the Rules

Draw the appropriate symbol for each of the following rules in the space provided. Decide whether each symbol should be drawn on the diagram or to the left of it.

1. Oranges and peaches are not sold at adjacent fruit stands.

2. Over the course of a week, two cars are serviced each day, one in the morning and one in the afternoon.
    The sedan is serviced in the morning.

	Mon	Tue	Wed	Thu	Fri
S Morning					
Aft					

3. If the action movie is shown on the fourth day, then the comedy is shown on the third day.

    $$A_4 \rightarrow C_3$$
    $$\sim C_3 \rightarrow \sim A_4$$

4. On a vacation, travelers visit exactly two areas each day.
    The travelers visit the ocean the same day they visit the plains.

    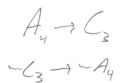

Mon	Tue	Wed	Thu	Fri

5. Either Leonard or Mildred presents first, and the other presents fourth.

    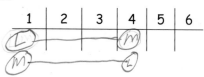

1	2	3	4	5	6

6. Freddie does not sit directly behind Erica.

7. Two repairs are made each day.
    The roof is not repaired on Thursday.

M	T	W	Th	F

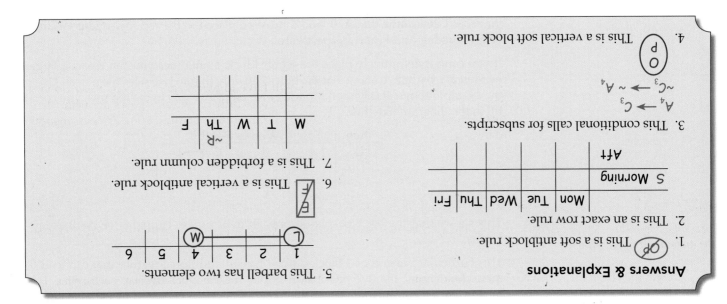

Answers & Explanations

1. This is a soft antiblock rule.

2. This is an exact row rule.

	Mon	Tue	Wed	Thu	Fri
S Morning					
A++					

3. This conditional calls for subscripts.

$$A_4 \rightarrow C_3$$
$$\sim C_3 \rightarrow \sim A_4$$

4. This is a vertical soft block rule.

5. This barbell has two elements.

	1	2	3	4	5	6

(L) and (W)

6. This is a vertical antiblock rule.

7. This is a forbidden column rule.

M	W	T	Th	F
			~R	

5.3 DEDUCE

5.3.1 COMBINING THE SYMBOLS

As with other games, the symbols you create in Grid games can be combined around common elements to produce more complete symbols that allow you to answer questions more quickly and more easily than you would be able to with individual symbols.

Blocks

You saw before that you can combine two horizontal blocks to form a larger block. The same can be done with two vertical blocks. You can also combine vertical blocks with horizontal blocks.

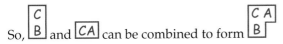

So, $\boxed{\begin{smallmatrix}C\\B\end{smallmatrix}}$ and $\boxed{CA}$ can be combined to form $\boxed{\begin{smallmatrix}C\,A\\B\end{smallmatrix}}$

This lets you know that whenever you place A, B, or C, you must place the remaining elements in the positions indicated by the block.

Antiblocks

Don't make deductions using antiblocks. Combining or making other deductions with antiblocks is not helpful and will often lead to confusion or mistakes.

For example, if you combined ⟨X/Y⟩ and ⟨Y/Z⟩ into one block, the result would be ⟨X/Y/Z⟩

While it is true that this exact configuration is not allowed, this symbol implies that Z cannot be below and to the right of X, which is actually allowed. It is more accurate and less confusing to leave antiblocks as separate symbols.

> In general, antiblocks, conditionals, and forbidden spot rules are stingy when it comes to allowing deductions. Don't spend too much time looking for deductions that can be made from these types of rules.

5.3.2 Placing Blocks

Creating larger block symbols can also help you make further deductions and may even enable you to place the blocks.

If you have a block consisting of three elements, then you need three consecutive open spaces in order to be able to place any of those elements. For example, if you had the block $\boxed{ABC}$ and a master diagram that looked like this:

Mon	Tue	Wed	Thu	Fri
	D			
		E		

you could determine that **A**, **B**, and **C** must be placed in the top row under Wednesday, Thursday, and Friday, respectively.

If you cannot definitively place the whole block, sometimes you can create a larger version of a barbell to show that the block can only fit into two possible places. Using the example above, if **D** was on Monday instead of Tuesday in the top row, you could fill in the diagram like this:

Mon	Tue	Wed	Thu	Fri
D	A	B	C	
		E		

This shows that the big block could only fit in Tuesday–Thursday or Wednesday–Friday.

This particular version of a block-barbell has an additional feature that can lead to more deductions: the two possible positions for the block overlap each other. This means that Wednesday and Thursday will definitely be occupied by elements in the block, and you can narrow those spots down to an either/or symbol. Tuesday is not as restricted, since it could hold **A** or a number of other elements, as could Friday. You can refine the diagram to look like this:

Mon	Tue	Wed	Thu	Fri
D		A/B	B/C	
		E		

5.3.3   Free Agents

Take special notice of **free agents**—elements that do not appear in any of the rules.

Big blocks like the one discussed above are important to focus on because they contain some of the most constrained elements—elements to which the rules give a very limited set of choices for where they could go. Since the choices are so limited, you should start each question by considering where the big block could be placed, or considering what could happen to elements that are highly constrained by the rules in other ways.

At the opposite end of the spectrum, many games contain an element that does not appear in any of the rules. It is completely unconstrained and can be placed absolutely anywhere in the diagram, as long as the other elements follow their rules. These completely unconstrained elements are called **free agents**, and it's important to notice them because you can use them to fill in parts of your diagram without having to worry about whether they are breaking any rules.

After you have finished symbolizing the rules, look at each element in your stock and determine whether it is constrained by any rules. If not, underline it in the stock to remind yourself that it is a free agent. For example:

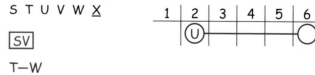

5.4   PUTTING IT ALL TOGETHER

5.4.1   Drill: Grid Games

Below is a situation with rules. Identify the type of game and set it up by drawing an appropriate diagram and symbolizing the stock and rules. Then make as many deductions as you can.

Five poets—Frida, Harlan, Minnie, Quentin, and Tabitha—will present their work, one at a time, during each of two reading sessions—session 1 and session 2. The scheduling of the reading sessions is subject to the following conditions:

Minnie presents first or last in each session.
Quentin presents last at least once.
Harlan presents immediately before or immediately after Quentin in each session.
If Frida presents before Tabitha in session 1, then she presents after Tabitha in session 2.

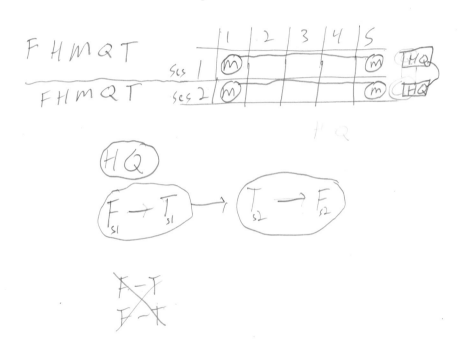

5.4.2 ANSWERS & EXPLANATIONS

Identify

Several features identify this as a Grid game. The situation asks you to *order* the five poets in *two different* sessions, meaning one row will not be enough to contain all the elements. The rules discuss sequential positions, such as *first* and *last*. They also state that certain people present *before* or *after* others. Additionally, the rules indicate that more than one order will have to be determined by mentioning that certain people present in a certain position *in each session* or *at least once*. Finally, no elements are left out of either of the sequences. This is a Grid game.

Set Up

The diagram for this game starts with a grid with five columns—numbered 1–5 to represent the first poet, the second poet, and so on—and two rows—labeled Session 1 and Session 2, to represent each of the two reading sessions.

The stock in this game is composed of the initials of the five poets: F H M Q T. Since the situation tells you that each poet presents in each reading session, write the entire stock to the left of each row.

		1	2	3	4	5
F H M Q T	Session 1					
F H M Q T	Session 2					

To complete the Set Up, symbolize each of the rules.

Rule 1 is a barbell rule that applies to both sessions. Put this on the diagram to show that **M** goes first or last in each session.

Rule 2 is another barbell rule that says that **Q** goes in at least one fifth spot. Put this on the diagram as well.

Rule 3 is a soft block rule. Symbolize it as $\boxed{HQ}$

Rule 4: If **F** goes before **T** in the first session, then their order is reversed for the second session. This is a wonderful example of an opportunity to think about what a rule *means* rather than what it says. When you do this, you can make symbols that are cleaner and more efficient, and you gain insight into how the elements will interact with the diagram. For example, if you tried to symbolize the literal wording of the rule, you might come up with

$$F_{S1} - T_{S1} \rightarrow T_{S2} - F_{S2}$$
$$F_{S2} - T_{S2} \rightarrow T_{S1} - F_{S1}$$

This is certainly correct, but it is a little hard on the eyes. It's not simple to glance at it and instantly recognize what the rule entails and whether the configuration you're working on at the moment follows the rule. A better way to symbolize the rule would be to figure out what is *not* allowed. You can see that any time **F** comes before **T** in one of the sequences, you can't let it happen again in the other sequence. So a different symbol could be

$$\frac{F - \cancel{T}}{\cancel{F} - T}$$

This is definitely cleaner. For those interested in ultimate efficiency, you can put the symbol in terms of what *must* happen:

$$\text{At least one } T - F$$

-OR-

$$1^+ \ T - F$$

That last one is really elegant, especially compared to the very first symbol. It's nicer on the eyes and gives a better understanding of the guidelines you'll need to follow as you put together different configurations. This is a thought process that you should practice frequently. When symbolizing a complicated rule, ask, "Is this the most efficient way to write this? How will this rule really work within the context of the game?"

At this point, your diagram should look like this:

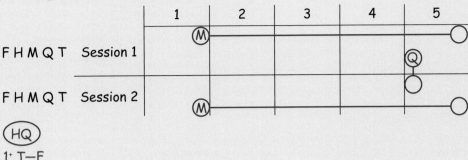

Deduce

A few simple deductions can be made. Since **Q** will be fifth at least once, then **H** will be fourth at least once. You can turn the barbell for **Q** into a barbell between two blocks for **H** and **Q**. Although the block for **H** and **Q** started off as a soft bock, you can convert it into a regular block here as the two elements will have to appear in that set order. You also know that when **Q** is fifth, then **M** will have to be first, but your symbols already make this pretty clear, so there is no need to go out of your way to make a new symbol for this.

These are all the deductions that you can make, so draw a box around this grid to signify that it is the master diagram to which you will refer when answering the questions and creating other grids for specific questions.

MASTER DIAGRAM

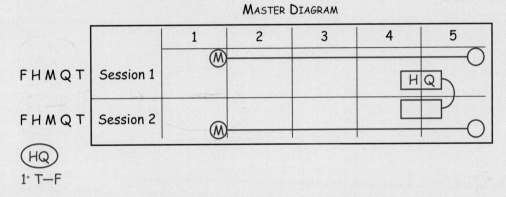

NOW MOVE ON TO THE SECOND CHAPTER OF LECTURE 3. WHEN YOU HAVE COMPLETED IT, YOU CAN GET FURTHER PRACTICE WITH GRID GAMES IN THE CORRESPONDING EXAM AT THE END OF THE BOOK.

LECTURE ③ CHAPTER 6

SPOT & ELEMENT QUESTIONS

Spot questions and **Element questions** have a lot in common with Truth questions in that their question stems are always concerned with what must, could, or cannot be true.

The difference is that Spot and Element questions have a much narrower scope. Instead of asking you about your deductions throughout the entire diagram, these questions ask where a *particular element* must be, or which element must fill a *certain spot*. Because the question stem is more specific, you can usually focus your work more efficiently and often predict the correct answer before looking at the answer choices.

6.1 IDENTIFY THE QUESTION

Element questions have stems that ask you about what happens to a particular *element*. They can come in Local or Universal varieties.

Here are some examples of Element question stems:

> If Bamforth's second appointment is with Ward, then Bamforth's appointment with Ovrahim must be the

> Which one of the following could be the bin holding apples?

> If Juvencio staffs the third booth, exactly how many different booths could be the booth staffed by Duane?

> Which one of the following CANNOT be the cage occupied by the liger?

Spot questions have stems that ask you about what happens in a particular *spot*. They can also come in Local or Universal varieties.

Here are some examples of Spot question stems:

> Which one of the following advertisements CANNOT be the one featured on billboard 4?

> Which one of the following is a pair of bicycles that, if assembled on the same day as each other, must be assembled on Tuesday?

> Which one of the following dishes could be served sixth?

> If Omnicorp is included in the audit, which one of the following companies must also be included in the audit?

6.2 WORK THE DIAGRAM

As with all Local questions, working the diagram on Local Spot and Element questions is a vital step. Since every Local question gives you a new rule, you should deal with that rule just as you do with the original rules of the game:

Everything you learned in Chapter 4 regarding Truth questions is also applicable to Spot and Element questions.

1. **Symbolize the new rule either directly on the diagram if you can or to the *right* of the diagram.** The overall rules of the game are symbolized to the *left* of the diagram. The new rule given in a Local question applies only to that question, so you don't want to get it confused with the overall rules of the game. Set aside a new row below your master diagram to work on the question at hand, and symbolize the new rule in or to the right of that row.

2. **Make as many deductions as you can with the new rule.** You will *always* be able to make deductions with the new rule, and the correct answer will *always* be concerned with these new deductions.

The new deductions you make could be anywhere on the diagram, but since Spot and Element questions are concerned with a particular part of the game, you should always pay particular attention to a spot or element named in the question stem. If you deduce something new about that spot or element, check the answer choices to see if you have done enough to find the correct answer. However, be aware that you may have to make deductions about other parts of the diagram before you can determine what's happening to the part you're focused on.

Take a look at this example. It comes from the Poets game that you worked on at the end of Chapter 5.

1. If Tabitha presents fifth in session 1, then Frida could present

    (A)   first in session 1
    (B)   third in session 1
    (C)   fourth in session 1
    (D)   first in session 2
    (E)   second in session 2

This is an Element question because it specifically asks you about **F**. It's also a Local question because it gives you a new rule. As you work the diagram, pay particular attention to where **F** could go.

First, fill in the new rule on a separate grid in your diagram by putting **T** fifth.

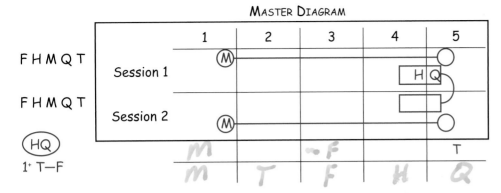

MASTER DIAGRAM

Then, make all the deductions you can. A lot can be determined with just this one piece of information.

Since **Q** didn't go last in session 1, it must do so in session 2. That means that **H** comes right before it. **M** therefore goes first in both sessions, and that leaves the second and third spots for **F** and **T** in session 2. Note that since **T** went last in session 1, it had to have gone after **F**. Therefore, it must go before **F** in session 2.

	1	2	3	4	5
Session 1	M				T
Session 2	M	T	F	H	Q

There are now only three spots left, all in session 1. The remaining elements, **H**, **Q**, and **F**, can go anywhere, as long as **H** and **Q** are not separated. That means that **F** is forbidden in the third spot, but anything else is allowed.

Your diagram should now look like this:

	1	2	3	4	5
Session 1	M		~F		T
Session 2	M	T	F	H	Q

Now you've done enough work to predict the correct answer. Since the stem asked you where **F** could go, you know there are only three correct answers: second or fourth in session 1, or third in session 2. All you have to do is look for an answer choice that matches what you predicted. Choice (C) looks like a winner.

Choice (C) is the correct answer.

6.3   ATTACK

In the last example, you were able to arrive at the answer directly. You didn't need to look at the answer choices until after you had already determined exactly where **F** was allowed to be. Not all Spot and Element questions are so easy. Sometimes you have to attack the answer choices.

6.3.1   ATTACKING LOCAL SPOT AND ELEMENT QUESTIONS

Imagine that you were unable to see the last deduction in the previous example (the one that told you that **F** could not be third in session 1). In that case, it would look like both choices (B) and (C) were correct. To figure out which one was really correct, you would have to try out the answer choices in the diagram.

You learned in Chapter 4 that to try out a question stem that asks you what *could be true*, you should try to prove it in your diagram by coming up with a configuration in which it's true. This question stem, in not so many words, is asking, "It *could be true* that Frida presents…" so try to make choices (B) and (C) true in your diagram.

First try choice (B). Place **F** third in session 1, keeping the other deductions you already made:

	1	2	3	4	5
Session 1	M		F		T
Session 2	M	T	F	H	Q

ILLEGAL

This is problematic because now there is no place for **H** and **Q**, which must be consecutive. Choice (B) is impossible, so eliminate it.

Now try choice (C). Here's one way to put **F** fourth:

	1	2	3	4	5
Session 1	M	H	Q	F	T
Session 2	M	T	F	H	Q

Choice (C) is possible, meaning it *could be true*. Thus, you have proven that choice (C) is correct by trying out the answer choice in your diagram.

6.3.2 ATTACKING UNIVERSAL SPOT AND ELEMENT QUESTIONS

When you encounter a Universal Spot or Element question, you have to go through the same process. Since the question stem of every Universal question gives you no new information to work with, the only tools at your disposal are your master diagram and the answer choices.

Sometimes, your master diagram is enough to get you the answer. You should always check there first. For example,

2. Which one of the following poets could present fourth in both sessions?

    (A) Frida
    (B) Harlan
    (C) Minnie
    (D) Quentin
    (E) Tabitha

This is a Spot question because it's asking you about the fourth spot. It's also a Universal question because the question stem gives you no new rules to follow. So, look to your master diagram. In the fourth spot you deduced that **H** has to appear at least once, so in order to have the same person fourth both times, that person has to be **H**.

Choice (B) is the correct answer.

Sometimes, however, your master diagram is not enough. This is often the case with Binary games or other games in which the rules usually don't allow you to deduce very much about definite placements on the diagram. In such cases, you have to attack the answer choices.

Here's another Universal Spot question that involves a more intense attacking of the answer choices.

3. Which one of the following pairs CANNOT exchange positions in the order between session 1 and session 2?

    (A) Frida and Quentin
    (B) Frida and Tabitha
    (C) Harlan and Minnie
    (D) Harlan and Tabitha
    (E) Minnie and Quentin

This question asks you to identify a pair that cannot exchange positions from session 1 to session 2. Your master diagram isn't much help here, so your second tactic is to use your previous work. Unfortunately, you don't have much to look back on at this point, so just get down to work and attack each answer choice.

In this case, the question stem is acting like a *must be false* question. You'll recall that your strategy for these is to try to come up with a complete configuration that proves the answer choice could be true. If you're successful, you should eliminate the answer choice. If not, pick it.

Choice (A): **F** and **Q** could possibly switch, as shown in this configuration, so choice (A) could be true. That means you should get rid of it.

	1	2	3	4	5
Session 1	M	F	T	H	Q
Session 2	M	Q	H	T	F

Choice (B): It's also possible for **F** and **T** to switch, so get rid of this choice too:

	1	2	3	4	5
Session 1	M	T	F	H	Q
Session 2	M	F	T	H	Q

Choice (C): There's a problem here. If **M** is going to switch between two spots, those spots will have to be first and last, per rule 1. That means **H** would also have to be first and fifth. But then you would have no way to put **Q** last.

	1	2	3	4	5
Session 1	H				M
Session 2	M				H

ILLEGAL

Choice (C) is impossible, and that's what the question stem tells you to look for.

Choice (C) is the correct answer.

To summarize, the techniques you should use to approach Spot and Element questions are exactly the same ones you already learned about for Truth questions. The only difference is that, since the question stem asks you to focus on a particular piece of the game, you can focus your attention there. Once you've deduced something about the particular spot or element in question, you've usually done enough to answer the question, so check the choices and save yourself some time.

Since, in the Analytical Reasoning section, one answer choice is 100% correct and the others 100% wrong, you can stop looking at the answer choices as soon as you're confident you've found the right one. This saves time. However, if you're not sure whether you're approaching a game correctly or if you think you may have missed something, it is safer to check every answer choice.

STOP. THIS IS THE END OF LECTURE 3. DO NOT PROCEED TO THE CORRESPONDING EXAM UNTIL INSTRUCTED TO DO SO IN CLASS.

LECTURE (4) CHAPTER (7)

GROUPING GAMES

7.1 IDENTIFY THE GAME

7.1.1 WHAT IS A GROUPING GAME?

A **Grouping game** is almost exactly like a Binary game, except that it has more than two groups.

A Grouping game requires you to sort elements into **three or more** groups. Just as in Binary games, **order doesn't matter**. The only thing that matters is which group an element is in.

7.1.2 HOW TO RECOGNIZE GROUPING GAMES

Any situation that requires you to sort the elements into three or more groups, within which order is not important, is a Grouping game.

Most Grouping games clearly tell you the names of all the groups. Take a look at this example:

> A company has nine officers who oversee its three divisions—marketing, production, and treasury. Three officers oversee each division.

In this example, the three groups are Marketing, Production, and Treasury.

Some Grouping games don't give the groups names, such as this example:

> Three trucks will be used to ship seven products. Each product will be shipped by exactly one truck.

In this case, the groups are the trucks, but they don't have names. You can give the trucks names such as 1, 2, 3, or A, B, C, or even just leave the top of the diagram empty.

The Grouping games that are hardest to spot are the ones that tell you about only *two* groups but have a feature that means the elements will actually be distributed across *three*. Here's an example:

> A company will choose from nine applicants a staff for its two new offices—the Oakley branch and the Fishtown branch. Three applicants will be selected for each office and no applicant will be selected for more than one office

In this case, the situation tells you about the Oakley group and the Fishtown group, but there's more going on. You know that *only six* of the nine applicants will be selected, so the remaining three applicants will not be chosen. So this game actually features three groups: the Oakley group, the Fishtown group, and the Not Selected group.

All of these are Grouping games because they all require you to place the elements into three or more groups without regard to any order within those groups.

> Grouping games are the least common of the four major types. About half of all tests feature a Grouping game.

7.2 SET UP

7.2.1 HOW TO DRAW A GROUPING GAME DIAGRAM

Before you can draw your diagram, you need to determine which of the things mentioned in the situation you are going to use as the groups and which you are going to use as the elements. It is usually easier to place a lot of elements into a few groups than it is to place a few elements into many groups. Therefore, you should usually use the smaller set of things as the groups, and the larger set of things as the elements.

In any Grouping game, you should take notice of how the elements fit into the diagram. Ask yourself these questions:

• How many elements fit into each group?

• Are any elements used more than once?

• Are any elements not used at all? (This may necessitate an additional group.)

Your **backbone** for a Grouping game should consist of headings for each group, plus any information you have about how many elements will be placed in each group. This information may come from the rules rather than the situation, so you should always read the rules before deciding how to design your diagram.

Write a solid line to show the number of spots that you know for sure will be in any group.

Each store carries at least two of the products.

Grocery	Farmer's Market	Discount Store
__ __	__ __	__ __

After you have drawn your backbone, write your **stock** to the left of it. Make your stock as complete as you can. If you know that each element is used twice, your stock should consist of each element written twice.

If you know that each element may be used more than once, but don't how many times each will be used, simply write the stock once in the upper left to indicate that you can reuse it. Then, note next to each element anything that you know about it. For example, a game may tell you that the elements may be reused, and there may be a rule that states that a specific element will be used exactly twice. In his case, note this next to that element in your stock.

J K L M$^{(2)}$ N   Molly stars in exactly two of the plays.

This will help you quickly recognize that Molly must be placed exactly twice.

7.2.2 CATEGORIES OF ELEMENTS

In many games, the situation tells you that the elements fit into different categories. This can happen in any type of game. For example, an Ordering game may ask you to create an order for a set of people, some of whom are adults, and some of whom are children. When the situation tells you exactly which category every element fits into, then you should include that information when you write the stock of elements. Use uppercase and lowercase if there are two categories, and script if there is a third category (there has never been a game with more than three categories of elements). For example, take a look at this situation:

> A restaurant's staff consists of four cooks— F, G, H, and J—three servers—M, N, and O—and three runners—V, W, and Y. The ten employees are assigned to three shifts—breakfast, lunch, and dinner—subject to the following conditions:

In this case, there are three categories of elements: cooks, servers, and runners. The situation tells you exactly which category every element fits into. The stock, therefore, would look like this:

COOKS: F G H J	Breakfast	Lunch	Dinner
servers: m n o			
runners: v w y			

Games in which the elements fit into different categories can be some of the most complicated ones. If you run across one, consider postponing it until you've completed any simpler games.

Writing the stock like this allows you to recognize the different categories when placing the elements, which is generally very important. When you place the elements into the diagram, you should write them the same way they appear in the stock. For example, if you placed the cook G into Lunch, you would write it in uppercase, and if you put the server m into Dinner, you would write it in lowercase.

Notice that writing the stock this way only applies when the situation has *already told you* exactly which category each element fits into. This is not the same as a game that requires you to *figure out* that information about the elements. For example, if the restaurant game above asked you instead to determine the order in which the employees take their breaks and *figure out* what kind of employee each person was, then the game would be a Grid game, with one of the rows in your diagram dedicated to figuring out what kind of employee each person was. The stock would then simply consist of the elements, without any information about their types.

When elements are separated into categories, there are often rules that dictate where elements of a certain category must be placed. Symbolize this by creating a reserved spot and writing below it which category must be placed there.

At least one cook is assigned to each shift.

Breakfast	Lunch	Dinner
__	__	__
C	C	C

Other rules state that elements from a certain category cannot be placed in a certain group. Symbolize this above the appropriate column.

No servers work during the breakfast shift.

Breakfast	Lunch	Dinner
~s		

7.2.3 Symbolizing the Rules

Many of the rules in Grouping games are conditionals, but when there are more than two categories, you will usually need to use subscripts to identify the relevant groups. So,

> If Matt lives in the third dorm, then Neil lives in the second dorm.

is symbolized

$$M_3 \longrightarrow N_2$$

To create the contrapositive, you still **Switch and Negate** the symbol to represent

> If Neil does not live in the second dorm, then Matt doesn't live in the third dorm.

$$\sim N_2 \longrightarrow \sim M_3$$

You don't have to create conditional symbols for rules that tell you that two elements must be placed in the same group or cannot be placed in the same group. Instead, use blocks or anti-blocks.

> Justin and Karyn do not attend the same concert.

$$\boxed{\text{J̸K}}$$

> Leah and Melissa must attend the same concert.

$$\boxed{\text{LM}}$$

Some rules state that certain elements may not appear together within a certain group. You still want to use an antiblock, but since it applies to only one of the groups, not all of them, put the antiblock in the appropriate column for that group.

The third stand does not sell both yams and zucchini.

1	2	3
		$\boxed{\text{Y̸Z}}$

> [!NOTE]
> Notice how the block symbol is used to mean slightly different things in Ordering games and Grouping games. In Ordering games, a block means two elements have to occupy consecutive spots. In Grouping games, a block means two elements have to occupy the same group.

7.3 DEDUCE

7.3.1 Reserved Spots

There is a certain kind of conditional rule that can usually lead to a very useful deduction in Binary games and Grouping games. When you see a conditional symbol in which the ~'s are lined up on one side in both the original and the contrapositive, you can usually reserve a spot in one of the groups for the elements in the conditional. Take a look at this example, from a Binary game:

If Shemika goes to Milan, then Tonia goes to Paris.

$$S \longrightarrow \sim T$$

$$T \longrightarrow \sim S$$

Milan	Not Milan (Paris)

Don't make the mistake of thinking this rule means S and T can't go to the same city. These are all the ways to arrange S and T:

Milan	Not Milan (Paris)	
S	T	Allowed
T	S	
	S T	
S T		Not allowed

Most people recognize the first two ways, but don't forget that it's also possible for both S and T to go to Paris. In fact, the only situation that is *not* allowed is for both of them to go to Milan.

The important deduction here is that in every legal way to arrange S and T, *at least one of them is always in Paris.* Thus, you can reserve a spot in the Paris group—set aside a spot that must be occupied by either S or T, and remember that it's also possible for both of them to be in Paris.

Milan	Not Milan (Paris)
	S/T

Why is this such a useful deduction? Because now you know a little more about *how many* elements must fit into the different groups, and how the elements must be arranged. If, for example, you saw a Rule Tester that asked you about acceptable configurations for the Paris group, you could easily eliminate any answer choice that didn't have either S or T.

The same process can be used when the ~'s line up on the left-hand side of the conditionals:

If Upton goes to Paris, then Vince goes to Milan.
$$\sim U \longrightarrow V$$
$$\sim V \longrightarrow U$$

In this case, these are the possible ways to arrange the elements:

Milan	Not Milan (Paris)	
V	U	⎤
U	V	⎦— Allowed
U V		
	U V ←	Not allowed

Again, in every legal case, at least one of them is always in Milan, so you can reserve a spot in Milan for at least one from the pair U and V.

Milan	Not Milan (Paris)
U/V	

> The test writers often find various ways to ask you about reserved spots, so understanding this concept is an important skill to master.

You can also make this kind of deduction in some Grouping games, but you have to be a little more careful. In general, look for cases in which at least one element from a certain pair must always be in a particular group. Specifically, this will most often occur when the ~'s line up on the left-hand side, and the rule only mentions *one* group. Consider this example:

If Jeb does not grow corn, then Marvin does.

$$\sim J_c \longrightarrow M_c$$
$$\sim M_c \longrightarrow J_c$$

Corn	Beans	Squash

If you think about this rule, you'll see that at least one of them must grow corn. So, you can reserve a spot in the Corn group for either J or M.

Corn	Beans	Squash
J/M		

7.3.1.1 When To Avoid Reserved Spots

There are some situations in which you should not create reserved spots. This would be when doing so is likely to lead to confusion, mistakes, or wasted time. In order to avoid this:

1. **Create reserved spots using the original rules only,** not deductions, chains, or linked rules.

2. **Don't create more that one reserved spot involving the same element.**

3. **Don't create reserved spots using conditionals with AND or OR.**

4. **Don't create a reserved spot when you're not sure if it's correct.**

7.3.2 Distribution and Scenarios

Many Grouping games don't explicitly tell you how many elements must fit into each group, but you can often make some deductions that allow you to figure this out, either partially or completely.

Discovering reserved spots is often the first step in this process. It also pays to look out for big blocks and rules that discuss the numerical distribution of the elements. Always keep in mind the total number of elements. Take a look at this example:

> Eight animals are housed in three habitats, numbered 1–3.
> Each habitat houses at least one animal and each animal is
> housed in exactly one habitat.
> Habitat 3 houses exactly twice as many animals as habitat 2.

There are only a few ways to distribute the animals and satisfy the rules. The smallest number of animals you could put in habitat 2 would be one. In that case, you know exactly how many have to be in the other habitats:

>   Habitat 1: five animals
>
>   Habitat 2: one animal
>
>   Habitat 3: two animals

What else could you do? You could put two animals into habitat 2:

>   Habitat 1: two animals
>
>   Habitat 2: two animals
>
>   Habitat 3: four animals

That's it! you can't put three animals into habitat 2, because you would need six in habitat 3, but there aren't enough animals to do that.

Therefore, you can narrow the distribution of the elements down to two scenarios:

	Habitat 1	Habitat 2	Habitat 3
Scenario ①	_ _ _ _ _	_	_ _
Scenario ②	_ _	_ _	_ _ _ _

> Splitting a game into scenarios can be tremendously useful in some games, but in others it's a waste of time. It's best used when one very constrained piece of a game affects a lot of other elements as soon as it's placed. In order to build your intuition for when this is a good technique to use, try doing it often in your untimed homework games, and evaluate after each game whether it helped you or not.

These two scenarios then form your master diagram. You should make as many deductions as you can for *each* scenario. Splitting the game into two scenarios can lead to tremendously useful deductions. For each question you encounter, the first thing you should figure out is which scenario you are dealing with. For example, if a question stem began by saying, "If the marmots and the weevils are in habitat 2..." then you could be sure that you're dealing with the second scenario, since that's the only one with enough room for two animals in habitat 2. Knowing this would allow you to work the question much more quickly.

CHAPTER 7: GROUPING GAMES • 85

Even if you are not able to determine that there are only a couple of possible scenarios for the distribution of the elements into the groups, you should make deductions to determine the number of times each element may be used. As an example, consider the following situation and rules:

> Five campers—Ken, Lisa, Meagan, Nathan, and Pam—
> participate in at least one of three activities: archery, basket-
> weaving, and canoeing, but do not participate in any other
> activities. The following conditions apply:
>> Ken participates in more activities than Meagan.
>> Ken and Nathan do not participate in any of the same
>> activities.

You can determine from the first rule that Ken participates in more than one activity and Meagan participates in fewer than three activities.

The second rule means that Ken does not participate in all three activities (because there is at least one activity in which Nathan participates and Ken does not).

So, Ken must participate in two activities, which means that Meagan—who participates in fewer activities than Ken—and Nathan—who does not participate in any activity in which Ken participates—each participate in one activity. Symbolize this in your stock.

This also allows you to determine that, since Nathan participates in the only activity in which Ken does not participate, every activity has either Ken or Nathan as a participant. Symbolize this on your master diagram.

$K^{(2)}$ L $M^{(1)}$ $N^{(1)}$ P

Archery	Basket-weaving	Canoeing
K/N	K/N	K/N

Copyright © 2007 Examkrackers, Inc.

7.4   PUTTING IT ALL TOGETHER

7.4.1   Drill: Grouping Games

Below is a situation with rules. Identify the type of game and set it up by drawing an appropriate diagram and symbolizing the stock and rules. Then make as many deductions as you can.

Seven teachers—Hector, Juan, Kira, Nell, Patrick, Ronnie, and Trent—work at a school. One of them teaches gym, three of them teach math, and three of them teach science. None of them teaches more than one of those subjects. The following conditions must apply:

    Kira and Patrick teach different subjects.
    If Nell teaches math, then Trent teaches science.
    Hector and Ronnie teach the same subject.
    Patrick teaches math.

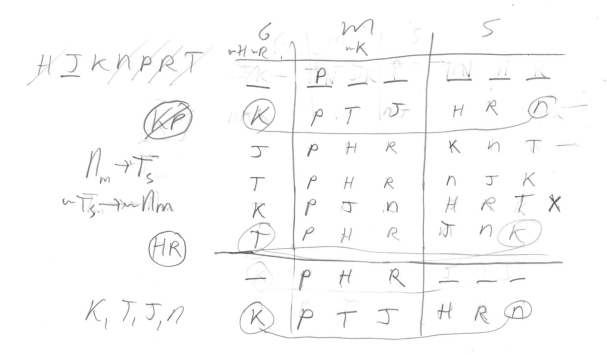

7.4.2 ANSWERS & EXPLANATIONS

Identify

Several features identify this as a Grouping game. The situation asks you to sort the elements into three groups. The rules discuss elements being in the same or different groups, and there is a conditional rule that references the groups. Finally, there is no mention of any order.

Set Up

The diagram for this game starts with columns for each group. Since you know the name of each group, label the columns by subject. The situation tells you how many elements are in each group, so set aside one spot under Gym, while Math and Science each have three spots.

The stock is composed of the initials of the seven teachers. Since each element will be used only once, write the stock to the left of the top row in the diagram.

HJKNRPT | Gym | Math | Science

To complete the Set Up step, symbolize each of the rules.

Rule 1 is an antiblock rule. Symbolize it as $\overline{KP}$

Rule 2 is a conditional rule. Use subscripts to identify the relevant groups:

$$N_M \rightarrow T_S \qquad \sim T_S \rightarrow \sim N_M$$

Rule 3 is a block rule. Symbolize it as $\boxed{HR}$

Rule 4 is an exact position rule, so add it directly to one of the Math spaces in your diagram.

At this point, your diagram should look like this:

HJKNRPT | Gym | Math (P) | Science

$\overline{KP}$ $N_M \rightarrow T_S$ $\sim T_S \rightarrow \sim N_M$ $\boxed{HR}$

Deduce

You can make a few deductions. Since H and R are always together, neither of them can teach Gym, since there is only one spot for that subject. And since P, who is always in Math, cannot teach with K, then K cannot teach Math. Your master diagram should look like this:

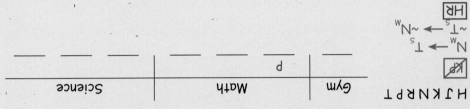

MASTER DIAGRAM

HJKNRPT | Gym (~H ~R) | Math (~K, P) | Science

$\boxed{KP}$ $N_M \rightarrow T_S$ $\sim T_S \rightarrow \sim N_M$ $\boxed{HR}$

NOW MOVE ON TO THE SECOND CHAPTER OF LECTURE 4. WHEN YOU HAVE COMPLETED IT, YOU CAN GET FURTHER PRACTICE WITH GROUPING GAMES IN THE CORRESPONDING EXAM AT THE END OF THE BOOK.

LECTURE 4 CHAPTER 8

LIST QUESTIONS AND SCENARIOS

List questions ask you to make a list of all the elements that could be (or cannot be) placed in a particular spot, or ask you to make a list of all the spots into which a certain element could be (or cannot be) placed.

8.1   IDENTIFY THE QUESTION

List questions have the following characteristics:

1. **The question stem asks for a *complete and accurate list* of elements that could occupy a particular spot or a *complete and accurate list* of spots that could be occupied by a particular element.**

2. **The question stem refers to either a specific element or a specific spot on the diagram.**

3. **The answer choices are composed of either a list of elements or a list of spots.**

Here are some examples of List questions:

> If Keri renovates the gymnasium, which one of the following is a complete and accurate list of buildings any one of which could be renovated by John?

> Which one of the following is a complete and accurate list of teams that CANNOT be ranked fifth?

> If the soybeans are planted third during the first cycle, which one of the following is a complete and accurate list of crops any one of which could be planted fourth during the second cycle?

All of these questions refer to a particular element or spot and ask for a *complete and accurate list* of spots or of elements, indicating the answer choices will be lists of spots or lists of elements. List questions can come in Local or Universal versions.

Don't confuse List questions with Rule Tester questions. Although both question stems often use the phrase "complete and accurate," the two question types are very different. Since there could be many possible legal configurations of the elements, Rule Testers ask you which answer choice *could be* a complete configuration. But there is only one accurate list of all the spots in which a certain element can go, so List questions ask you which answer choice *is* the complete list of those spots. Compare:

Rule Tester:	Which one of the following could be a complete and accurate list of the crops planted by the farmer, in order from first to seventh?
List question:	Which one of the following is a complete and accurate list of the crops any one of which may be planted fifth?

> The techniques for solving Rule Testers and List questions are very different, so make sure you can tell the two question types apart.

8.2 WORK THE DIAGRAM

As with all Local questions, working the diagram on Local List questions is a vital step.

Generally, you should deal with new rules just as you do with the original rules of the game:

1. **Symbolize the new rule either directly on the diagram if you can or to the *right* of the diagram.**

2. **Make as many deductions as you can with the new rule.**

Take a look at this example, which comes from the Teachers game at the end of Chapter 7:

1. If Trent teaches math, which one of the following is a complete and accurate list of the teachers, any one of whom could teach science?

    (A) Hector, Kira, Nell
    (B) Hector, Ronnie, Juan
    (C) Hector, Ronnie, Kira
    (D) Hector, Ronnie, Kira, Nell
    (E) Hector, Ronnie, Juan, Kira, Nell

The new rule in this question puts H in Math. That means you must put H and R in Science, the only place with enough room. You also know that N cannot teach Math as long as T teaches something other than Science, per rule 2. Since neither K nor N can teach Math, one of them must be in Gym, and the other one must be in Science. That leaves J to take the last Math spot.

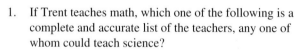

HJKNRPT   Gym | Math | Science

$N_M \rightarrow T_S$
$\sim T_S \rightarrow \sim N_M$
[HR]

The question stem asks for a list of everyone who could possibly teach Science. Remember, they don't all have to teach Science at the same time—just find the answer choice that contains everyone who could teach Science and that contains no one who is forbidden to teach Science. In this case, H and R will definitely teach Science, and K and N are also allowed to do so. P, T, and J are forbidden because they are stuck in Math.

Choice (D) is the correct answer.

8.3 ATTACK

The **process of elimination** is a powerful tool that you can use on List questions. You don't have to figure out the entire list all at once. You can figure out one thing at a time and let the answer choices guide you.

First, use your master diagram and previous work to discover just one element or spot that *must be included* in the correct answer choice. Then eliminate any answer choices that don't contain that element or spot. Keep repeating the process for every element or spot that you know for sure must be included in the correct answer.

Next, repeat the process for any elements or spots that *must be excluded* from the correct answer choice and eliminate the answer choices that contain those elements or those spots.

Finally, look at the remaining answer choices and find the differences between them. The answer choices will generally be very similar, with only one or two differences. Explore those differences and you will find the correct answer choice. For instance, if you were down to these two lists:

> (A) W, X, Y
> (B) W, X, Y, Z

you would not need to pay any attention to W, X, and Y, since both answer choices have those elements in common. Instead, all you have to do is determine whether Z should be included in the correct choice. If so, pick choice (B), and if not, pick choice (A).

Take a look at this example, also from the Teachers game:

> 2. Which one of the following is a complete and accurate list of the teachers, any one of whom could teach gym?
>
> (A) Hector, Kira, Nell, Trent
> (B) Juan, Kira, Nell, Trent
> (C) Juan, Kira, Nell   J or T
> (D) Juan, Kira, Trent
> (E) Kira, Nell, Trent

First, take a look at your master diagram:

MASTER DIAGRAM

H J K N R P T	Gym	Math	Science
$N_M \rightarrow T_S$	~H ~R	~K	
$\sim T_S \rightarrow \sim N_M$			
[HR]	___ P	___ ___	___ ___ ___

It's clear that H and R can't teach Gym, and P is stuck in Math class, so eliminate any answer choices that contain H, R, or P. That gets rid of choice (A).

Next, use your previous work. In Question 1, you saw that K or N could teach Gym. Thus, the correct answer must include both K and N. This allows you to get rid of choice (D), which is missing N.

Now, compare the remaining choices. In addition to Kira and Nell, they all include J, T, or both. So, check if they can teach Gym by trying to create a legal configuration with each of them in Gym. Here's one that shows J could teach Gym:

Gym	Math		Science		
J	P	H	R	K	N	T

So you can get rid of choice (E), which is missing J. And here's one that shows T could teach Gym:

Gym	Math			Science		
T	P	H	R	J	K	N

So you can get rid of choice (C), which is missing T.

Choice (B) is the correct answer.

8.4 CREATING SCENARIOS WHEN WORKING ON QUESTIONS

You saw in Section 7.3.2 that it's possible to narrow down your options to a few major scenarios when setting up a game. This is a skill that you frequently need to use when working on questions as well.

This usually occurs on Local questions when the new rule given by the question stem is rather vague. In such cases, there may be several possible ways to satisfy the new rule, and you have to explore each one. Here's an example:

3. If Juan and Nell teach the same subject, which one of the following must be false?

This is a Local Truth question. The new rule tells you that J and N have to be together, but the problem is that you don't know exactly *where*. They could be together in Math or together in Science. So, to work the diagram, you have to explore both scenarios. Create two new lines in your diagram. In one of them, put J and N in Math. In the other, put J and N in Science. Then make as many deductions as you can in each of the scenarios.

	Gym	Math			Science		
Scenario ①	K	P	J	N	H	R	T
Scenario ②	(K)	P	H	R	J	N	(T)

In Scenario ①, H and R must be in Science because that's the only group with enough room. Rule 2 forces T into Science, and K takes the final remaining spot, Gym.

In Scenario ②, H and R can fit only in Math, but K and T could each be in either Gym or Science.

Now that you have explored all the possible scenarios, you are ready to attack the answer choices. Since the question stem asks for something that *must be false*, you should eliminate any answer choice that *could be true*. If something was true in *either* of the scenarios, you can eliminate it.

(A) Hector teaches science.

Choice (A) was true in the first scenario. Eliminate this choice.

(B) Kira teaches science.

Choice (B) was true in the second scenario. Eliminate this choice.

(C) Kira teaches gym.

Choice (C) was true in the both scenarios. Eliminate this choice.

(D) Ronnie teaches math.

Choice (D) was true in the second scenario. Eliminate this choice.

(E) Trent teaches math.

Choice (E) was not true in either scenario. Since you mapped out *every single legal configuration* that follows the new rule in the question stem, and since none of them included T in Math, then you know choice (E) must be false, which is what you're looking for.

Choice (E) is the correct answer.

Here's another example of a question in which you need to explore two scenarios:

> 4.   If Hector and Trent teach different subjects, which one of the following pairs CANNOT teach the same subject?

This question follows the same pattern as the last one. It presents a new rule, that H and T are not together, but is vague in that it doesn't tell you where to put them. You have to explore all the possibilities. **It's best to organize your scenarios around the most constrained elements.** In this case, instead of exploring the *three* scenarios of trying out T in each of the groups, explore the *two* scenarios of trying out H (and its companion R) in Math and Science.

	Gym	Math			Science		
Scenario ①	Ⓚ	P	J	T	H	R	Ⓝ
Scenario ②		P	H	R			

In the first scenario, T cannot teach Science because of the new rule in the question stem. **Rule 2** tells you that N must therefore avoid Math. At this point, there are only two teachers left, J and T, to fill the two remaining Math spots.

In the second scenario, the remaining letters, J, K, N and T, are free to fill the remaining spots in any configuration. You don't have to worry about breaking the new rule in the question stem because there's no room left in Math for T.

Now take a look at the answer choices, and eliminate the pairs that could teach the same subject.

> (A)   Juan and Nell

Choice (A) could be true in the second scenario. Eliminate this choice.

> (B)   Kira and Ronnie

Choice (B) could be true in the first scenario. Eliminate this choice.

> (C)   Nell and Patrick
> (D)   Nell and Ronnie
> (E)   Patrick and Ronnie

Choice (C) was not possible in either scenario. Since you mapped out *every single legal configuration* that follows the new rule in the question stem, and since none of them allowed N and P to teach together, then you know that this is the pair that cannot teach together.

Choice (C) is the correct answer.

STOP. THIS IS THE END OF LECTURE 4. DO NOT PROCEED TO THE CORRESPONDING EXAM UNTIL INSTRUCTED TO DO SO IN CLASS.

When you construct a *master diagram*, it can be helpful in some games to split the game into two scenarios, but you can always work a game successfully even if you don't do so. However, that's not the case when it comes to a *question* like this one. Here, you absolutely **must** explore both scenarios, because each one allows you to eliminate only some of the incorrect answer choices.

LECTURE 5 CHAPTER 9

HYBRID GAMES

9.1 IDENTIFY THE GAME

9.1.1 WHAT IS A HYBRID GAME?

A **Hybrid game** is a mix of other game types. It includes some grouping aspects and some ordering or grid aspects. Hybrid games require you to bring together all the skills you use on different game types in a single game, and thus they are usually more difficult than the average game.

Hybrid games are rare. Only about one in every four or five tests contains a Hybrid game.

9.1.2 HOW TO RECOGNIZE HYBRID GAMES

Once you know how to recognize the four major game types, recognizing a Hybrid game should not be too difficult. As the name implies, a Hybrid game combines aspects of two or more game types. Hybrid games require you to arrange elements into a specific order or grid *and* to divide elements into two or more groups.

As you read the situation and rules, there are several telltale signs that will alert you to the fact that you are dealing with a Hybrid game:

1. **An Ordering or Grid game in which not all the elements can fit into the order or grid.** If this is accompanied by rules or questions that discuss what happens when certain elements *are* or *are not* included in the grid, then you are dealing with a Hybrid game.

2. **A Binary or Grouping game in which the elements must be ordered within the groups.**

3. **A Binary or Grouping game in which you need to create several rows.** For example, you may need to sort the elements into groups in two different years, each needing its own row.

There are two basic types of Hybrid games. The first type looks like a normal Ordering or Grid game, with one added feature: not all of the elements fit into the order or the grid. These elements are therefore left out and should be placed in a "Not Used" group. This group works just like a group in a Binary game. Order is not important within the Not Used group; you only care about whether an element is there or not. Many times, the rules in this kind of game will include conditionals that reference both *whether* an element is placed on the grid (as in a Binary game) and *where* an element is placed on the grid (as in a Grid game).

For example:

> Exactly six of eight athletes—Jason, Kyle, Lance, Mark, Nathan, Olin, Ricky, and Tommie—compete in three consecutive events at an athletic meet. Exactly two athletes compete in each event and no athlete competes in more than one event. The following conditions also apply:

Since this game consists of three consecutive events, each with two athletes, it resembles a Grid game. However, there are also two athletes who do not compete, so you will need a Not Used group.

The other major type of Hybrid game looks like a normal Binary or Grouping game, with an added feature. Sometimes the added feature is that the elements in each group are ordered or ranked. For example,

> Each of six people—Ursula, Victor, Wendy, Xavier, Yusuf, and Zelda—enters exactly one of two dance contests—modern and traditional. At least two people enter each contest, and the people who enter each contest are ranked in order of dancing ability from best to worst, with no ties. The following conditions must apply:

Other times the feature added to the Grouping game is that you have to create two rows. This may happen if you need to sort the same elements twice or sort two separate stocks (as in a Grid game). For example,

> In each of two years, at least three of the exactly seven members of the Busse family—Martha, Noel, Oren, Paul, Stephanie, Travis, and Zachary—will attend a music conference. Any member that does not attend the conference in the first year must attend in the second year. Attendance of the conference must conform to the following conditions:

9.2 SET UP

All Hybrid games can be diagrammed using the same techniques you use for the four major game types, but they require you to combine features from different game types in a single diagram. The most important decision you have to make when diagramming a Hybrid game is **whether the most important part of the game is the grouping feature or the ordering feature**.

9.2.1 Hybrid Diagrams Based on Grouping

If there is no ordering feature, then the most important feature of the game is of course the grouping, and your diagram will be based on that of a Grouping game, with whatever adjustments you need to make to accommodate the Hybrid element. For example, in the Music Conference example you saw above, the diagram would look like this:

Hybrid games call on you to combine the skills that you developed on the other game types.

In each of two years, at least three of the exactly seven members of the Busse family—Martha, Noel, Oren, Paul, Stephanie, Travis, and Zachary—will attend a music conference. Any member that does not attend the conference in the first year must attend in the second year. Attendance of the conference must conform to the following conditions:

		Attend			Do Not Attend
M N O P S T Z	1st yr:	__	__	__	
M N O P S T Z	2nd yr:	__	__	__	

As in a Grid game, this diagram contains two rows, and each row is basically a Binary game.

Another case in which your diagram should be organized around the groups is when you don't know how many elements will make up each order. For example, in the Dance Contest game you saw above, you know that the elements in each contest will be ranked, but the number of people in each contest is not constant. Therefore, it would be very difficult to draw a typical Grid or Ordering diagram, since you would not know how many spots to put on each diagram. If you knew someone was the worst in a particular contest, you might not know whether to put that person in the second, third, or fourth spot because you might not know exactly how many people will end up in each contest. Therefore, a better diagram would look like this:

Each of six people—Ursula, Victor, Wendy, Xavier, Yusuf, and Zelda—enters exactly one of two dance contests—modern and traditional. At least two people entered each contest, and the people who enter each contest are ranked in order of dance ability from best to worst, with no ties. The following conditions must apply:

U V W X Y Z	Modern	Not Modern (Traditional)

You probably noticed that this diagram looks identical to the normal Binary diagram, and it is. The only difference is how you use it. As you place elements into the diagram, you have to **pay attention to the order**. Within each group, place higher-ranked elements to the left of lower-ranked elements. You may not be able to tell who is second (because there might be unplaced elements), but you will be able to tell who is better or worse than someone else.

9.2.2 HYBRID DIAGRAMS BASED ON AN ORDER OR GRID

Other Hybrid games are much more focused on a specified order or grid, and the only hybrid element of the game is the fact that some of the elements are left off the diagram. In such cases, draw the Ordering or Grid diagram as you normally would and create a Not Used group to the right of the diagram.

Consider the following situation:

A television executive is setting a station's weekly line-up for the eight o'clock time slot. From nine shows—I, J, K, L, M, N, O, P, and Q—the executive will select exactly one to air each day, Monday through Saturday. No show will air on more than one day.

The situation tells you there are nine elements, but that only six of them will be placed in the described order. So, create a normal Ordering diagram for Monday–Saturday, and add to it a Not Selected group for the three remaining elements.

I J K L M N O P Q	M	T	W	Th	F	S	Not Selected
							__ __ __

9.2.3   Drill: Identify and Set Up

For each of the following situations, identify the type of game and set it up by drawing the appropriate diagram.

Situation

1. A track team consists of seven athletes—O, P, Q, R, S, T, and U—exactly five of whom will compete in a relay race. Each consecutive leg of the relay will be run by exactly one athlete and no athlete will run more than one leg. The following conditions must apply:

   Game Type: _____Binary -Ordering_____

2. Each of eight dogs—Koosh, Lucky, Max, Nibbler, Oso, Princeton, Shana, and Wrigley—competes in one of two competitions—talent and appearance—at a dog show. Each competition consists of four dogs, each of which is ranked from first to fourth in a manner consistent with the following conditions:

   Game Type: _____Binary - Ordering - grouping_____

3. A business conglomerate conducts evaluations to determine the profitability of each of its seven subsidiaries—media companies J, K, L and M, and services companies N, O, and P. On the basis of the evaluations, each subsidiary is assigned a different rank, from first (most profitable) through seventh (least profitable). The ranking is consistent with the following conditions:

   Game Type: _____

4. A building superintendent will inspect exactly six of eight apartments—F, G, H, I, J, K, L, and M—over a three day period, Monday through Wednesday. The superintendent will inspect exactly two apartments per day—one in the morning and one in the afternoon—subject to the following conditions:

   Game Type: _____

5. On Saturday night, exactly eight planes—S, T, U, V, W, X, Y, and Z—arrive at an airport. Each plane arrives at either the domestic terminal or the international terminal. The planes arrive consecutively and one at a time at each terminal. The arrivals are consistent with the following conditions:

   Game Type: _____

6. Each of exactly six of a company's nine employees— Osgood, Peavy, Quentin, Rodriguez, Saldovar, Tuttle, Utter, Vasquez, and Weasley—is to be transferred to exactly one of two new offices—the West Coast office or the East Coast office. The following conditions must apply:

   Game Type: _____

Diagram

run   not
— — — — — | ﹏ —

T   — — — — — | — — —

A   — — — — — | — — —

Answers & Explanations

1. This is a Hybrid game. The situation indicates that the elements will be ordered, but that some elements will be excluded from the order.

OPQRSTU

1	2	3	4	5	Not Competing
					— —

2. This is a Grid game. The situation indicates that the elements will need to be ranked in two groups and tells you that exactly four elements will be ranked in each group.

KLMNOPSW

	1	2	3	4
Talent				
Appearance				

3. This is an Ordering game. The situation indicates that the elements will be ranked from first through seventh, with no elements left out of the order. *Media* and *services* are the two categories that the elements fit into, not something that you must figure out.

MEDIA: JKLM   services: n o p

1	2	3	4	5	6	7

4. This is a Hybrid game. The situation indicates that the elements will need to be arranged into a grid, but that some elements will be excluded from the grid.

FGHIJKLM

	M	T	W	Not Inspected
Morning				— —
Afternoon				

5. This is a Hybrid game. The situation indicates that the elements will need to be divided into two groups and that they must be ordered within each group. Since the situation does not indicate how many elements will be placed in each group, the diagram is organized around the groups.

STUVWXYZ

Domestic	Not Domestic (International)

6. This is a Grouping game. The situation indicates that the elements will be divided into three groups and that there is no order within the groups.

OPQRSTUVW

East Coast	West Coast	Not Transferred
		— — —

9.3   SYMBOLIZE THE RULES AND DEDUCE

Just as Hybrid games require you to create diagrams that combine concepts from different game types, the rules in Hybrid games often require you to create combined symbols.

While these rules are more common in Hybrid games, you may encounter strange rules in any type of game. Symbolizing these rules will sometimes require you to invent your own symbols. Just remember that the symbols you create should be

1. **Complete.** Each symbol should contain exactly the same information as the rule. The more complicated a rule, the more careful you have to be to make sure the symbol captures the full meaning of the rule.

2. **Compact.** Although you may have to create some clever symbols to capture all of the information in a new rule, don't waste time symbolizing every implication of the rule. Instead, use compact symbols that capture the rule's meaning and make deductions as needed for individual questions.

3. **Standardized.** Just because you have to invent new symbols doesn't mean you can't use familiar pieces to create them.

Occasionally, you will run into a rule that is so unique that you won't be able to use any of the standard symbols to express it. In such a case, come up with something that makes sense to you, whether that means creating a new symbol, writing a few words to capture the meaning of the rule, or even just putting a big star next to the rule as it is written to remind you to follow it. In the end, don't spend too much time trying to determine the *best* way to symbolize every strange rule. Just pick a way that works with your diagram and allows you to recognize the full meaning of the rule.

Here are some examples of the strange rules you may encounter on the LSAT. Although it is impossible to come up with an exhaustive list, the techniques used to symbolize the rules below can also be used to symbolize any new rules you may come across.

Combining Conditionals with Blocks

Some rules combine conditional statements with block rules. For example,

> If J is selected, then K must be aired on the day
> immediately following the day on which L is aired.

Symbolize this rule and its contrapositive just as you would a normal conditional, but use the blocks instead of individual elements:

$$J \rightarrow \boxed{LK}$$
$$\boxed{\cancel{LK}} \rightarrow \sim J$$

Combining Conditionals with Relative Order Rules

Some rules combine conditional statements with relative order rules. For example:

> If Oliver and Tom both take the exam, Oliver scores
> higher than Tom.

To symbolize a rule like this, simply write the relative order rule on the appropriate side of the arrow:

$$O \text{ AND } T \rightarrow O-T$$

Creating the contrapositives for these rules can still be done by **Switching and Negating** the rule, but sometimes the contrapositive is not the best way to express the additional implications of the rule. For example, the contrapositive for the above rule is

$$T-O \rightarrow \sim O \text{ OR } \sim T$$

which basically means

> If Tom scores higher on the exam than Oliver, then either
> Oliver or Tom doesn't take the exam.

As you can probably see, this doesn't make much sense and wouldn't be much help in answering questions. It's better to deduce as much as you can about what this *means*.

If Oliver scores higher than Tom whenever they both take the exam, then there is *no way* that Tom can score higher than Oliver. The following makes for a more useful symbol:

$$\cancel{T-O}$$

Here's another example of a rule that combines a conditional statement with a relative order rule:

> If Ursula enters the modern dance contest, then Victor and
> Wendy enter the modern dance contest, Ursula ranking
> lower than Victor but higher than Wendy.

This symbol ignores the possibility that Tom and Oliver have the same score. If the game allowed for that possibility, you would also create another symbol, such as a vertical antiblock, that would be determined by your diagram.

To symbolize this rule, you would again put the relative order symbol on the right-hand side of the conditional symbol:

$$U \longrightarrow V-U-W$$

This incorporates all of the information in the rule. Don't simply write "$U \longrightarrow V$ AND W" because the rule gives you more information than that. In addition to telling you that Victor and Wendy are also in the modern dance contest, it tells you the specific order of the three.

Again, it is more beneficial when creating the contrapositive of this rule to focus on the group aspect of the rule without regard to order.

$$\sim V \text{ OR } \sim W \longrightarrow \sim U$$

This lets you know that if either Victor or Wendy doesn't enter the modern dance contest, then Ursula doesn't enter it either.

Combining Conditionals with Placement Rules

Some rules combine conditional statements with exact or forbidden row, column, and spot rules. For example:

If Emily attends the wedding, she is seated in the first seat at one of the tables.

	1	2	3	Not Attending
Bride				__ __
Groom				

Use your diagram to help you determine how to symbolize these rules.

You could use subscripts, such as

$$E \longrightarrow E_1$$
$$\sim E_1 \longrightarrow \sim E$$

But you may find it clearer to simply symbolize the rule as a forbidden row or column. For example, since there are only three seats at each table, you could write a $\sim E$ above the second and third columns:

	1	$\sim E$ 2	$\sim E$ 3	Not Attending
Bride				__ __
Groom				

Of course, this won't work for conditional placement rules that state that the row of one element will dictate the column of another (or vice versa). For example,

If Frank is seated at the groom's table, Pat is seated in the
first seat at one of the tables.

could not be symbolized using forbidden row or column symbols because Pat could be in another seat as long as Frank isn't at the groom's table.

Instead, symbolize this using a different subscript on each side of the arrow:

$$F_G \longrightarrow P_1$$
$$\sim P_1 \longrightarrow \sim F_G$$

Other conditional placement rules refer to exact or forbidden spots. The same technique can be used for symbolizing these rules, so

If Cori attends the wedding, she is seated in the
first seat at the bride's table.

can be symbolized with forbidden row and column symbols:

There are more deductions that can be made in forming the contrapositive, such as $W-V \longrightarrow \sim U$ and $U-V$ and $W-U$, but it is probably too time-consuming to try to come up with all of the possible deductions, so just symbolize the most important ones and plan to discover the rest as you approach the questions.

		~C	~C		
	1	2	3	Not Attending	
Bride					
~C Groom					

but, since there are only two spots that C could occupy, it is better symbolized with a barbell:

	1	2	3	Not Attending
Bride	Ⓒ			◯
Groom				

There are many times—not just on conditionals in Hybrid games—when you may be able to symbolize the same rule in several different ways. Keep an open mind and practice finding the most efficient way to express every rule.

Special Status

In some games, there is a special status that must be bestowed upon one of the elements. This status is not tied to a particular spot or element, so it can be a little tricky to deal with, but you can still symbolize it. For example, take a look at this game:

> From a group of seven company employees—F, J, K, O, R, S, and V—exactly four will be selected to serve on a project team. One of the members of the project team will be designated team leader.

In this case, the special status is the *team leader*. The diagram for this game is the normal Binary diagram, with exactly four spots in the Selected group. You may be tempted to set aside one of those spots for the team leader, but this is problematic. Imagine that a question informs you that K is on the team. Should you put K in the team leader spot or not? There is no way to know until you have worked through the question, and immediately assuming that K either is or is not the leader can lead to overlooked possibilities.

The best approach is to use a symbol that is not tied to a particular spot to denote the team leader. An asterisk is perfect. You can freely place elements onto teams and come back later and add an asterisk next to the team leader when you determine which element it is. You can symbolize that rule with a bit of text next to your diagram:

* = team leader

9.4 PUTTING IT ALL TOGETHER

9.4.1 Drill: Hybrid Games

Below is a situation with rules. Identify the type of game and set it up by drawing an appropriate diagram and symbolizing the stock and rules. Then make as many deductions as you can and answer the questions that follow.

Of eight students—Marcy, Otis, Rachelle, Scott, Tanya, Ursula, Warren, and Zed—exactly two will be elected in each of three grades—sixth, seventh, and eighth—as the class president and vice president. Each student can be elected only in his or her own grade. The following conditions apply:

> If Scott is elected to be a president, then Rachelle is elected to be a vice president.
> Otis is in the eighth grade.
> If Tanya is elected in the seventh or eighth grade, then Ursula and Zed are both elected in the next lowest grade.
> Marcy is not elected to be a vice president.

1. If Rachelle, Tanya, and Warren are elected to be presidents, not necessarily in that grade order, then which one of the following is a complete and accurate list of students any of whom could be elected in the seventh grade?

   (A) Marcy, Rachelle, Scott, Ursula, Warren, Zed
   (B) Otis, Rachelle, Scott, Ursula, Warren, Zed
   (C) Rachelle, Scott, Ursula, Tanya, Warren, Zed
   (D) Rachelle, Scott, Ursula, Warren, Zed
   (E) Scott, Ursula, Warren, Zed

2. If neither Ursula nor Warren is elected in any grade, then which one of the following must be true?

   (A) Marcy and Scott are elected in different grades.
   (B) Otis and Zed are elected in different grades.
   (C) Rachelle and Zed are elected in different grades.
   (D) Rachelle is elected in the sixth grade.
   (E) Tanya is elected in the sixth grade.

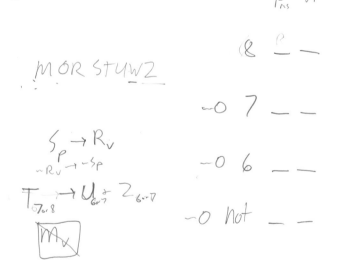

9.4.2 Answers & Explanations

Identify

Initially, this appears to be a Grid game—the situation names consecutive spots with two elements placed in each ordered spot—but, upon closer examination, one important feature identifies this as a Hybrid game: there are two elements that will not fit into this grid. Therefore, this game combines a Grid game with a Binary game. This is a Hybrid game.

Set Up

The diagram for this game starts with a grid with three columns for each of the three grades and two rows, one each for president and vice president. Added to this grid is a Not Elected group for the two students who will not be elected.

The stock in this game consists of the initials of the eight students: M O R S T U W Z. Write this to the left of the diagram.

M O R S T U W Z	Sixth	Seventh	Eighth	Not Elected
Pres				— —
VP				

To complete the Set Up step, symbolize each of the rules.

Rule 1 is a conditional rule. Symbolize it with subscripts as

$$S_P \rightarrow R_{VP}$$
$$\sim R_{VP} \rightarrow \sim S_P$$

Rule 2 cannot be symbolized the way it is written because, although you know O is in the eighth grade, you don't know whether he will be elected. Instead, think about the implications of this rule.

Since O is in the eighth grade, you know he will not be elected in either the sixth or the seventh grade. So, symbolize it as a forbidden column rule. Write ~O above both the sixth grade and the seventh grade columns.

Rule 3 is rather complicated, but the best way to handle it is to separate the symbol out into two scenarios: one if T is elected in the seventh grade, and one if T is elected in the eighth. Each symbol will combine a conditional with a soft block.

$$T_7 \rightarrow \begin{pmatrix} U \\ Z \end{pmatrix}_6 \qquad T_8 \rightarrow \begin{pmatrix} U \\ Z \end{pmatrix}_7$$
$$\sim U_6 \text{ OR } \sim Z_6 \rightarrow \sim T_7 \qquad \sim U_7 \text{ OR } \sim Z_7 \rightarrow \sim T_8$$

Rule 4 is a forbidden row rule. Write it next to the Vice President row as ~M.

At this point, your diagram should look like this:

M O R S T U W Z	Sixth ~O	Seventh ~O	Eighth	Not Elected
$S_P \rightarrow R_{VP}$ $\sim R_{VP} \rightarrow \sim S_P$	Pres			— —
	VP ~M			

$$T_7 \rightarrow \begin{pmatrix} U \\ Z \end{pmatrix}_6$$
$$\sim U_6 \text{ OR } \sim Z_6 \rightarrow \sim T_7$$

$$T_8 \rightarrow \begin{pmatrix} U \\ Z \end{pmatrix}_7$$
$$\sim U_7 \text{ OR } \sim Z_7 \rightarrow \sim T_8$$

After symbolizing the rules, you should look for deductions. Unfortunately, the only rules you have in this game are **conditionals and forbidden spot rules. Those two types of rules, along with antiblocks, tend to be the least productive types when you are looking for deductions**. If you find yourself dealing with a game that includes only these types of rules, chances are that you won't be able to find many (or any) deductions to make, and you shouldn't spend a lot of time trying to find something that isn't there.

In this game, there are no new deductions other than the ones you made as you were initially symbolizing the rules. Put a box around your diagram to show that it is the complete master diagram, then move on to the questions.

Question 1

This is a Local List question. You can deduce a couple of things from the new rule. First, **M** has no room to be president and is forbidden to be VP. Therefore **M** is not elected. Eliminate choice (A). Next, you already deduced that **O** cannot be seventh, so choice (B) is incorrect as well. Finally, you know that **U** and **Z** don't have room to be together in any grade, so rule 1 says that **T** cannot be seventh or eighth (it must be sixth). Get rid of choice (C). You are now left with two answer choices. What is the difference between choices (D) and (E)? The only difference is that choice (E) has **R**. So all you have to do is figure out whether or not **R** could be in the seventh grade.

	Sixth	Seventh	Eighth	Not Elected
Pres	T	R	W	M O
VP	S	U	Z	

According to this possible configuration, **R** can be seventh. So the correct answer choice should include **R**.

Choice (D) is the correct answer.

Question 2

This Local Truth question puts **U** and **W** in the Not Elected group. That means everyone else is elected. It also means that, according to rule 4, **T** must be in the sixth grade, since you will be unable to have **U** and **Z** together. That's good enough to let you pick choice (E).

	Sixth	Seventh	Eighth	Not Elected
Pres	T		O	U W
VP	◯		◯	

Choice (E) is the correct answer.

NOW MOVE ON TO THE SECOND CHAPTER OF LECTURE 5. WHEN YOU HAVE COMPLETED IT, YOU CAN GET FURTHER PRACTICE WITH HYBRID GAMES IN THE CORRESPONDING EXAM AT THE END OF THE BOOK.

LECTURE **5** CHAPTER **10**

RULE CHANGERS

Rule Changers are questions that change the rules of the game. They may remove a rule, change a rule, or replace one rule with another.

10.1 IDENTIFY THE QUESTION

Rule Changers have the following characteristics:

1. **The question stem *changes*, *replaces*, *removes*, or *suspends* one of the original rules of the game.** The question stem usually explicitly tells you this, but sometimes it simply adds a new rule that contradicts one of the original rules of the game.

2. **The question stem tells you that all of the other rules remain in effect**.

3. **When they appear, Rule Changers are always the last question in a particular game.**

Here are some examples of Rule Changer question stems:

> Assume that the condition is removed that prevents sequoias from being planted next to willows. If all other conditions remain the same, each of the following could be true EXCEPT:

> If L is presented immediately before K but all the other conditions remain in effect, which one of the following could be an accurate list of presentations, listed in order from first through seventh?

> If the condition that exactly three persons attend the festival is changed to require that exactly five persons attend the festival, but all other conditions remain the same, then which one of the following persons CANNOT attend the festival?

Fortunately, Rule Changers are becoming quite rare.

> Suppose that the condition requiring that Reta speaks more languages than Silvia is replaced by a new condition requiring that Reta and Silvia speak exactly two of the same languages. If all of the other original conditions remain in effect, which one of the following must be true?

All of these question stems change, replace, remove, or suspend one of the original rules and state that the other rules remain in effect.

Be careful not to mistake Local questions for Rule Changers. The LSAT sometimes includes Local questions that resemble Rule Changers. For example, you may see a question that reads something like this:

> Suppose that the condition is added that football and hockey are not played on the same day. If all the other conditions remain in effect, then each of the following could be a complete and accurate list of the sports played on Tuesday EXCEPT:

While this is worded like a Rule Changer, none of the original rules is changed or removed. This question simply adds a new rule. Thus, it can be approached in the same manner as any other Local question.

10.2 WORK THE DIAGRAM

As with Local questions, working the diagram is a vital step in Rule Changer questions, but it is often much more time-consuming.

Since Rule Changers change or remove one of the rules that you used to create your initial diagram, you need to remove that rule from your diagram. In addition, you will need to remove any deductions you made as a result of that rule. As such, the best way to deal with a rule changer is generally to create a new diagram reflecting the information from the new rule. Since the new diagram will only apply to the Rule Changer, you should answer any Rule Changer last so you won't be tempted to consult the new diagram to answer other questions.

To create the new diagram:

1. **Copy the backbone used for the master diagram. DO NOT COPY ANY OF THE DEDUCTIONS THAT YOU MADE.**

2. **Symbolize the new rule.**

3. **Determine which of the original rules are still valid and copy the symbols for them.**

4. **Make as many new deductions as you can with the new rule and the remaining original rules**. (You can now copy any original deductions that still apply.)

As always, the new deductions you make could be anywhere on the diagram. After you make deductions that seem particularly relevant to the question at hand, check the answer choices to see if you have done enough to answer the question, but be aware that you may have to make other deductions before you can determine which answer choice is correct. Pay special attention to the new deductions that result from the changed rule.

Take a look at this example that comes from the Students game in chapter 9:

1. If Marcy is elected to be vice president in the eighth grade but all other conditions remain in effect, which one of the following CANNOT be true?

    (A) Otis is elected to be a president.
    (B) Otis is elected to be a vice president.
    (C) Rachelle is elected to be a president.
    (D) Rachelle is elected to be a vice president.
    (E) Scott is elected to be a vice president.

Begin by copying the backbone used for the master diagram.

M O R S T U W Z		Sixth	Seventh	Eighth	Not Elected
	Pres				— —
	VP				

Next, symbolize the new rule. This is an exact spot rule. Symbolize it by placing **M** directly in the eighth grade vice president spot.

Now, look at the rules to see which of them still apply. Rule 1 is not violated by the new rule. Copy the conditional symbols onto your diagram.

Rule 2 is not violated by the new rule either, but the new rule does allow you to symbolize it differently. Since **O** is in the eighth grade, and **M** is elected vice president in the eighth grade, you know that **O** will either be elected president in the eighth grade or he will not be elected. Symbolize this with a barbell.

M O R S T U W Z		Sixth	Seventh	Eighth	Not Elected
$S_P \rightarrow R_{VP}$	Pres			◎———◯	—
$\sim R_{VP} \rightarrow \sim S_P$	VP			M	

This is an interesting deduction that resulted from the changed rule. So, pause for a moment and look at the question and answer choices to see if this deduction has already done enough to allow you to answer the question.

Choice (B) has **O** as vice president, but the barbell shows that **O** is either president or he is not elected. Thus, you've already found the correct answer.

Choice (B) is the correct answer.

10.3 ATTACK

As with other questions, it is sometimes necessary to attack the answer choices in Rule Changers to arrive at the correct answer.

Take a look at the following example:

2. If the condition that Otis is in eighth grade is suspended, but all other conditions remain in effect, then each of the following could be an accurate list of the students elected to be vice president in sixth, seventh, and eighth grades, respectively, EXCEPT:

    (A) Otis, Scott, Rachelle
    (B) Otis, Warren, Tanya
    (C) Scott, Otis, Zed
    (D) Ursula, Tanya, Rachelle
    (E) Tanya, Otis, Ursula

This just tells you that a rule is suspended; it doesn't give you any new information. Start by redrawing the diagram.

Here are the remaining original rules:

If Scott is elected to be a president, then Rachelle is elected to be a vice president.

Otis is in the eighth grade.

If Tanya is elected in the seventh or eighth grade, then Ursula and Zed are both elected in the next lowest grade.

There is no way to symbolize this new rule, so move on to the remaining original rules.

Rules 1, 3, and 4 aren't affected by the information in the question stem, so they can be copied onto the new diagram.

There are no new deductions that result from removing the second rule, so now you have to use the master diagram to answer this question.

Now that you have removed one of the original rules, the rest of the question stem works just like a normal Rule Tester question: you are asked to find the one list of vice presidents that violates one of the remaining rules. So you can attack the answer choices just as you do on a normal Rule Tester question. Look at each rule and try to find an answer choice in which it is broken.

First, take a look at rule 1. You know that **R** must be vice president if **S** is president (and that **S** can't be president if **R** is not vice president), but the answer choices don't mention who is elected president. Check another rule.

Rule 4 looks like it may be important because it also concerns vice president placement. You know **M** can't be vice president, but none of the answer choices include it as vice president. Move on.

Rule 3 doesn't mention vice presidents, but it does mention grades, so see if this rule is broken in any of the answer choices. Choice (B), which has **T** elected president in the eighth grade and **W** elected president in the seventh grade, doesn't leave enough room for both **U** and **Z** in the seventh grade. This choice contains a series of elements that *cannot* be the list of vice presidents, which is what you're looking for.

Choice (B) is the correct answer.

VPs in 6, 7, and 8:

(A)   Otis, Scott, Rachelle
(B)   Otis, Warren, Tanya
(C)   Scott, Otis, Zed
(D)   Ursula, Tanya, Rachelle
(E)   Tanya, Otis, Ursula

10.4 SECTION STRATEGY

In the introduction, you learned three general principles for section strategy:

> If you are getting more than one question wrong per game, then you're not working accurately. You can improve your accuracy by going back and reviewing techniques, reworking old games, slowing down, and doing as many homework games as possible.

1. **Work as quickly as you can *without sacrificing accuracy*.** You have limited time, so you need to work quickly, but it makes no sense to blaze through the section carelessly. You should find a pace at which you can work quickly but comfortably enough to remain accurate. Understand that you may not finish the entire section.

2. **Work the games that will give you the most points in the shortest time first.** While there is no simple formula for what makes a game difficult, you should be developing a sense of what makes a game take a long time. In general, if the diagram is complicated or there are lots of elements, then the game might take a long time. If a time-consuming game is accompanied by only a few questions, skip it and return to it if you have time later. There's no

reason to spend twelve minutes answering five questions when you could spend that same amount of time answering eight questions.

3. **Work each game as a unit**. Skipping around between different games is a bad idea. Each time you change games, you have to refamiliarize yourself with the rules and how the game works. This can be a significant waste of time. When you begin a game, keep working on it until you have finished all the questions associated with that game. Only if a question has you completely stumped should you guess and move on to the next game. Return to it if you have extra time remaining after answering everything else.

Now that you are more familiar with the Analytical Reasoning section, you can add some specific details to these general principles.

Remember: never leave a question blank!

10.4.1 HOW TO CHOOSE GAMES

Before you begin a section, you should know approximately how many games you will get through. You should have practiced a number of timed sections before the official test day arrives, and your performance on those timed sections will give you a good indication of how fast you can *accurately* work. This knowledge determines how picky you should be about which games to attempt.

For example, if you can regularly finish or come close to finishing all four games in an Analytical Reasoning section, then you should approach the section with the expectation that you will work all the games in order. Don't waste much time putting the games in a different order. Only if a game appears particularly evil should you skip it and return later.

On the other hand, if you are in the majority of people who cannot accurately finish all four games, then you should be a little pickier. When you first approach a game, read the situation and rules carefully and glance at the questions. Then ask yourself:

1. Can I clearly envision what the diagram will look like?

2. Will the diagram be simple, and not complicated or unusual?

3. Are there a manageable number of elements, and will the stock be easy to symbolize?

4. Do I understand the rules, and can I envision how I will symbolize them?

5. Do the questions seem straightforward, and not unfamiliar or time-consuming?

6. Are there more than five questions attached to the game?

The more of these questions you can answer "yes" to, the more likely it is that you're dealing with a good game to attempt.

The process of reading a situation and rules, asking yourself these questions, and deciding whether to attempt the game should take you no longer than 30 seconds, and it depends on practice. As you work on homework games, go through these same questions and predict how hard you think a game will be. After you complete the game, return to your predictions. Did you accurately anticipate the difficulty of the game? Why or why not? Did you accurately predict what the best diagram should look like and how the game would work? If not, keep refining your prediction skills—they will help you avoid time-wasting games on the official test day.

10.4.2 WHEN TO SKIP A QUESTION

You should work on each game's questions in roughly the order in which they are presented, since they usually start easier and get harder. However, it can be useful to put certain questions off until later in the game.

If you see a Universal question, first determine whether you have already deduced enough to answer it. If not, and if it appears that looking back on previous work would be helpful, then put off the question until you have answered all the Local questions. Then use your previous work to get to the answer more quickly.

If you see a question that looks particularly tricky, it can again be helpful to put it off until later, when you will have become more comfortable with the game and how it works.

When you do return to questions you have put off, they will usually be the most time-consuming questions, often requiring you to grind through each answer choice. However, it is in your best interest to take the extra time to get them right, not skip them completely. Each game requires a significant investment of time to draw the diagram and make deductions, and you want that investment to produce as many points as possible.

What if you're in the middle of a question that seems to be taking a very long time? The last thing you want to do on the LSAT is get stuck on a question, and you should develop an internal mental timer that alerts you when a question is taking much longer than normal. When this happens, you have to make a decision: Are you completely lost, just staring at the page, or spinning your wheels? If so, get out. Guess and move on. However, if a question is taking a long time but you are making steady progress toward the correct answer, then you should take the time to get the question right.

10.4.3 When To Fill In The Answer Bubbles
The most efficient way to fill in the answer bubbles is to wait until you have finished a game completely before you transfer the answers to your answer sheet. You can use the opportunity to give your mind a little break before you move on to the next game. You should also take that time to close your eyes, sit up straight, take a few deep breaths, and prepare your mind to focus on the next game. Taking little breaks throughout the section will help your brain stay fresh longer and help you avoid careless mistakes.

10.4.4 What To Do In The Last Few Minutes
When you have only a few minutes left in the section, you should start transferring each answer to the answer sheet as soon as you get it. This ensures you won't get caught with half a dozen questions done but not filled in on your answer sheet, which would be a disaster. If you know you are not going to finish the section, you should answer the remaining questions with your chosen Guess Letter, and if you complete any more questions after doing so, erase the Guess Letter and put in the answer you worked out.

If you are in the middle of a game and making progress, stick with it. However, if you have just finished a game or if you are stuck on some very time-consuming questions, you can usually grab an extra point or two by looking for Rule Tester questions in the game(s) you haven't tried. Many times, you won't need a diagram or symbols to get the Rule Tester correct. Just look at each rule and find an answer choice in which it is broken.

However, not every Rule Tester is that easy. For example, in some Grid games you are presented with the complete configuration of only *one* of the rows on the grid, and you would have to make deductions about the other row in order to get the question right. Such a question would require you to go through the entire process of setting up the game, so if you had any questions remaining in games for which you already had the diagram, it would be better to work on those in the last few minutes.

Your proctor is required to give you a warning when five minutes remain in a section, but there are lots of stories of incompetent proctors failing to do so. You may not bring a timer or digital watch to the test, but you can use your own analog watch to keep time. It's helpful to write down your own "5-minute warning" time at the top of each section you work on. (Hint: it's 30 minutes after the section begins.)

STOP. THIS IS THE END OF LECTURE 5. DO NOT PROCEED TO THE CORRESPONDING EXAM UNTIL INSTRUCTED TO DO SO IN CLASS.

LECTURE **6**   CHAPTER **11**

RARE GAME TYPES

11.1 CIRCULAR GAMES

Circular games feature a circular diagram. Circular games are very similar to Ordering games, but there are important distinguishing features that result from their shape.

Pure circular games are quite rare: Fewer than five of them have appeared on official LSATs since 1991. However, other some games over the years have contained features that resemble circular games.

11.1.1 IDENTIFY

A game that requires you to arrange elements in a circle is a Circular game.

The situation will likely tell you explicitly that the elements must be arranged in a circle. All Circular games that have appeared on past LSAT tests have described people seated around a circular table, so be particularly aware if you encounter this situation, but also look out for any other situation that describes elements arranged in a circle.

In general, the situation and rules for a Circular game will resemble those for an Ordering game—all elements will be arranged in a single order—but the elements will be arranged in a circle instead of a straight line. This shouldn't be hard to spot because the situation should tell you that the elements are arranged circularly.

11.1.2 Set Up

11.1.2.1 How to Draw a Circular Game Diagram

Your initial reaction when you see a Circular game will probably be to draw a circle. That's understandable! But it turns out that the best diagram looks more like this:

This diagram is simpler and faster to draw, and it makes some features of the rules and questions much easier to see.

You will need a new "asterisk" diagram for each new configuration that you work with. Luckily, you can draw it quickly and without using a lot of space.

Just set aside your master diagram and indicate that it is your master diagram by drawing a box around it. Then consult it as needed for individual questions. As you need to explore a possible configuration, quickly sketch out a copy of the diagram and fill in the new rules and deductions on the new diagram.

11.1.2.2 Symbolizing the Rules

All past Circular games have contained at least one of the following three types of rules:

1. **A rule indicating that one element is required or forbidden to be *adjacent* to another element.** These rules can be symbolized using normal soft block or soft antiblock symbols.

2. **A rule indicating that one element is required or forbidden to be *across* from another element.** This requires a new symbol, but the "asterisk" diagram provides the perfect suggestion. People opposite from each other at the table will be placed at opposite ends of a "spoke" in the asterisk. Thus, you should use a spoke symbol for these rules. As an example,

   Maurice sits directly across from Leanna.

   is symbolized

   This works simply and intuitively with the diagram to represent elements that must be across from one another.

3. **A rule indicating that one element is required or forbidden to be immediately *clockwise* or *counterclockwise* from another element.** These can be symbolized using normal blocks and antiblocks, but be careful when reading these blocks to not mistake their meaning.

   As an example, consider the following:

   Jody sits immediately next to, and immediately clockwise from, Kristin.

   You may be tempted to symbolize this rule as

   But this is a mistake because it doesn't correspond to the diagram. It tells you that **J** is *to the right* of **K**, which is not the same as *clockwise* from **K**. Instead, use a symbol that matches the diagram. Since the diagram is circular, use a block that's also circular.

Make sure the asterisk has the right number of spokes—it needs to match the number of elements in the game.

This will remind you to turn the block to keep **K** and **J** correctly oriented, no matter where you put them on the diagram.

It's *always* important to make sure your symbols match the diagram, no matter what type of game you're dealing with.

11.1.3 Deduce

Circles have some peculiar features that can lead to important deductions. For the most part, the elements can be thought of as inhabiting a line, just as in an Ordering game. Elements can be next to each other or forbidden to be next to each other. But elements arranged in a circle have these additional traits:

1. **The first element is next to the last element.** This important feature will be tested in the questions, so make sure to consider it when reading lists of the elements (especially in the answer choices).

2. **Elements can be across from each other.** So, at a 10-person table, the person seated in chair 1 has a special relationship with the people in chairs 2 and 10 (adjacent) *and* a special relationship with the person in chair 6 (across).

3. **There is generally no starting or ending point.** Elements cannot usually be *before* or *after* another. This also means that you won't be able to make any deductions about the "ends" of your diagram.

   Most past Circular games have not focused on fixed positions within the order—that is, the spots in the circle weren't numbered. The only thing relevant to the questions was who was next to whom. So, if you have a Circular game, check to see whether fixed positions are important.

   If they're not, then you don't have to worry about where the *first* element is placed each time you are starting a new diagram. Just decide which element you want to start with and place it anywhere you want on the diagram. Then figure out the other relationships from there.

4. **There may be a mirror image.** In Circular games that refer strictly to adjacent relationships, every scenario has a mirror image.

   This means that the same elements will be next to each other regardless of the direction in which the scenario is constructed. Thus, if no order is mentioned and no distinction is made between clockwise and counterclockwise by the question or any of the rules, then you won't have to explore both scenarios.

   If any of the rules or the question does mention order or distinguishes between clockwise and counterclockwise, you will have to investigate two scenarios for elements that are said to be *next to* each other. For example, if a Local question directs you to place **Y** next to **Z**, you will have to explore what happens when **Y** is immediately *clockwise* from **Z**, and what happens when **Y** is immediately *counterclockwise* from **Z**.

11.1.4 PUTTING IT ALL TOGETHER

11.1.4.1 Drill: Circular Games

Below is a situation with rules. Identify the type of game and set it up by drawing an appropriate diagram and symbolizing the stock and rules. Then make as many deductions as you can and answer the questions that follow.

Six people—Galahad, King Arthur, Lancelot, Merlin, Palamedes, and Tristan—meet at a circular table called the Round Table, and each of them sits in a different one of six chairs, which are evenly spaced around the table. The following conditions apply:

Tristan sits immediately next to Merlin.

King Arthur sits immediately next to Lancelot, Merlin, or both.

Galahad does not sit immediately next to Lancelot.

If Palamedes sits immediately next to Tristan, Palamedes does not sit immediately next to Lancelot.

1. If Galahad sits directly between King Arthur and Tristan, then Lancelot must sit directly between

   (A) King Arthur and Merlin
   (B) King Arthur and Palamedes
   (C) Merlin and Palamedes
   (D) Merlin and Tristan
   (E) Palamedes and Tristan

2. If Merlin sits immediately next to Lancelot, then Galahad could sit directly between

   (A) King Arthur and Tristan
   (C) Merlin and Palamedes
   (D) Merlin and Tristan
   (E) Tristan and Palamedes

11.1.4.2   Answers & Explanations

Identify

You can identify this as a Circular game because the situation asks you to arrange people around a circular table. All of the rules concern who is sitting *next* to whom. Finally, there is just one circular arrangement into which all the elements are arranged.

Set Up

The diagram for this game starts with a six-point asterisk symbol to represent each of the six chairs.

The stock for this game consists of the initials of the six people: **G K L M P T**. Write this to the upper left of the diagram.

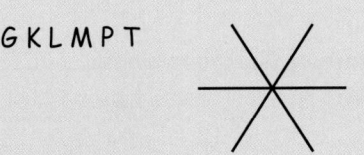

To complete the Set Up step, symbolize each of the rules.

Rule 1 is a soft block rule. Symbolize it as (TM)

Rule 2 is an alternate soft block rule. Symbolize it as (KL) OR (KM)

Rule 3 is a soft antiblock rule. Symbolize it as (G̶L̶)

> There is no need to symbolize the "or both" part of the rule because, on the LSAT and in your symbols, the word "or" always already includes the possibility of both.

Rule 4 combines a conditional with a soft block rule. You could symbolize it this way

$$(PT) \rightarrow \sim(PL)$$
$$(PL) \rightarrow \sim(PT)$$

This is correct, but it's a little bit complex and confusing. You can create a better symbol by considering the implications of the rule. If P is next to T, then it's not next to L and if it's next to L, then it's not next to T. So, it's simpler to just say that P cannot be next to *both* T and L. Symbolize this by showing that P cannot be between T and L:

Remember that this only means that the complete antiblock is not allowed. You could still put T next to P or L next to P, just not both.

Deduce

None of these elements can be definitively placed, so you can't begin to fill in the diagram. When you encounter a question, you can just put the first element wherever you wish and fill in the remaining elements around it.

MASTER DIAGRAM

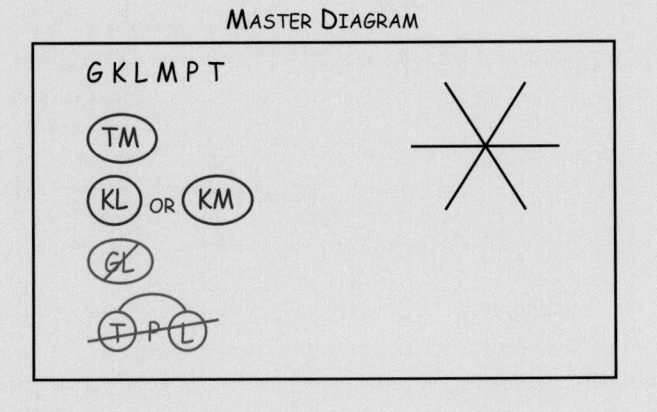

Question 1

This Local question puts **G** between **K** and **T**. You may wonder which order to put them in or where they should go on the diagram, but since the game does not mention numbered seats or make any distinction between clockwise and counterclockwise, then it doesn't matter. Just put them anywhere on the diagram.

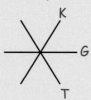

Now make some deductions. You know that **T** must be next to **M**, and that means **K** needs **L** next to it. The only element left is **P**. Thus you have the complete diagram:

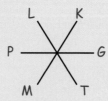

Now look at the answer choices. **L** has to be between **K** and **P**.

Choice (B) is the correct answer.

Question 2

This is another Local question. It puts **M** next to **L**, so insert that into a new spoke diagram.

Since the rules tell you that **T** is next to **M**, you can deduce that **K** is next to **L**. The two elements left are **G** and **P**, but it doesn't look like there are any rules restricting these two:

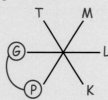

You can see that **G** can be either between **T** and **P** or between **P** and **K**. Choice (E) matches the first of these possibilities.

Choice (E) is the correct answer.

11.2 MAP GAMES

Map games rely on a map or diagram that has spatial or directional elements to it. Many Map games appear to be unique but are really only slight variations of Grouping or Grid games.

Map games were once common but have declined sharply in frequency. Since 1995, the LSAT has featured only one Map game, which appeared on PrepTest 40 in June 2003.

11.2.1 IDENTIFY

Map games can show up in a variety of forms. The most obvious Map games are those in which the test writers draw a map for you. Other Map games give you instructions on how to draw the map yourself. Finally, there have been a couple of Map games in which the situation simply describes five elements (either cities or islands) and asks you to determine which of them are *connected* by bridges or airline flights.

If a Map game appears on your test, it may not look anything at all like Map games from the past, but that isn't necessarily a problem. The whole reason you identify a game's type is so you can quickly determine the best standard diagram; with some of these rarer game types, precise identification is not as important because the diagram is unique to the individual game. The key is to recognize that you may need to use a diagram that is somewhat different from the four major diagrams. For Map games, just be aware that if a game seems to require the use of a map diagram, then you should feel comfortable going ahead and constructing an appropriate map.

11.2.2 SET UP

Since Map games can vary so much, there is no one consistent approach that works for all of them. But there are a few major points to keep in mind when approaching them, most of which also apply to other games that don't initially seem to resemble one of the major game types.

1. **Look for the ways in which a game resembles something familiar rather than something unfamiliar**. Even when the test writers provide you with a map, ask yourself whether the game can be worked using a more familiar diagram. Sometimes students get nervous when they encounter a map drawn for them. They think that they have encountered a rare game type that requires a completely different set of skills. This is generally not true. For example:

These principles apply to all games, not just Map games.

In October 1993, test takers were presented with a map of cities into which they had to place institutions like hospitals and jails. But the cities were simply arranged in a 2x3 grid, and the rules focused on what could happen in adjacent cities. While using the map was the most effective way to solve the game, the map was itself nothing more than a Grid game diagram that allowed for more than one element to be placed in each spot.

In June 1995, test-takers saw a game in which the situation described overlapping circles of radar detection areas and planes that occupied one or more of the circles. Mapping out these detection areas was certainly helpful in displaying the areas that a plane could simultaneously occupy, but, aside from that, the game was just a normal Grouping game.

2. **Don't be afraid to use the tools provided for you by a specific game**. It is a good idea to approach games using familiar tools, but that doesn't mean that you have to avoid features provided to you by the test writers. If the game provides you with a map or describes how to draw a map, use the map. It may not solve the game for you, but it won't hurt to have as a reference.

3. **If you're fairly sure you are dealing with a completely unique game, take the time to make sure you create a diagram and symbols that work well for all the questions**. Read the entire situation and all the rules carefully, and even glance at the questions and answer choices, before you start setting up the game.

Reading the situation and rules as a whole often allows you to make deductions that can help you determine how to create the appropriate diagram and how to reduce strange or unfamiliar rules into recognizable and usable symbols. The extra time you spend here will be less than the time you would have spent trying to figure out how to incorporate new information into an awkward diagram or repeatedly redrawing a diagram to accommodate new information.

11.2.3 Putting It All Together

Below is a situation with rules. Identify the type of game and set it up by drawing an appropriate diagram and symbolizing the stock and rules. Then make as many deductions as you can and answer the questions that follow.

The city of Mudville has a rail system that connects its five boroughs: P, Q, R, S, and T. The rail lines do not serve any areas other than the five boroughs, and each line runs directly from one borough to another borough without servicing any other borough along the way. The following conditions must apply:

No two boroughs are connected by more than one line.
No borough is directly serviced by more than three lines.
P, Q, and R are each directly connected with S, T, or both.
Exactly two lines run directly to P.
Exactly one line runs directly to Q.
One line directly connects P with T, and another directly connects S with T.

3. If a rail line directly connects Q with T, then which one of the following could be true?

(A) No rail line directly connects R with S.
(B) A rail line directly connects P with R.
(C) A rail line directly connects R with T.
(D) There are exactly three rail lines directly connecting R with other boroughs.
(E) There are exactly two rail lines directly connecting T with other boroughs.

4. Which one of the following could be true about the rail system?

(A) Rail lines directly connect P with both R and S.
(B) Rail lines directly connect Q with both S and T.
(C) Rail lines directly connect R with both P and S.
(D) Rail lines directly connect S with P, Q, and R.
(E) Rail lines directly connect T with Q, R, and S.

11.2.3.2 Answers & Explanations

Identify

This situation describes five places and asks you to determine connections between them. All of the rules are concerned with these connections. This is a Map game.

Set Up

This diagram consists of a map made up of the initials of the five boroughs. To make it easy to draw connections between the elements, arrange the elements, evenly spaced, in a pentagon formation:

P

Q   T

S   R

Next, you have to think about how you will show connections between the cities. Here is one good solution: when two cities are connected, draw a line between them to connect them. When two cities are forbidden to be connected, draw a broken line between them. When you aren't sure whether or not two cities are connected, don't draw anything between them.

By reading the rules before setting up the game, you should notice that they get increasingly specific. So symbolize the last rules first to avoid the need to symbolize some of the earlier rules.

The last rule describes definite connections. Symbolize it directly on your diagram by drawing a line connecting P and T and another connecting S and T.

The two previous rules are distribution rules. Symbolize them directly on your map by placing a (2) next to P and a (1) next to Q.

The third rule can be treated differently for each of P, Q, and R. Since you already know that P and T are connected, you don't have to worry about P. It has already satisfied this rule.

Since you know that Q is connected to only one city, which must be S or T, then it can't be connected to P or R. Symbolize this directly on the map with a broken line.

To complete this rule, you can make a note on your map that R must connect to either S or T.

Finally, the second rule is a distribution rule. The easiest way to deal with this rule is simply to write a note next to the diagram that tells you that the maximum number of connections any city could have is three.

Max: 3 connections
per city

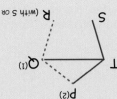

Deduce

You already made a number of deductions as you were symbolizing the rules, and there aren't any more that you can make. Take a look at the questions.

Question 3

This is a Local question, so put the new rule on your diagram by connecting Q and T.

At this point Q has its one connection, so you know it won't be connected to S. You can also see that T has reached its maximum of 3 connections, so it won't be connected to R. That means R will have to connect to S.

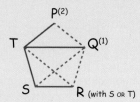

The only thing that's unknown at this point is what's going on with P. It needs one more connection, but there's no way to know if it's to S or R.

As you look at the answer choices, remember that you're looking for something that could be true—that is to say, something with some uncertainty surrounding it. Since P is the only borough that's not completely determined, the correct choice will probably have something to do with P, so focus your energy on looking for a choice involving P. Sure enough, only choice (B) contains P, and according to the diagram, it could be true.

Choice (B) is the correct answer.

Question 4

This is a Universal question, so your first line of attack is to try to use your master diagram and previous work so see if you have already proven that one of the choices is possible.

Choice (A): This contradicts the master diagram. Since P is already connected to T, and since it can only have two connections, it can't connect to both R and S. Eliminate this choice.

Choice (B): This contradicts the master diagram. Q is only allowed to have one connection. Eliminate this choice.

Choice (C): This seems to work with the master diagram, and look at the final diagram from Question 3. If you completed it by connecting R to P and making P and S not connected, then you would have a complete legal diagram showing that choice (C) could be true.

Choice (C) is the correct answer.

11.3 PATTERN GAMES

Like Map games, Pattern games are rare, and the few Pattern games that have appeared on past LSATs have not had that much in common with each other. Thus, it's hard to make too many generalizations about them.

However, there are a couple of important features that make Pattern games noteworthy, so keep an eye out for these.

11.3.1 IDENTIFY

Pattern games come in two main families. In the first, the LSAT writers actually give you the *full* configuration of *all* the elements before you start. In such a game, your task is then to rearrange the elements according to certain rules. Here's an example:

> Before the first inning of a baseball game, the members of the Rose family—Mark, Nancy, Ophelia, Pete, Rusty, Sarah, and Taq—are seated, in that order, in a single row of seats, numbered 1 to 7. After each inning, the family members switch seats, in accordance with exactly one of the following schemes:
>
> Scheme 1: Each family member in an even-numbered seat switches places with the person in the seat numbered exactly one higher than his or her own.
>
> Scheme 2: Each family member in an even-numbered seat switches places with the person in the seat numbered exactly one lower than his or her own.
>
> Scheme 3: The family member in seat 1 switches places with the family member in seat 7.

In this example, you are told the original order of the elements, so that's not something you need to figure out. Instead, you are asked to switch the elements around according to certain rules. The situation doesn't tell you how many times you'll have to switch things around. That information must be found in the questions, and different questions may ask you to perform more or fewer switches than others.

The other major family of Pattern games is one in which you have to put the same elements in order over and over again, and each new order is influenced by what happened in the previous orders. Here's an example:

> A chef is creating a schedule of the dishes to be featured as a restaurant's specials for the upcoming year. The restaurant is open Wednesday through Sunday each week, and each evening will feature exactly one dish chosen from the chef's seven specialties—mahi mahi, noodles, ostrich, pork, rhubarb, seitan, and tofu. The following conditions apply:
>> If a dish is not featured in a given week, then it must be featured in the following week.
>> No dish may be featured in any three consecutive weeks.
>> No dish may be featured on the same night of the week in any two consecutive weeks.
>> If a dish is featured on a Saturday night, then it may not be featured on any night in the following week.

In this example, you have to keep coming up with weekly schedules of the specials, and each schedule is influenced by what came before it. The situation doesn't tell you how many weeks you'll have to determine (though it certainly won't be a whole year). That information must be found in the questions, and different questions may ask you to determine more or fewer weeks than others.

Another noteworthy characteristic of this example is that none of the rules mentions any specific element by name. All of the dishes are created equal. The only thing you have to worry about for each one is what happened to it in previous weeks. This is a common feature in Pattern games.

11.3.2 SET UP

11.3.2.1 Diagram

There is no one diagram that works for every Pattern game, but if you encounter a Pattern game, you'll probably be able to use one of the four major diagram types you have already learned about. In fact, it's very likely that your diagram will be a grid, since the game will likely call for multiple rows to contain the multiple different arrangements of the elements in each question. If the game happens to have a grouping feature, then you'll probably need to construct some sort of hybrid diagram, but it will still have multiple rows for each question.

Here are a couple of things to think about as you construct your diagram:

1. **Sometimes you can deduce additional information that clarifies what your diagram should look like.** For example, perhaps the situation doesn't tell you how many rows you need, but it does dictate that each of the six elements needs to appear twice, and that each row contains three elements. A little simple math tells you that you'll need four rows.

2. **Look ahead at the questions**. Often, looking at the questions can better equip you to draw a diagram that works well once you start answering those questions.

11.3.2.2 Symbolizing the Rules

When a Pattern game (like the Rose Family example above) gives you rules that tell you how to rearrange an existing order, then it's very unlikely that you'll be able to symbolize those rules using the standard symbols you use on other games. That's okay—just come up with something that works. That could mean drawing arrows on the diagram to show which spots switch with each other, or it could mean rewriting all the rules in a shorthand list next to the diagram. It may even mean just putting a big star next to the rules as they are written for you and returning to read the originals every time you need them.

When a Pattern game (like the Restaurant Specials example above) gives you a lot of generic rules that apply to *every* element, not just a specific one, remember that you can create generic symbols using **X**'s to represent any element. You may also need to put some symbols or arrows directly on the diagram to show you what happens when an element occupies a certain spot. For example, perhaps a game tells you that the element that's *first* in one row has to be *last* in the next row. In that case, you could draw an arrow on your master diagram showing how the element (whatever it happens to be) has to move between the consecutive rows.

11.3.3 Deduce

There is one extremely powerful type of deduction that you can use on *some* Pattern games. That deduction is to **map out every single possibility in the entire game**.

You'll probably have the opportunity to do this only if you see a Pattern game that gives you an original configuration that must be rearranged. In such a case, consider whether you could write out *all* the possible rearrangements before you look at any questions. For example, if you never have to make more than two rearrangements, then it could be manageable. But if the game calls for you to rearrange things three or more times, then it would probably be a waste of time to write out everything.

The advantage to doing this is that you won't have to do any work on any of the questions. Just look at your diagram and follow what's written. In a way, this is the ultimate deduction.

As always, use your best judgment. Anything you do on the LSAT should be directed toward getting you the most points, in the shortest amount of time, with the highest degree of accuracy. But if something (like mapping out every possibility) is likely to confuse you or use up too much time, then skip it.

11.3.4   PUTTING IT ALL TOGETHER

11.3.4.1   Drill: Pattern Games

Below is a situation with rules. Identify the type of game and set it up by drawing an appropriate diagram and symbolizing the stock and rules. Then make as many deductions as you can and answer the questions that follow.

A hospital has exactly four intake employees—Isabel, Julia, Katya, and Laura—who begin a certain year working the morning shift, the day shift, the evening shift, and the graveyard shift, respectively. The morning shift is the earliest shift, and the graveyard the latest. The hospital has a rotating schedule system, in which the employees swap shifts with each other once a month, according to one of the following changes. No change may be used twice in any two consecutive months.

> Change 1: The employee who works the morning shift swaps shifts with the employee who works the evening shift, and the employee who works the day shift swaps shifts with the employee who works the graveyard shift.
> Change 2: The employee who works the evening shift swaps shifts with the employee who works the graveyard shift.
> Change 3: Isabel and Julia swap shifts with each other.

5. Which one of the following could be true after the first shift change of the year?

    (A)   Isabel works the graveyard shift.
    (B)   Katya works the day shift.
    (C)   Laura works the morning shift.
    (D)   Isabel and Katya each remain working the same shifts as before.
    (E)   Katya and Laura each remain working the same shifts as before.

6. If the first shift change is made according to change 1, which one of the following must be true?

    (A)   Isabel works the graveyard shift as a result of the second shift change.
    (B)   Julia works the morning shift as a result of the second shift change.
    (C)   Julia works the graveyard shift as a result of the second shift change.
    (D)   Laura works the evening shift as a result of the second shift change.
    (E)   Laura works the graveyard shift as a result of the second shift change.

11.3.4.2 Answers & Explanations

Identify

You can identify this as a Pattern game because the situation tells you the initial arrangement of the elements, and the rules all describe methods for rearranging the elements.

Set Up

The diagram for this game is basically a grid, consisting of four columns, one for each shift.

The stock consists of the initials of the four employees. Since the situation provides their original arrangement, write them, in order, in the first row of the diagram.

Morning	Day	Evening	Graveyard
I	J	K	L

The rules in this case simply describe possible ways to rearrange this initial configuration. Since they are so unique, you have to come up with a unique way to deal with them. In this case, it's best to simply rewrite them next to the diagram.

1: Switch morn & eve
   Switch day & grave

2: Switch eve & grave

3: Switch I & J

Morning	Day	Evening	Graveyard
I	J	K	L

Deduce

There are no deductions you can make about the elements' placement, since you already know where they all start. You have to wait for the questions to tell you how to switch the elements around.

However, you can consider mapping out every possible rearrangement of the elements. The wisdom of this depends on how many times you will have to rearrange them. The situation doesn't give you any limit on the number of rearrangements, but the questions deal only with a maximum of two changes. So it may be worth it in this case, and it would look like this:

		Morning	Day	Evening	Graveyard
Original:		I	J	K	L
After one change:	1	K	L	I	J
	2	I	J	L	K
	3	J	I	K	L
After two changes:	1, 2	K	L	J	I
	1, 3	K	L	J	I
	2, 1	L	K	I	J
	2, 3	J	I	L	K
	3, 1	K	L	J	I
	3, 2	J	I	L	K

As you can see, mapping out even just two changes starts to get complicated, so if you are working on a Pattern game in the future, you have to carefully consider whether this is the right thing to do. However, in this case, doing so makes the questions considerably easier, so it's probably worth the effort.

Question 5: This question asks you about the possibilities after just one shift change, so you can inspect the three rows in your diagram that show the arrangements after one change.

The first four answer choices are not true in any of those rows. But choice (E) is true after change 3.

Choice (E) is the correct answer.

That was not too hard, right?

Question 6: This Local question tells you that the first rearrangement was change 1. All the answer choices refer to what's required after the second change, so look at the two rows on the diagram that show "1, 2" and "1, 3." Choice (A) is true in both of these rows. Since you know these two rows are the *only* possibilities, then you know choice (A) *must be true.*

Choice (A) is the correct answer.

Again, very simple, so this should illustrate the value of mapping out all the possibilities when it's manageable.

NOW MOVE ON TO THE SECOND CHAPTER OF LECTURE 6. WHEN YOU HAVE COMPLETED IT, YOU CAN GET FURTHER PRACTICE WITH RARE GAME TYPES IN THE CORRESPONDING EXAM AT THE END OF THE BOOK.

LECTURE (6) CHAPTER (12)

MINIMUM/MAXIMUM QUESTIONS

Minimum/Maximum questions are concerned with determinations you can make about the extreme possibilities in a game. In an Ordering or Grid game, a Min/Max question might ask for the earliest spot in an order that an element could occupy or the largest number of spots that could separate two elements. In a Binary or Grouping game, a Min/Max question would more likely be concerned with the minimum or maximum number of elements that could occupy a certain group.

12.1 IDENTIFY THE QUESTION

Min/Max questions all have one thing in common.

1. **The question stem asks for a *minimum* or *maximum* number of elements or spots, or for the *earliest* or *latest* spot an element could occupy.**

Here are some examples of Min/Max question stems:

> If the guitar solo is ranked fourth, then the highest ranking that the jazz ensemble could have is

> What is the minimum number of people who could attend the ballet?

> If the couch is not moved, what is the greatest possible number of furniture pieces that could be moved?

> There could be at most how many days between the day the physics lecture is given and the day the neurology lecture is given?

All of these question stems ask for a minimum or maximum number of elements or spots or for the most extreme position on the diagram an element could occupy. Min/Max questions can come in Local or Universal (or even Rule Changer) versions.

12.2 WORK THE DIAGRAM

As with all Local questions, working the diagram on Local Min/Max questions is a vital step.

As always, you should deal with the new rule just as you deal with the original rules of the game:

1. **Symbolize the new rule either directly on the diagram if you can or to the *right* of the diagram.**

2. **Make as many deductions as you can with the new rule.**

The deductions you make can still be anywhere on the diagram and, since Min/Max questions are concerned with a minimum or maximum number of spots or elements or with a spot near the extremities of your diagram, you will usually have to make all possible deductions before you can determine the correct answer.

Take a look at the following example, which comes from the Shifts game in Chapter 11.

1. If the first shift change of a year was change 2, what is the latest possible shift Isabel could work after the second shift change of that year?

   (A) morning
   (B) day
   (C) evening
   (D) graveyard

If you mapped out all the possibilities for the rearrangements (as was done at the end of chapter 11), you could just refer to your diagram for this question. If you didn't map everything out, here's how you can work the diagram to determine the correct answer:

1: Switch morn & eve
   Switch day & grave

2: Switch eve & grave

3: Switch I & J

Morning	Day	Evening	Graveyard
I	J	K	L

If the change made was change 2, that means K, who started the year working the evening shift, switched with L, who started the year working the graveyard shift.

Morning	Day	Evening	Graveyard
I	J	L	K

The next change must be different. If it is change 1, then I will switch with L and J will switch with K:

	Morning	Day	Evening	Graveyard
Scenario 2, 1	L	K	I	J

If it is change 3, then I and J will switch:

	Morning	Day	Evening	Graveyard
Scenario 2, 3	J	I	L	K

In the first scenario, I is in Evening and in the second, it's in Day. So, the latest I could be is in Evening.

Choice (C) is the correct answer.

12.3 ATTACK

If you can't directly figure out the answer to a Min/Max question, then work on the answer choices. There is a very specific way in which to attack the answer choices for this type of question. Your strategy is to try out each choice, starting with the **biggest** number on a Maximum question, or the **smallest** number on a Minimum question

Likewise, when a question stems asks you to find the earliest or latest spot, start with the earliest or latest answer choice, respectively.

For example, if you saw a question asking you to find the maximum number of people that could attend the conference, try putting *all* the people in the conference. If that doesn't work, try leaving out just *one* (and choose well—don't pick someone who will drag others out with him). Doesn't work? Try leaving *two* people out, and so on, until you find the highest number that works.

For a question asking you to find the minimum number of days in between X and Y in an Ordering game, try putting X and Y immediately next to each other (you may have to try putting them in several different places). Doesn't work? Try putting them only one spot apart (again, in several places). Keep going until you find the minimum.

Take a look at the following example from the Round Table game in Chapter 11.

> 2. If Tristan sits immediately next to Palamedes, what is the maximum possible number of people sitting between Merlin and Galahad, counting clockwise from Merlin to Galahad?
>
> (A) zero
> (B) one
> (C) two
> (D) three
> (E) four

Since this question is asking for the maximum, start with the largest answer choice, which is four. That means trying to put G all the way around so it's next to M on the *counter*clockwise side. Then use the rule in the question stem and the other rules of the game to try to make a complete configuration.

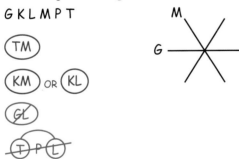

The first rule tells you that T has to be next to M, and the question stem tells you that P is next to T.

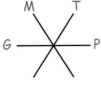

ILLEGAL

This is where the trouble starts. You can't put L next to G, nor can you put it next to P without breaking the last rule. Thus, it's impossible to put G four clockwise seats away from M. Eliminate choice (E) and try choice (D).

Looking at choice (D), G will be in a different place, but T and P are in the same places for the same reason.

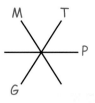

ILLEGAL

Again, it's impossible to place L so it's not next to G. Choice (D) is also impossible, so get rid of it and try choice (C).

Choice (C) entails putting G across from M. You can put T and P in the same spot, and now you finally have a safe place for L: next to M. K can take the last remaining spot, leading to this valid complete configuration:

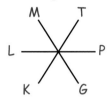

If you use this method, you can confidently pick the first answer choice that works; you don't need to bother trying the rest.

Since choice (C) works and anything larger than choice (C) doesn't work, you have found the maximum.

Choice (C) is the correct answer.

STOP. THIS IS THE END OF LECTURE 6. DO NOT PROCEED TO THE CORRESPONDING EXAM UNTIL INSTRUCTED TO DO SO IN CLASS.

ADVANCED TECHNIQUES

Every LSAT game has its own idiosyncrasies and unique twists. Most of the time, you can deal with these twists using the same techniques you have used on countless other games. However, you should realize that some games call for you to improvise or create new techniques on the spot. It is impossible to anticipate everything that could appear in the games on your LSAT, but reviewing the quirks that have appeared on past LSAT games and the proper way to deal with them will prepare you to deal with any new variations you may encounter.

13.1 IDENTIFYING THE BEST DIAGRAM

13.1.1 TRY TO USE FAMILIAR DIAGRAMS

When you come across a game that does not appear to fit into one of the four major diagrams, your first impulse should be to try to make it fit. Often, games that appear to require new diagrams are really only unique in the way they're presented. They can still be approached with a familiar diagram. Take a look at the following example:

> There are exactly eight shops on the Main Street Promenade.
> On one side of the street, the shops are numbered
> consecutively 1, 3, 5, 7, and 9. On the opposite side of the
> street, the shops are numbered consecutively 2, 4, 6, 8, and 10.
> The shops numbered 1, 3, 5, 7, and 9 face the shops numbered
> 2, 4, 6, 8, and 10, respectively. Each shop sells food, gifts, or
> housewares, subject to the following constraints:
>
> No shop sells the same product as any shop adjacent to it.
> No shop sells the same product as any shop directly across
>   the street from it.
> Exactly one shop on each side of the street sells
>   housewares.
> Shop 5 sells housewares.
> Shop 8 sells gifts.

This situation discusses ordered shops being *across* from one another, but that doesn't mean a typical Grid diagram can't be used. The diagram will have to be altered slightly, but, in essence, it is just a Grid diagram with a sequence that's numbered differently on the top row than it is on the bottom row. You can simply number the spots 1, 3, 5, 7 and 9 in the top row of your diagram and 2, 4, 6, 8 and 10 in the bottom row, leaving room in each spot to put the element (the type of merchandise the shop sells). Just remember when reading the diagram that the vertically aligned spots face each other.

The first two rules can be symbolized with generic antiblocks. The third can be symbolized by putting a (1) next to the H in each stock, and the last two are exact spot rules. At this point, the diagram looks like this:

Now, use this diagram to make as many deductions as you can. Shop 6 has an H directly across from it and a G adjacent to it, so an F must be placed there because of Rules 1 and 2. An F must also be in shop 7 because it has an H next to it and a G across from it. Shop 9 can't have an F per Rule 1 and it can't have an H because there is already one H on that side of the street. Place a G in 9.

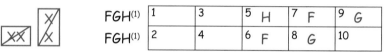

You can make some final deductions about forbidden spots. You know shops 1 and 3 can't have an H because there is already one H on that side of the street. And because of Rule 1, shop 3 can't have an F and shop 10 can't have a G.

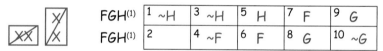

13.1.2 Unspecified Size

Other times, you may have trouble drawing a diagram because you can't completely determine how big the diagram should be. If you come across a situation like this, don't worry about it. Simply draw what you can of the diagram and move on to the questions to help you determine the rest. As an example, consider the following situation:

A DJ's playlist consists of songs that are each classified as exactly one of five genres of music—funk, house, jazz, rap, and trance. The order in which the DJ plays songs is subject to the following constraints:

If a jazz song and a funk song are played consecutively, any song that immediately follows and any song that immediately precedes that pair must be a trance song.

No two songs of the same genre can be played consecutively unless the genre is rap.

A trance song and a house song cannot be played consecutively.

Every sequence of eight consecutive songs must include at least one song of each genre.

This looks like an Ordering game, but it doesn't tell you how many elements are in the order, so it is difficult to come up with a good diagram. The rules can still be symbolized because none of them refers to a specific position in the order, but you can't determine an appropriately sized diagram. So just symbolize the rules and move on to the questions.

Rule 1 is a little complicated. You know that anything that precedes (FJ) or follows it must be T, but that doesn't mean that T has to precede and follow every (FJ). That's because F and J could be the first two or last two songs played without violating a rule. The easiest way to deal with this is just to write yourself a little note next to your conditional.

$$\text{(FJ)} \rightarrow \boxed{\text{T (FJ) T}} \text{ (except on the ends)}$$

A contrapositive in this case seems like it would be weird and confusing, so don't bother.

Rule 2 could be symbolized by creating antiblocks for each pair of consecutive elements besides R, but it's easier to create a generic antiblock and again write the exception next to the symbol.

 (except RR)

Rule 3 is a soft antiblock. Symbolize it as

$$\text{(H̶T̶)}$$

Rule 4 is difficult to symbolize. Rather than trying to create a complicated symbol, it is again best just to make a quick note of what the symbol means, such as

8 songs → all genres

Now, try to answer the following question.

1. If in an eight-song sequence the second, third, and fourth songs are trance, rap, and jazz, respectively, and the sixth and seventh songs are funk and trance, respectively, then which one of the following must be true?

   (A) The first song is funk.
   (B) The fifth song is rap.
   (C) The fifth song is house.
   (D) The eighth song is house.
   (E) The eighth song is jazz.

The original situation never told you how many songs were in the sequence, but for this particular question, there are eight. Start by drawing the eight-song sequence described by the question.

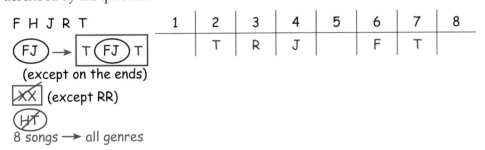

Then make deductions to fill in as much of the sequence as possible. Per Rule 4, every genre must be played at least once in this sequence. The only genre that is not in the sequence is H. Because of Rule 3, it can't be next to T, so the fifth spot is the only place you can put it.

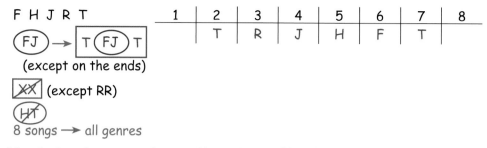

Now look at the answer choices. Choice (C) has H in the fifth spot.

Choice (C) is the correct answer.

Other questions in the game may involve sequences that are shorter or longer than eight songs. Don't worry—if a question tells you how long a sequence you have to deal with, just draw a row in your diagram that has that many songs, even if it's a different length from rows that came before it.

13.1.3 USE THE RULE TESTER TO DETERMINE THE GAME TYPE

The first question in a game can often tell you how to diagram the game. You will usually be able to answer any Rule Tester question without a diagram, but the Rule Tester can often show you a good way to approach the game. As an example, consider the following situation:

> Before the first round of training, a restaurant's employees consist of managers Odessa and Shawn, cashier Tracy, and cooks Nancy, Phillip, Quincy, Ralph, Vivian, and Wayne. Each month, there is a round of training in which each cashier and cook may be trained to be able to move to a different position, and at least one person from each position moves to a different position. A cook is moved to a cashier when a majority of the cashiers and managers trains him or her. A cashier is moved to a manager when a majority of the managers trains him or her. No new employees are hired, and no current employees leave the restaurant.
>   Tracy never trains Nancy, Phillip, or Vivian.
>   Shawn never trains Quincy or Ralph.
>   Odessa never trains Phillip or Wayne.

There are several options for a diagram for this game, and the choice may not be completely clear. Is it a Binary game that revolves around Trained and Not Trained? Should it revolve around who is in each position? Or maybe around who trains whom? If you're not sure, take a look at the Rule Tester question.

2.   Which one of the following could be the distribution of the employees after the first month's round of training?

	Manager	Cashiers	Cooks
(A)	Odessa, Tracy, Shawn	Nancy, Phillip, Quincy	Ralph, Vivian, Wayne
(B)	Odessa, Shawn	Quincy, Tracy, Ralph	Nancy, Phillip, Vivian, Wayne
(C)	Odessa, Tracy, Shawn, Ralph	Nancy, Quincy, Vivian, Wayne	Phillip
(D)	Odessa, Tracy, Shawn		Nancy, Phillip, Quincy, Ralph, Vivian, Wayne
(E)	Odessa, Tracy, Shawn	Nancy, Quincy, Ralph, Vivian	Phillip, Wayne

All of the answer choices in this question list the people, grouped by which position they hold. So you should diagram this as a Grouping game with the positions as the groups and the people as the elements. To start, fill in the initial arrangement of the elements as provided by the situation.

Managers	Cashiers	Cooks
O S	T	N P Q R V W

You also have to find some way to deal with the information about who trains whom. Instead of trying to invent some crazy symbols, just make a list that summarizes the information next to the diagram.

T: M̶ P̶ N̶
S: O̶ R̶
O: P̶ N̶

Managers	Cashiers	Cooks
O S	T	N P Q R V W

Can you answer questions 2 and 3 on these pages? For answers, see page 151.

13.1.4 USE THE QUESTIONS TO DETERMINE THE BACKBONE

Sometimes you can easily tell what type of game you're dealing with, but it's not obvious what should form the backbone of the diagram and what should be the elements.

Again, a Rule Tester question can provide this answer for you; use those things listed in the Rule Tester answer choices as the elements, and use the headings as the backbone. Even if the game doesn't include a Rule Tester, the first question can often tell you how to set up a game. Take a look at the following example:

> In a residential treatment center, there are exactly six patients—Uma, Vance, Wade, Xander, Yvette, and Zoe—who will each receive at least one of the following three types of therapy—physical therapy, occupational therapy, and mental therapy—and no other type of therapy. The following conditions apply:
> Yvette and exactly three other patients receive physical therapy.
> Vance receives both occupational and mental therapy.
> Xander does not receive any therapy that Vance receives.
> Wade receives more types of therapy than does Vance.
> Zoe does not receive any therapy that Xander receives.
> Uma receives exactly two types of therapy.

The desirability of more elements and fewer groups is a great rule of thumb, but it's also better for elements to be *assigned* to groups, and it's better for groups to *receive*, *have*, or *contain* elements, so keep an eye out for concepts such as these.

This is a Grouping game. You learned previously that it's usually better to choose a diagram so that you have fewer groups and more elements. The first rule seems to be in line with that approach, but the rest of the rules look like they would be easier to symbolize with the patients as the groups and the types of therapy as the elements. To determine which is the best approach, look at the first question.

> 3. For exactly how many of the six patients is it possible to determine exactly which of the three types of therapy each receives?
>
> (A) one
> (B) two
> (C) three
> (D) four
> (E) five

This question concerns what you can determine about the therapies that are received by each of the patients. Thus, it is better to organize the diagram around the patients and use the types of therapy as the elements.

13.1.5 Use the Questions to Determine the Game Type

If you come across a game in which neither the situation nor the rules can provide you with enough information to determine what kind of game you're looking at, the questions can again be a valuable tool. Take a look at the following situation:

> The Mitavech Corporation will spend a total of $14 million on six advertisements for its three new products—X, Y, and Z.
> The corporation will create at least one advertisement for each of the three products.
> The corporation spends at least $2 million on each advertisement.
> The corporation spends money on each advertisement in increments of one million dollars.

This game mentions a few factors, but it is hard to determine what to use as the elements and how to set up the diagram. You know that $14 million will be spent, so you could use dollar amounts to set up the diagram, but that would create a larger diagram than most games you have seen.

There are only three products, so you could use those to create the diagram and place the six advertisements in them as the elements, but the advertisements aren't named, so it is difficult to place them.

The products are named, so they could be used as the elements and the six ads could make up the backbone. But the amount of money spent also looks important; what do you do with that? The reason you create the diagram is to help you with the questions, so quickly glance at the question stems to determine what kind of diagram would be the most helpful. Here are all the question stems for this game:

> If Mitavech spends exactly $8 million advertising X, then which one of the following CANNOT be true?
>
> If Mitavech spends $3 million advertising Y and $7 million advertising Z, then which one of the following must be false?
>
> If Mitavech spends as much as possible on the first advertisement it creates for X and as little as possible on each of the other advertisements it creates, then which one of the following must be true?
>
> If Mitavech creates equal number of advertisements for each of the three products, what is the greatest amount of money it can spend advertising X?
>
> If Mitavech creates a combined total of four advertisements for X and Y, what is the greatest amount it can spend advertising Y?

Can you answer the last two question stems on this list? The answers are on page 151.

All of these question stems concern the amount of money spent on each product, so this should be a focus of your diagram. You'll want to create a diagram in which you can match up the products to the dollar amounts. Since you have three factors to figure out (the ad, the product, and the dollar amount), you will need two rows in the diagram below the backbone. The number of times each product is advertised could change, as could the dollar amounts, but the total number of ads must always be six, so, because this is the most predictable factor, you should use it as the backbone of the diagram. The columns won't have labels, but there will always be six of them.

Use the products and the dollar amounts as the elements and make sure every configuration adds up to fourteen. A typical configuration might look like this:

Product:	X	X	X	Y	Y	Z
Amount:	3	2	2	3	2	2

13.2 SET UP: ADVANCED STOCKS

13.2.1 PUTTING THE STOCK ON THE DIAGRAM

While it is generally not a good idea to clutter your diagram with lists of every element that could possibly occupy every spot, doing this will sometimes help you make important deductions. If the situation gives you a specified list of elements for each spot, then it wouldn't make sense to extract the elements from those spots in order to create a stock. Instead, note for each spot the elements that could occupy it and make deductions from there. As an example, consider the following situation:

> While running errands, Allison stops at exactly five shopping centers. At each shopping center, Allison visits exactly one business. She does not visit any two businesses of the same kind. Each shopping center has a limited number of businesses, which are listed below:
> The first shopping center contains a grocery, a laundromat, a shoe store, and no other businesses.
> The second shopping center contains a grocery, a laundromat, a shoe store, a nail salon, and no other businesses.
> The third and fourth shopping centers contain a shoe store, a nail salon, and no other businesses.
> The fifth shopping center contains a nail salon, a post office, a repair shop, and no other businesses.

You can think of these rules as giving you a "menu" of elements available for each spot in the order.

This situation lists the elements that could occupy each spot. There is no need to write the stock to the left of your diagram. Just write in each spot a list of the elements that occupy it.

1	2	3	4	5
G/L/S	G/L/S/N	S/N	S/N	N/P/R

Now look at the elements in your diagram to see what deductions you can make. Notice the third and fourth spots. The same two elements are the only two elements in those spots, which means that either S or N will be in the third spot and the other will be in the fourth spot. Thus, S or N cannot be in any other spot. Eliminate S from the first and second spot and N from the second and fifth.

1	2	3	4	5
G/L	G/L	S/N	S/N	P/R

Now either G or L will have to be in the first spot and the other will be in the second. The fifth spot will have either P or R. Knowing this will be essential to answering the questions.

1	2	3	4	5
Ⓖ—Ⓛ		Ⓢ—Ⓝ		P/R

Take a look at the following question.

4. Which one of the following statements could be true?

(A)   Allison stops at the shoe store in the first shopping center.

(B)   Allison stops at the shoe store in the second shopping center.

(C)   Allison stops at the nail salon in the second shopping center.

(D)   Allison stops at the nail salon in the fifth shopping center.

(E)   Allison stops at the post office in the fifth shopping center.

Looking at your diagram, you'll see that choice (E) is the only possibility.

Choice (E) is the correct answer.

By writing the available elements in each spot and making deductions on your diagram, you were able to answer a question without doing any more work.

There are other games that do not list the elements by spot, but nonetheless let you know that only certain elements can occupy each spot. For these, you should still write the stock directly in the appropriate spots in the diagram. Take a look at the following example:

> Evan attends school no more than three days per week and is enrolled in five courses. His schedule is, in order: writing, math, science, history, gym. Each of Evan's courses is taught by exactly one of seven teachers, who are listed below with the courses each can teach:
>   Fuller: science
>   Juelch: history, gym
>   Kline: writing, gym
>   Lewis: writing, history
>   Newman: math, science
>   O'Connor: history
>   Painter: math, gym
> The following conditions must apply:
>   Evan attends at least one course each day he attends school.
>   Science and gym are not taught on the same day.
>   None of Evan's teachers teach more than one course per day.
>   Each of Evan's courses is taught at a separate time on exactly one day of the week.

> This is a very complex game. If you saw something like this on your test, it would be a great one to postpone until after you've done any simpler games.

This game does give you an order, but it also names more teachers than courses, and it says that there is only one teacher for each course, so some teachers won't teach a class—they will be left out of the order. Therefore, it is a Hybrid game.

> Use an artificially imposed order as your diagram's backbone, just as you would use a natural order.

When a game contains a natural order, such as first through last, you always use that as the backbone of your diagram. Classes don't have a natural order, but in this case the situation imposes an order upon them, so you should still use that order as the backbone of your diagram.

For each class, you have two things to figure out: the teacher and the day. Because of this, you'll need two rows. You'll also need a Not Teaching group to contain the teachers who don't get assigned to any class.

Just like the last game, this situation lets you know that there are only certain elements that can fill each spot. Place each element in the spots it could occupy.

	Writing	Math	Science	History	Gym	Not teaching
Teacher:	K/L	N/P	F/N	J/L/O	J/K/P	
Day:						

The elements in this game can be used more than once, so you can't make deductions to eliminate elements from certain spots, but listing the available elements in each spot can still help you make some important deductions. Look at the first question.

5. Which one of the following could be a complete and accurate list of Evan's teachers?

    (A) Fuller, Juelch, Kline, Lewis
    (B) Fuller, Juelch, Lewis, Newman
    (C) Juelch, Kline, Lewis, Painter
    (D) Juelch, Kline, O'Connor, Painter
    (E) Fuller, Juelch, Newman, O'Connor, Painter

This is a Rule Tester question that does not reference the order of the elements. It only matters *whether* the elements are included in the order, not *where* they are in the order. In that way, it's a little like a Binary game. But you can still use the order to make deductions. Look back at the diagram you created. You know that there are only certain elements that can occupy each spot in the order, so you can deduce that any acceptable selection of elements must include at least one of the elements from each spot in the order.

Start with Writing: Evan needs to have either K or L as one of his teachers, since they are the only two who know how to teach writing. Choice (E) doesn't have either K or L, so eliminate it.

Now look at Math: Choice (A) has neither N nor P; get rid of it.

Science needs either F or N; both choice (C) and choice (D) are lacking both of them, so they can be eliminated.

That leaves only choice (B). Just to make sure, check it against the remaining two spots. It has both J and L, so it works.

Choice (B) is the correct answer.

13.2.2 VAGUE STOCKS

Some games do not provide you with a clear stock of elements. Instead of giving you particular elements, they tell you that each element fits into one of two categories, and there could be multiple elements in each of the categories. Even more complicated versions of these games have overlapping sets of categories. Still, you should try to turn these games into something familiar.

As an example, take a look at the following:

A school has five available lockers—numbered one through five—for its seven new transfer students. Five of the transfer students are sophomores and two are juniors. Four of them are female and three are male. The school will assign them to the five lockers in a manner consistent with the following constraints:

No more than two students can be assigned to any locker.
Any shared lockers must be shared by two students of the same gender.
No junior male can be assigned a locker immediately next to a sophomore female.

Here there are three factors to figure out: which locker, which year, and which gender. Having three things to figure out means you're dealing with a Grid game. Use the natural order, 1–5, as the backbone, and create two rows for the other two factors.

	1	2	3	4	5
Year: SSSSS JJ					
Gender: FFFF MMM					

One strange thing about this game is that some of the ordered spots will have two people in them. Normally, you would deal with that by creating two rows, one for each person, but you can't do that in this case because you already have two rows for the different categories. As a result, just put the two people side by side in the same ordered spot when two people share a locker.

For example, in a game in which each spot can hold more than one element, [O P] means O and P are in the same spot, and [O][P] means they must be in adjacent spots.

However, when you symbolize the rules, you will have to deal with this somehow. Usually, two things next to each other in a block means that they are in *consecutive* spots in the order, but you also need a way to symbolize two things together in the *same* spot. Because of this, you can draw vertical lines inside your blocks to symbolize things that are consecutive, and leave the lines out to symbolize things that are in the same locker. The vertical lines in the blocks mimic the vertical lines separating the spots on your diagram.

As a result, your symbols will look like this:

Rule 1: You can't have three or more students in the *same* locker:

Rule 2: You can't have a male and a female sharing the *same* locker:

Rule 3: This particular configuration of *consecutive* lockers is not allowed:

Now use your diagram to answer the following question.

6. If at least one sophomore female is assigned to locker 2 and two junior males are assigned to locker 4, then which one of the following could be true?

(A) Two students are assigned to locker 3.
(B) Two students are assigned to locker 5.
(C) A sophomore male is assigned to locker 1.
(D) A sophomore male is assigned to locker 2.
(E) A sophomore male is assigned to locker 5.

Begin by filling in the new rule in your diagram.

	1	2	3	4	5
Year: SSSSS JJ		S		J J	
Gender: FFFF MMM		F		M M	

Now there are only four people left to place, and they are all sophomores. That means you have three sophomore females to place, and none of them can be in lockers 3 or 5 because of rule 3. They must all be crowded into lockers 1 and 2, and the remaining sophomore male must be in either 3 or 5.

		1	2	3	4	5
Year:	SSSSS JJ	S S	S S	S	J J	
Gender:	FFFF MMM	F F	F F	M	M M	

Did you notice the possibility in this game that one of the lockers could be empty? That's a rare feature, but you should always consider whether a game allows for it.

According to the diagram, only choice (E) is possible.

Choice (E) is the correct answer.

13.2.3 VAGUER STOCKS

Other games can get even more difficult because they don't tell you how many elements of each classification exist. Take a look at the following example:

> A video rental store is selling some of its inventory. In one day, it sells exactly six movies. Each of the movies is exactly one of three genres: romance, science fiction, or western, and each is either new or used. The following conditions apply:
>> The store sells at least two genres of movies.
>> The store does not sell more than three science fiction movies.
>> The store does not sell a used western.
>> The store sells at least one used romance.
>> If the store sells two or more used movies, then at least one of the used movies it sells is a science fiction movie.

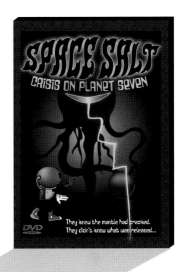

This states that only some of the elements are sold, so it's basically a Binary game, but it is difficult to set it up as a Binary game because it's possible that one element will be sold multiple times.

As a result, your diagram should just consist of six spots for the six movies that are sold. Since each spot will have two factors—the genre and whether it's new or used—give yourself two rows. Symbolize that movies are not sold by creating anti-blocks. Also notice that the six spots are not in any particular order, so block symbols in this case work just as they do in grouping games: they refer to things that are together in the same group, not consecutive in an order.

Remember to read all of the rules before symbolizing, and start with the easiest ones.

Rule 4 is an exact position rule. Place it directly in your diagram.

This makes it easier to symbolize rule 1. You already know that **R** is one of the genres sold, so at least one of the other five movies sold must be something other than **R**. Place a ~R in one of the remaining spots on your diagram (there is no order to this game, so it doesn't matter which spot).

Rule 2 is an antiblock. Symbolize it as

Rule 3 is another antiblock. Symbolize it as

Rule 5 combines a conditional with a block rule. Since you already know that one used movie was sold and it was a romance, that means that if a second used movie is sold, then it must be a used science fiction movie. Symbolize this as

second U →

The final diagram ends up looking like this:

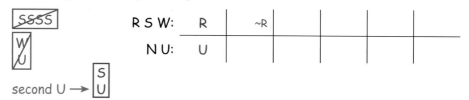

13.2.4 Overlapping Categories

Other games do identify specific elements by name, but still classify the elements according to two different sets of categories, resulting in overlapping categories for each element. In order to symbolize these effectively, your stock starts to resemble a miniature diagram. Use rows to show one of the classifications and columns to represent the other. The rows and columns overlap, just as the categories overlap for each element. Take a look at this example:

> A bookstore will select exactly four books from its eight bestsellers to display. Four of the bestsellers—I, J, K, and L—are fiction and four—M, O, P, and T—are nonfiction. I, M, P, and T are printed in paperback whereas J, K, L, and O are printed in hardcover. The bookstore will select which books to display according to the following conditions:
>> Exactly two fictions and two nonfictions will be displayed.
>> Exactly two paperback books and two hardcover books will be displayed.
>> Either M or J or both are selected.

In this case, each book is either fiction or nonfiction, so separate the elements in those categories into two different rows. In addition, each book is either paperback or hardcover, so separate the elements in those categories into two different columns. The result is that your stock looks like this:

	Paperback	Hardcover
Fiction	I	J K L
Nonfiction	M P T	O

Remember, this is just the stock, not the diagram on which you'll do your work! Since this game revolves around Displayed and Not Displayed, it's a Binary game, with the normal Binary diagram.

Take a look at the rules.

Rule 1: You have to display two books from each row. You can put this on our diagram by setting aside spots for each category. A little note next to the categories table might also be helpful:

Two from each row

Rule 2: You have to display two books from each column. This will be harder to put on the diagram, especially with your spots already reserved for fiction and nonfiction. You have no way of knowing which fiction books will be paperback, etc., so just stick with a note similar to the last one.

Two from each column

Rule 3 is best symbolized as a conditional. If one isn't displayed, the other must be.

$$\sim M \rightarrow J$$
$$\sim J \rightarrow M$$

The diagram now looks like this:

	Paperback	Hardcover
Fiction	I	J K L
Nonfiction	M P T	O

Displayed | Not Displayed

— — — —
F   F   N   N

— — — —

Two from each row
Two from each column
~M → J
~J → M

One interesting deduction to be made here is to think about how you will be able to satisfy the first two rules. If you display the paperback fiction **I**, then you will have to display exactly one hardcover fiction (in order to have two fictions) and exactly one paperback nonfiction (in order to have two paperbacks), which then leaves you needing to display **O**, the hardcover nonfiction. The same chain of reasoning could be used if you start with **O**. That is to say, if you pick either **I** or **O**, you will need to display one book from each quadrant of the categories diagram.

The only other way to satisfy the rules is to have two hardcover fictions and two paperback nonfictions. So you will have to make your selections like this:

1	1
1	1

OR

	2
2	

Realizing this makes the game significantly easier.

13.2.5 CONNECTIONS

Sometimes when a game's elements have overlapping categories or multiple features, it's better to symbolize them as blocks instead of trying to come up with creative way to write the stock.

Take a look at the following example:

> A town is repainting each of its five schools—the grammar school, the middle school, the high school, the junior college, and the university. The schools are painted one at a time, in the school colors. Each school has exactly two colors: the grammar school's colors are white and purple, the middle school's colors are yellow and orange, the high school's colors are red and yellow, the junior college's colors are white and red, and the university's colors are purple and orange. The following conditions also apply:
>> Each school will be painted using one of the colors used to paint the school painted immediately before it or the school painted immediately after it (or both).
>> Either the grammar school or junior college is painted fourth.

In this case, you have to figure out the order of the schools, but you *don't* have to figure out each school's colors. The situation already told you every color for every school. Thus, you won't need two rows in your diagram—it's a regular Ordering game—but you do need some way to deal with the colors. Use blocks.

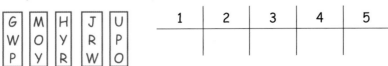

1	2	3	4	5

When it comes to the rules, the first one is pretty strange. Each school has to have a color in common with one of its adjacent schools. You could try to create some generic symbol to capture this idea, but it's better to figure out which schools share a color so that you know which consecutive combinations will satisfy the rule. Make a little list next to your diagram of which schools can "connect":

> G: next to J or U
> M: next to H or U
> H: next to M or J
> J: next to G or H
> U: next to G or M

Rule 2 can be symbolized with an either/or symbol in the fourth spot.

Use the stock to make deductions. Since there is no school painted after the fifth school, the fifth school must be connected to either G or J. G is connected to J and U; J is connected to G and H. Neither is connected to M, so M cannot be the fifth school painted. Symbolize this in your diagram.

1	2	3	4	5
			G/J	~M

> G: next to J or U
> M: next to H or U
> H: next to M or J
> J: next to G or H
> U: next to G or M

13.3 SYMBOLIZE

13.3.1 THE SIMPLE HIDES THE COMPLEX

Make sure you get all of the information that you can out of the rules, and try to symbolize them in the simplest way possible. The LSAT writers love to say simple things in a convoluted way, but they sometimes try to trick you by using a simple sentence to mask rules with complicated implications.

As an example, take a look at the following situation and rules:

> A bookshelf holds five books—M, N, O, P, and R. Each
> book is exactly one of the following types: journal, textbook,
> or encyclopedia. Only the encyclopedia does not cite any of
> the other books. The other books each cite exactly one book,
> which is either the encyclopedia or a textbook. Each book that
> cites another is of a different type from the book it cites. The
> following conditions apply:
> There is exactly one encyclopedia.
> At least one of the books that cites the encyclopedia is a
>   textbook.
> Each textbook is cited by at least one book.
> M is not cited.
> N is cited by exactly two books.

Diagram this situation as a Grouping game, with the three types of books as the groups. Draw one spot in the Encyclopedia group because Rule 1 tells you there is exactly one encyclopedia.

M N O P R	Journal	Textbook	Encycl.
			___

By the time you get to rule 2, you should be thinking about what to do about this "citing" feature. This is an idiosyncratic twist that is unique to this game, so you have to invent some way to indicate what is citing what. Anything will do as long as it's easy, makes sense to you, and won't be confused with other symbols. One possible solution is a curved, dashed arrow. In that case, one book citing another would look like:

Z | X

Rule 2 looks like it is saying something relatively unimportant: you know from the rest of the situation that the encyclopedia is the only one that can be cited by a textbook. The important piece of information to take from this is that there is at least one textbook. The fact that the textbook cites the encyclopedia is not particularly informative, but it is important that a textbook exists. Create a spot in the Textbook group.

Journal	Textbook	Encycl.
	__	__

There are also deductions you can make as you symbolize the other rules. Look at rule 3. This means that there must be at least as many journals as textbooks. So, by combining this with rule 2, you know that there must be at least one journal.

Journal	Textbook	Encycl.
__	__	__

Now you know the distribution of all but two of the elements. Where can the final two go? You know from the situation that there can't be any more encyclopedias. So, the final two elements must be either journals or textbooks. They can't both be textbooks because then there won't be enough journals for each textbook to be cited by at least one. So, at least one of these last two elements has to be a journal. Could the other be a textbook?

Journal	Textbook	Encycl.
__ __	__ __	__

This seems to work. Could the final book be a third journal instead?

Journal	Textbook	Encycl.
__ __ __	__	__

This also works. So, there are two possible scenarios for distributing the elements.

	Journal	Textbook	Encycl.
Scenario ①	__ __	__ __	__
Scenario ②	__ __ __	__	__

Now examine the final two rules. If **M** is not cited, then it must be a journal, since every textbook is cited, and the encyclopedia is as well.

If **N** is cited twice, then it can't be a journal because no journal can be cited. Can you figure out what it must be? In Scenario ①, you know **N** can't be a textbook, because if it were cited by both journals, then there would be nothing left to cite the other journal. However, in Scenario ②, it looks like **N** could be either the textbook or the encyclopedia. You should also make some kind of note to remind you that it's cited exactly twice.

The final diagram looks like this:

M N O P R
Each cites once
(except encycl.)
Each txtbk cited
N: cited exactly
twice

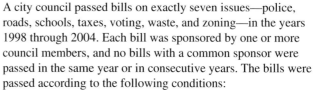

13.3.2 The Complex Hides the Simple

The LSAT writers also like to use complex rules to disguise relatively simple relationships between elements. Don't let them confuse you. Try to see if the complex language is concealing familiar features. Take a look at the following situation and rules:

> A city council passed bills on exactly seven issues—police, roads, schools, taxes, voting, waste, and zoning—in the years 1998 through 2004. Each bill was sponsored by one or more council members, and no bills with a common sponsor were passed in the same year or in consecutive years. The bills were passed according to the following conditions:
>
> The police bill was passed in 2002, and the voting bill was passed in 2000.
>
> There is at least one council member that sponsored the police bill, the school bill, and the zoning bill
>
> One council member sponsored both the roads bill and the voting bill.
>
> The tax bill and the waste bill were each passed at least one year before the police bill was passed and at least one year after the roads bill was passed.
>
> The school bill, which shares a sponsor with the waste bill, was passed in 1999.

This is a rather complicated game because multiple elements could be placed in the same spot in the order, and not all spots will necessarily be filled. Even worse, you have no idea who the sponsors are and how many of them there are! But the game looks more complicated than it really is.

While all these sponsor rules may look difficult or strange, they are really just block rules. The rule that no bills with a common sponsor were passed in the same or consecutive years lets you know that any bills that share sponsors simply cannot be in the same year or consecutive years. These rules are really just antiblocks in disguise.

Rule 1 contains two exact position rules. Symbolize it by placing P and V directly on your diagram.

Rule 2 is three soft antiblocks. If the same council member sponsored all three of these bills, then none of them can be in the same or consecutive years. Symbolize them as

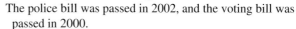

Rule 3 is another soft antiblock. Symbolize it as

Rule 4 is a relative order rule. Symbolize it as

Rule 5 is an exact position rule and a soft antiblock. Symbolize it by placing S directly on your diagram and as

So the diagram looks like this so far:

PRSTVWZ	98	99	00	01	02	03	04
		S	V		P		

Now you can make deductions and place almost all of the elements. Use the soft antiblocks and the relative order rules to eliminate elements from certain spots. Remember that the antiblocks apply to the same spot as well as to adjacent spots.

98	99	00	01	02	03	04
~Z	~Z	~Z	~R	~Z	~Z	~T
~T	~R	~R	~Z	~T	~T	~W
~W	~W	~W		~W	~W	~R
				~R	~R	
	S	V		P		

Now place the elements that have only one possible spot left.

98	99	00	01	02	03	04
~T				~T	~T	~T
R	S	V	W	P		Z

T is the only element left, and it can only be placed in one of three spots. After a strange looking situation, this game turns out to be very simple, and the questions can be answered with lightning speed.

13.4 DEDUCE

13.4.1 USE THE QUESTIONS TO HELP YOU DEDUCE

No matter how thorough you are, you may still miss some deductions. This doesn't have to be a problem. Occasionally the test writers are kind enough to write questions that guide you to important deductions. You can add those deductions to your master diagram.

Universal questions concern the rules that apply throughout the entire game, so whatever you discover on a Universal question can be used on any other question. For example, imagine you saw this question in a typical Ordering game:

> 8. Which one of the following must be true?
>
> (A) M is first.
> (B) N is second.
> (C) O is third.
> (D) P is fourth.
> (E) Q is fifth.

Always try to make as many deductions as you can before you start on the questions, but don't get bogged down. Develop an internal mental timer that tells you when it's time to get started on the questions.

With luck, you would have already deduced the answer when you set up the game, but if you hadn't, then you could still find the answer by using your previous work or plugging in the answer choices. However, once you do determine the correct answer—imagine it's choice (C)—then you can put O in the third spot in your master diagram and use it throughout every subsequent question.

The same can be done for other types of Truth questions. For example, imagine you saw this question in a typical Grid game:

9. Which one of the following must be false?

(A) R has green eyes.
(B) S has brown eyes.
(C) T has brown eyes.
(D) U has blue eyes.
(E) V has hazel eyes.

If you worked through the question and discovered that (A) was the correct answer, then you could create an antiblock

that you could use throughout the rest of game.

You can even use the *incorrect* answers to add new deductions to your master diagram. For example,

10. Which one of the following could be true?

(A) X teaches math.
(B) Y teaches nutrition.
(C) W teaches the fourth class.
(D) Z teaches the class immediately after the class that X teaches.
(E) Y teaches the class immediately after the class that W teaches.

If you determined that choice (D) was the correct answer, then you could also infer that all the other choices must be false. This would lead you to be able to put ~W in the fourth spot (because of choice (C)) and add some antiblocks to your master diagram:

It's likely that you would have already deduced some of these, but maybe not all of them.

However, don't take this technique too far—don't let it start to waste your time. For example, if you discover new deductions on the last question in a game, then there's no need to modify the master diagram. Just get moving on to the next game. Likewise, you should only be concerned with new deductions that seem like they could be useful elsewhere. For example, imagine you saw this (rather difficult) question in a typical Binary game:

11. Which one of the following could be false?

(A) If L and P are selected, then either M or O must be selected.
(B) If M and O are selected, then either Q or R must be selected.
(C) If N and P are selected, then either M or Q must be selected.
(D) If N or Q, but not both, are selected, then both M and O must be selected.
(E) If L or O, but not both, are selected, then both R and N must be selected.

While it's true that all of the incorrect answer choices are things that must be true, it is very unlikely to be worth your time to add them as new deductions to your master diagram. They all are far too specific, and it's unlikely that any of those situations would come up again on other questions.

13.5 ATTACK THE CHOICES EFFICIENTLY

When you're working on a Local question, you always put the new information in your diagram and then try to fill in as many new deductions as you can. When you have your diagram as complete as you can get it, you will typically have some things in definite positions and others up in the air. Then glance at the question stem. Is the question asking you about the definite things or the indefinite ones? This can save you a little time as you attack the answer choices. For example, imagine you have this diagram:

Stock: G H J L K M with one element repeated	1	2	3	4	5	6	7
	J	G/K		L	H	G/K	M

If the question stem asks you what *must be true*, skip over any answer choices with the elements G or K, or spots 2, 3 or 6. Those elements and spots are indefinite. Focus instead on finding answer choices regarding elements J, L, H and M, and spots 1, 4, 5 and 7.

On the other hand, if the question stem asks you what *could be true* or *could be false*, then seek out answer choices that include elements G or K, or spots 2, 3 or 6, since those are the things that could vary.

This strategy can be a time-saver, but it's not foolproof. For example, the correct answer to a *must be true* question stem with this diagram could be: "Either G or K is second."

NOW MOVE ON TO THE SECOND CHAPTER OF LECTURE 7. WHEN YOU HAVE COMPLETED IT, YOU CAN GET FURTHER PRACTICE WITH ADVANCED TECHNIQUES IN THE CORRESPONDING EXAM AT THE END OF THE BOOK.

LECTURE 7 CHAPTER 14

COMPLETE CONFIGURATION QUESTIONS

Complete Configuration questions are concerned with broad conclusions you can reach about the entire configuration of the elements.

14.1 IDENTIFY THE QUESTION

Complete Configuration questions ask one of three things:

1. **How many elements can be definitely placed or how many groups or spots are completely determined.**

2. **How many different configurations are possible.**

3. **What additional information would lead to only one possible configuration or no possible configurations.**

Here are some examples of Complete Configuration question stems:

Which one of the following, if known, would allow one to completely determine the order in which the movies were presented and identify the director of each?

If Mike finishes the race before Katie, then exactly how many different orders are there in which the seven runners could finish the race?

For how many cars is it possible to determine exactly when each was built?

Which one of the following conditions, if added to the existing conditions, would result in a set of conditions to which no arrangement of pictures could conform?

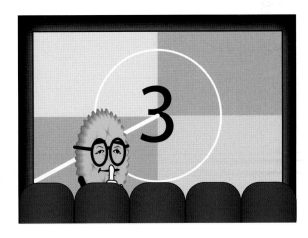

14.2 WORK THE DIAGRAM

As always, working the diagram on a Local Complete Configuration question is a vital step, and you should deal with the new rule just as you deal with the original rules of the game:

1. **Symbolize the new rule either directly on the diagram if you can or to the *right* of the diagram.**

2. **Make as many deductions as you can with the new rule.**

The deductions you make can still be anywhere on your diagram and with these questions, you will have to make all possible deductions before you can arrive at the correct answer. For questions that ask how many of the elements can be definitely placed or how many of the groups or spots can be definitely filled, making these deductions will be enough to lead you to the correct answer.

As an example, consider the following question which comes from the Music game you diagrammed in Chapter 13.

12. If in a nine-song sequence the first and fourth songs are funk, and the second and fifth songs are jazz, then one can determine the genres of exactly how many of the other songs in that sequence?

    (A) one
    (B) two
    (C) three
    (D) four
    (E) five

Start by drawing nine spots on your diagram and filling in the spots as described by the new rule.

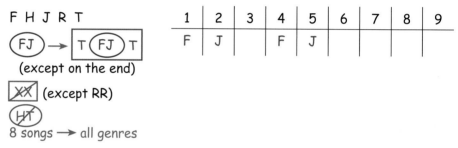

Now make deductions to fill in as many of the remaining spots as you can.

Rule 1 tells you that T's must be in 3 and 6 to surround F and J.

Because of Rule 4, all of the genres need to be in every eight-song sequence. So H and R must be placed in 7 and 8, and H can't be next to T, so it must be in 8 and R must be in 7.

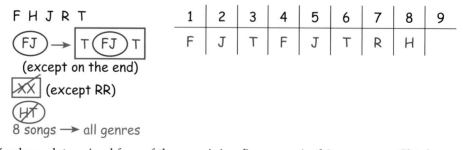

You have determined four of the remaining five songs in this sequence. Check to see if you can also determine what element is in the last spot. It can't be H per Rule 2, and Rule 3 tells you that it can't be T, but it still could be F, J, or R. Thus, only four of the remaining five spots can be determined.

Choice (D) is the correct answer.

Working the diagram allows you to answer this kind of question, but for questions that ask you how many configurations are possible, you will often have to do more than just make deductions. You have to explore every possible scenario.

For example, consider the following question from the Main Street Promenade question from chapter 13.

13. If shop 3 sells food, then exactly how many different arrangements of the types of shops on the Main Street Promenade are possible?

(A) two
(B) three
(C) four
(D) five
(E) six

Start by symbolizing the new rule on your diagram and making deductions just as you would for any other Local question.

| FGH⁽¹⁾ | 1 ~H | 3 F | 5 H | 7 F | 9 G |
| FGH⁽¹⁾ | 2 | 4 ~F | 6 F | 8 G | 10 ~G |

If **F** is in 3, then **G** must be in shop 1—**F** can't be there per Rule 1 and **H** can't per Rule 3. Now the second spot can't have a **G**, so it must have either an **F** or an **H**. Shop 4 can't have an **F**, so it must have either a **G** or an **H**. Finally, shop 10 similarly must have either an **F** or an **H**.

| FGH⁽¹⁾ | 1 G | 3 F | 5 H | 7 F | 9 G |
| FGH⁽¹⁾ | 2 F/H | 4 G/H | 6 F | 8 G | 10 F/H |

An **H** can be placed in any of the three remaining spots, but it can only be placed in one of them because of Rule 3. So, explore what happens if you place it in each spot.

If an **H** is placed in 2, then a **G** must be placed in 3 and an **F** must be in 10.

| 1 G | 3 F | 5 H | 7 F | 9 G |
| 2 H | 4 G | 6 F | 8 G | 10 F |

This is the only possible scenario with the **H** in the second spot.

There is similarly only one scenario with the **H** in each of the other two spots.

| 1 G | 3 F | 5 H | 7 F | 9 G |
| 2 F | 4 H | 6 F | 8 G | 10 F |

| 1 G | 3 F | 5 H | 7 F | 9 G |
| 2 F | 4 G | 6 F | 8 G | 10 H |

These are the only three scenarios that are possible with the new rule in the question stem.

Choice (B) is the correct answer.

Permutations!? You probably thought there wasn't any math on the LSAT, right?

14.3 ATTACK

Working the diagram generally allows you to solve the above types of Complete Configuration questions, but not all types of Complete Configuration questions can be solved this way. In questions that ask you to determine what would lead to there being a single possible configuration or no possible configuration, working the diagram is not enough. You have to attack the answers.

Take a look at the following example from the School Colors game you diagrammed in Chapter 13.

14. If each school (except the fifth) shares one color with the school painted immediately after it, then the order in which the schools are painted is completely determined if which one of the following is true?

(A) M is painted first.
(B) G is painted fourth.
(C) U is painted third.
(D) M is painted second.
(E) J is painted fourth.

In this case, the only approach is to plug each answer choice into the diagram and see if it leads to the entire configuration being completely determined. Start with choice (A).

G	M	H	J	U
W	O	Y	R	P
P	Y	R	W	O

1	2	3	4	5
M			G/J	~M

G: next to J or U
M: next to H or U
H: next to M or J
J: next to G or H
U: next to G or M

Because of the new rule in the question stem, the school painted second has to share a color with M. It could be H (which shares yellow), or it could be U (which shares orange). Check both of these options to make sure they really work and allow you to "connect" each school to the next.

1	2	3	4	5
M	H	J	G	U

1	2	3	4	5
M	U	G	J	H

Yes, they both work with the overall rules of the game and with the new rule. Since there could be two possible orders in which M is first, this is not the piece of information that allows the order to be completely determined. Get rid of (A) and try choice (B).

Choice (B) puts G fourth. You know that it has to share a color with the schools painted third and fifth, so those two schools will have to be J and U. Could they go in either order?

1	2	3	4	5
M	H	J	G	U

1	2	3	4	5
H	M	U	G	J

Yes. Again, either order could work, so choice (B) also fails to pin down a completely determined order. Eliminate choice (B) and try choice (C).

Choice (C) puts U third. Thus, the schools on either side of U have to be G and M. However, only J or G is allowed to be fourth. That means G will have to be fourth and M second. The rest of the order must work like this:

1	2	3	4	5
H	M	U	G	J

This means that when you put U third, then there is only one possible order, and every spot is completely determined.

Choice (C) is the correct answer.

STOP. THIS IS THE END OF LECTURE 7. DO NOT PROCEED TO THE CORRESPONDING EXAM UNTIL INSTRUCTED TO DO SO IN CLASS.

LECTURE 8   CHAPTER 15

ANALYTICAL REASONING REVIEW

By now, you have seen everything the LSAT writers can throw at you in the Analytical Reasoning section. The most important thing you should now realize is that 95% of all LSAT games can be completed using one of (or a combination of) the four major types of diagrams: Ordering, Binary, Grid, or Grouping. You should also realize that, although the test writers can present situations, rules, and questions in a seemingly unending variety of ways, you can actually solve every question using just a small set of techniques. Things that *look* drastically different often aren't.

15.1 THE MAJOR GAME TYPES

15.1.1 ORDERING GAMES

1. Identify the Game

An **Ordering game** requires you to put the elements into an order of consecutive spots. The consecutive spots could go from earliest to latest, most popular to least popular, shortest to tallest, or any other attribute that can be ordered.

The one characteristic that sets Ordering games apart from all other types of games is that all the elements fit into a single order. While there may be some elements repeated, there are no elements left out of the order, there is no ordering within two separate groups, and there is no more than one order to be determined.

You can also identify an Ordering game by looking at the rules. Ordering games typically feature:

- **Relative order** rules, which require or forbid one element to come before or after another element in the order.

- **Block** rules, which require or forbid two elements to be adjacent or consecutive.

2. Set Up

The diagram for an Ordering game simply consists of the natural order. This will usually be 1, 2, 3…, or it may be the days of the week or the hours of a day. Write this backbone near the top of your working space and draw vertical lines to keep the spots in the order separate. Below the backbone, leave room for a collection of rows. Each row will contain a possible order of the elements.

1	2	3	4	5	6

15.1.2 Binary Games

1. Identify the Game

A **Binary game** requires you to sort the elements into two groups.

Some Binary games explicitly name two groups and require you to divide all of the elements between those groups.

Other Binary games do not explicitly identify two groups, but instead ask you to select some (but not all) of the elements and use them to create one smaller group. In this case, your two groups are the Selected and Not Selected groups.

In Binary games, **order is irrelevant**. Binary games do not contain any feature that puts the elements in an order, that refers to elements being adjacent to each other, or that mentions any element being before or after another element.

You can also identify a Binary game by looking at the rules. Binary games typically feature:

- **Conditional** rules.
- **Block** rules, which require or forbid two elements to be in the same group.
- **Distribution** rules, which tell you how many elements or what type of elements must be in each group.

2. Set Up

Start your diagram for a Binary game by writing the names of the two groups near the top of your working space. Draw a vertical line to separate the groups. Below this backbone, leave room for a collection of rows.

The two groups should always be thought of in terms of *yes* and *no*. Even if the groups are given names, reorient how you look at the groups and simply designate one group as the *yes* group and the other as the *no* group. For example, instead of having a Red group and a Green group, label the groups Red and Not Red.

If you have any information about the size of a group, place an underlined spot in each group for each element you know must be there.

Selected	Not Selected
__ __ __ __	__ __ __ __

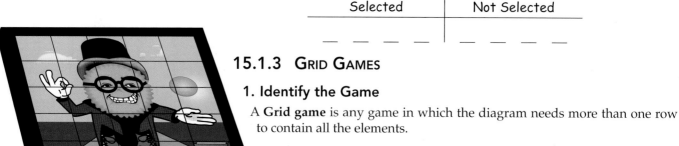

15.1.3 Grid Games

1. Identify the Game

A **Grid game** is any game in which the diagram needs more than one row to contain all the elements.

Grid games have a lot in common with Ordering games, since the spots are usually part of a natural order, and elements can be adjacent to, before, or after other elements.

The difference is that the elements in Ordering games can all fit into one row. In Grid games, you need several rows to contain all the elements. Thus, your diagram will be a grid with both rows and columns.

There are three common types of Grid games:

- **Spatial arrangement.** Elements can be next to each other *and* in front of or behind each other. Examples of this would include several rows of seats or pictures arranged in a rectangle on a wall.

- **Ordering with more than one element per ordered spot.** When you know each spot in the order will contain two or more elements, use several rows and arrange the elements vertically as well as horizontally.

- **Games with more than two factors to figure out.** For example, in an Ordering game, you have only two factors to consider, such as 1) the person and 2) the place in the order. On the other hand, in a Grid game, you may have three factors to figure out: 1) the person, 2) the person's eye color, and 3) the place in the order.

2. Set Up

The diagram for a Grid game is a grid of rows and columns. Since most Grid games involve an ordering feature, the columns should be labeled with the names of the spots in the order. This will usually be 1, 2, 3…, or it may be the days of the week or the hours of a day.

The rows will usually need labels too. For example, one row may contain the names of songs, while the second contains the artists.

Set aside the first grid to contain your master diagram with all the overall rules for the game and any deductions you make. Leave room below the master diagram to draw new grids to contain the work for individual questions.

	1	2	3	4	5
Song:					
Artist:					

15.1.4 GROUPING GAMES

1. Identify the Game

A **Grouping game** requires you to sort the elements into three or more groups. Just as in Binary games, order doesn't matter. The only thing that matters is which group an element is in.

Most Grouping games tell you the names of all three (or more) groups. However, a few situations name just *two* groups but indicate that some elements will not be placed into either of the named groups. These are also Grouping games because you will have to create a third, "Not Selected" group.

2. Set Up

Before you draw your diagram, you need to determine what to use as the groups and what to use as the elements. It is usually easier to place a lot of elements in a few groups than it is to place a few elements into many groups. Therefore, you should usually draw your diagram so that you have fewer groups and more elements.

However, there are a few exceptions. It's better for elements to be *assigned to* groups, and it's better for groups to *have* or *contain* elements. So if the questions revolve around concepts such as these, then organize your diagram to work best with the questions.

Your backbone for a Grouping game consists of the names of all the groups plus any information you have about how many elements will be placed in each group. This information may come from the rules rather than the situation, so you should always read the rules before deciding how to design your diagram.

Draw underlined spots to show the number of elements that you know for sure will be in any group.

Cincinnati	Davis	Ithaca
_ _ _	_ _ _	_ _ _

15.1.5 HYBRID GAMES

1. Identify the Game

A **Hybrid game** is a mix of other game types. It requires you to arrange elements into a specific order or grid *and* to divide elements into two or more groups.

There are several signs that can alert you to a Hybrid game:

- **An Ordering or Grid game in which not all the elements can fit into the order or grid.** If this is accompanied by rules or questions that discuss what happens when certain elements are or are not included in the grid, then you are dealing with a Hybrid game.

- **A Binary or Grouping game in which the elements must be ordered within the groups.**

- **A Binary or Grouping game in which you need to create several rows.** For example, you may need to sort the elements into groups in two different years, each needing its own row.

2. Set Up

All Hybrid games can be diagrammed using the same techniques you use for the four major game types, but they require you to combine features from different game types in a single diagram. The most important decision you have to make when diagramming a Hybrid game is whether the central feature of the game is the grouping feature or the ordering feature.

If there is no ordering feature, or if you don't know how many elements will occupy each order, then the most important feature of the game is the grouping. Your diagram will be based on that of a Grouping game, with whatever adjustments you need to make to accommodate the hybrid aspect.

Other Hybrid games are much more focused on a specified order or grid, and the only hybrid element of the game is the fact that some of the elements are left off the diagram. In such cases, draw the Ordering or Grid diagram as you normally would, and create a Not Selected group to the right of the diagram.

M	T	W	Th	F	S	Not Selected
						_ _ _

15.2 THE MINOR GAME TYPES

Only about 5% of games fall into one of these minor types, and they are becoming increasingly rare.

15.2.1 CIRCULAR GAMES

1. Identify the Game

A **Circular game** requires you to arrange the elements in a circle.

In general, the situation and rules for a Circular game will resemble those for an Ordering game—all elements will be arranged in a single order—but the elements will be arranged in a circle instead of a straight line. This shouldn't be hard to spot because the situation should tell you that the elements are arranged circularly.

2. Set Up

The best diagram for a Circular game looks like an asterisk:

This allows you to deal with elements that are seated opposite each other by placing them at either end of one of the "spokes."

Use a new asterisk diagram for each new configuration that you work with.

15.2.2 MAP GAMES

1. Identify the Game

A **Map game** is based on a map. The test writers may either draw the map for you or give you instructions on how to draw the map yourself.

2. Set Up

Since Map games can vary so much, there is no one consistent approach that works for all of them. But there are a few major points to keep in mind when approaching them:

- **Look for the ways in which the game resembles something familiar rather than something unfamiliar.** Even when the test writers provide you with a map, ask yourself whether it can be solved using a more familiar diagram.

- **Don't be afraid to use the tools provided for you by a specific game.** It's a good idea to approach games using familiar tools, but that doesn't mean that you have to avoid features provided to you by the test writers. If the game provides you with a map or describes how to draw a map, use the map. It may not solve the game for you, but it won't hurt to have it as a reference.

- **Take the time to make sure you create a diagram and symbols that work well for all the questions.** Read the entire situation and all the rules carefully, and even glance at the questions and answer choices, before you start setting up the game.

15.3 STOCKS

Once you have the diagram, the next order of business is to symbolize the stock. There are several ways in which you may have to do this:

Perfect Match

Sometimes, the number of elements matches perfectly with the number of spots, and each element is used exactly once. This is the easiest case, and all you have to do is write a list of the elements (or their first initials) to the left of the diagram.

Repeats

Sometimes, elements will be used more than once. If any element can be used any number of times, then you should still just write a list of the elements to the left of the diagram and make a note that they could be repeated.

If each element will be repeated a precise number of times, then you should write each element exactly that number of times in the stock. For example:

$$GGGHHJJK$$

If most of the elements can be repeated any number of times, but one element must be used a certain exact number of times, then use a superscript.

$$TW^{(2)}XY$$

Dummy Elements

If any spot will be left empty, it can be useful to invent a dummy variable such as X to symbolize "empty." Then you can just treat it like any other element to be placed in the diagram.

One Stock, Repeated for Each Row

In some Grid games, the same stock will be repeated, in a different order, in each row. In these games, you should write the stock to the left of each row it will be used to fill. This signifies that you have to place the entire stock in each row. The diagram will contain two of each element, but no element can appear twice in the same row.

Different Stocks for Different Rows

There are also Grid games that contain different stocks for different rows. Write each stock to the left of the row that those elements will occupy.

Other Situations

Since every game comes with its own unique idiosyncrasies, you have to be ready for unique ways in which the stock will have to be symbolized. Your guiding principle, however, is that when a row has certain elements that must fill it, you should write the stock for that row next to the row.

15.4 SYMBOLIZING THE RULES

Here of the most commonly used symbols:

Blocks

Blocks are used to show that two elements must be adjacent and in a specified order in an Ordering or Grid game.

They can also be used in Binary and Grouping games to show that two elements must be in the same group. You can use them in several variations:

Adjacent in the same row

Adjacent in the same column

In the same group

In adjacent groups (in a Hybrid game)

Antiblocks

Antiblocks are used to show that two elements are forbidden to be adjacent in a specified order in an Ordering or Grid game.

They can also be used in Binary and Grouping games to show that two elements are forbidden to be in the same group. They can have the same variations as blocks.

Soft Blocks

Antiblocks, like blocks, are used to show that two elements must be adjacent in an Ordering or Grid game, but they allow the elements to appear in any order. They can have the same variations as blocks.

Soft Antiblocks

Soft antiblocks are used to show that two elements are forbidden to be adjacent in an Ordering or Grid game, regardless of order. They can have the same variations as blocks.

Relative Order

Relative order symbols show that one element precedes another by an undetermined number of spots.

W—Z

They can also branch to show that one element precedes or follows *two* others.

Tilde (~)

Tildes are used to show that an element is forbidden in a particular spot, column, row, or group.

~L

Either/Or Spot

A slash shows that a spot must be filled by one of two elements.

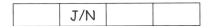

Barbell

A barbell can show that an element must fill one of two spots.

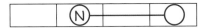

Or that two elements must fill two nonconsecutive spots, in an unspecified order.

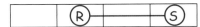

Menu

This is a subset of the stock, written next to a row or above a column or group, indicating which elements may be placed there.

Free Agent

Within the stock, use an underline to denote a *free agent*, which is an element unrestricted by any rules.

UVW̲XYZ

Uppercase/Lowercase/Script

Use different cases to show elements that belong to different categories.

Adults: HJKL
Children: mnop

Subscript

You can also use subscripts to denote an element's category. This can be useful in conditional symbols or when a rule says something about categories but not about specific elements.

Canaries: $P_c \, Q_c \, R_c$
Goldfinches: $T_G \, U_G$
Wrens: $X_W \, Y_W \, Z_W$

Reserved Spots

These can be used for several things. For example, you can show how the elements are distributed across the groups.

Main Dish (4 or 5)	Appetizer (2 or 3)
— — — —	— — ......

You can also use them to show information about the placement of a certain category of element.

E.g. *An element of the canary category must be in the second cage.*

First	Second	Third
— — —	— —	— — —
	C	

You can also use a reserved spot to show the existence of a spot in a group that must be filled by one of two elements.

E.g. *At least one of elements X and Y must be chosen.*

Chosen	Not chosen
X̲/Y̲	

Conditionals

Conditionals are a very common type of rule in the Analytical Reasoning section, usually expressed in "If... then..." language. A strong mastery of conditionals is vital to your success on the LSAT.

- **If... then...**
  When you see a sentence with *if*, the part of the sentence immediately following the *if* goes on the left-hand side of the conditional symbol.

Sentences:	If A, then B.
	If A, B.
	B if A.
Conditional Symbol:	A ⟶ B

- **Only if**
  The phrase *only if* works completely differently from the word *if*. So ignore the fact that they contain the same word. Cross out the entire phrase *only if* and replace it with an arrow. Whatever the arrow points to goes on the right-hand side of the conditional symbol.

- **Unless**
  When you see a sentence with *unless*, cross that word out and replace it with *if not*. Remember, if the *if not* applies to two things linked with AND or OR, you'll have to negate both of them and turn the AND into OR or vice versa.

- **All, every, whenever**
  Whatever follows one of these words goes on the left-hand side of the conditional symbol.

- **No, none, never**
  When you see a sentence with one of these words, make sure the "~" is on the right-hand side of the conditional symbol.

- **The contrapositive**
  You should construct the contrapositive of every conditional symbol. To do so, Switch and Negate. When negated, AND becomes OR, OR becomes AND.

  Original Symbol: $A \longrightarrow B$ AND C
  Contrapositive: $\sim B$ OR $\sim C \longrightarrow \sim A$

- **Making chains**
  When you see something identical on the left-hand side of one conditional symbol and on the right-hand side of another conditional symbol, then you can link them together into a chain.

  $$\begin{array}{c} B \longrightarrow C \\ \sim C \longrightarrow \sim B \end{array} + \begin{array}{c} A \longrightarrow B \\ \sim B \longrightarrow \sim A \end{array} = \begin{array}{c} A \longrightarrow B \longrightarrow C \\ \sim C \longrightarrow \sim B \longrightarrow \sim A \end{array}$$

  If the identical thing is involved in an AND or OR, you can make a chain only when the AND is on the right-hand side and the OR is on the left-hand side.

  $$\begin{array}{c} D \longrightarrow F \text{ AND } G \\ \sim G \text{ OR } \sim F \longrightarrow \sim D \end{array} + \begin{array}{c} F \longrightarrow H \\ \sim H \longrightarrow \sim F \end{array} = \begin{array}{c} D \longrightarrow F \text{ AND } G \\ \searrow \\ H \\ \sim G \text{ OR } \sim F \longrightarrow \sim D \\ \nearrow \\ \sim H \end{array}$$

15.5 MAKING DEDUCTIONS

You have seen that being able to quickly and correctly answer questions in the Analytical Reasoning section of the LSAT is largely dependent on your ability to make important deductions. Here's a review of some of the most common deductions you can make:

- **Combining symbols**
  A great general rule of thumb when trying to combine symbols is to look for two symbols that contain the same element. It is very common to be able to combine relative order symbols with each other and with blocks. However, don't try to combine antiblocks.

- **Endpoint deductions**
  Both blocks and relative order clues can lead to deductions about the ends of your diagram. For example if you have G—H, then you know G can't be last and H can't be first.

You should also look for places that blocks can't fit:

XY	1	2	3	4	5	6
	~X ~Y	T	~Y			~X

- **Reserved spots**

  When you see a conditional symbol in which the ~'s are lined up on one side in both the original and the contrapositive, you can usually reserve a spot in one of the groups for the elements in the conditional. Look for the group that cannot contain both of the elements, and then reserve a spot in the *other* group.

  There are some situations in which you should not create reserved spots. This would be when doing so is likely to lead to confusion, mistakes, or wasted time. Don't create reserved spots using deductions, chains, or linked rules, using conditionals with AND or OR, or when you're not sure if the spot is correct. Also don't create more that one reserved spot involving the same element.

- **Distributions**

  Many Grouping games don't explicitly tell you how many elements must fit into each group, but you can often make some deductions that allow you to figure this out, either partially or completely.

  Discovering reserved spots is often the first step in this process. It also pays to look out for big blocks and for rules that discuss the numerical distribution of the elements. Always keep in mind the total number of elements.

  In games when the elements can be repeated, it also pays to try to figure out more about how many times each one can be used.

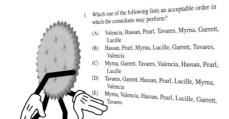

1. Which one of the following lists an acceptable order in which the comedians may perform?

   (A) Valencia, Hassan, Pearl, Tavares, Myrna, Garrett, Lucille
   (B) Hassan, Pearl, Myrna, Lucille, Garrett, Tavares, Valencia
   (C) Myrna, Garrett, Tavares, Valencia, Hassan, Pearl, Lucille
   (D) Tavares, Garrett, Hassan, Pearl, Lucille, Myrna, Valencia
   (E) Myrna, Valencia, Hassan, Pearl, Lucille, Garrett, Tavares

15.6 APPROACHING THE QUESTIONS

15.6.1 THE GENERAL APPROACH

In general, you want to complete the questions in order, unless you encounter a question that would greatly benefit from an extensive set of previous work to refer back to.

This typically means:

- Do any Rule Testers first.

- Do any Rule Changers last.

- For all the questions in between, use this process:

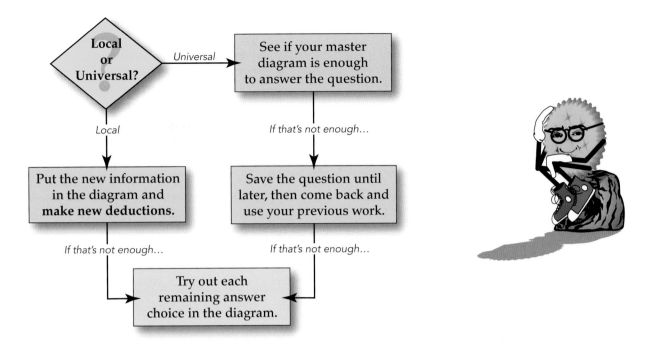

Here's some specific discussion about each of these steps.

15.6.2 PUT NEW INFORMATION ON THE DIAGRAM

15.6.2.1 Make Vague Information More Specific

All Local questions give you a new rule, but sometimes it's not in a form that you can put directly into your diagram—it's too vague. When you see a question like this, ask yourself questions that make the information more concrete. For example:

> If songs 3 and 4 are by the same composer…
>
> > **Which** *composer are they by?*
>
> If there are only two adults in one of the groups…
>
> > **Which** *group has only two adults?*
>
> > **Which** *two adults are in the group?*
>
> If Trey and Page are in adjacent rooms…
>
> > **Which** *adjacent rooms are they in?*

Often, there will be only one or two possible answers to your question, and you will then be able to work with the information in a more concrete way, including possibly splitting the question into two scenarios.

15.6.2.2 Scenarios

When there are several possible ways to satisfy a new rule, you often have to explore each one.

Create two (or three) new lines in your diagram. It's best to organize your scenarios around the most constrained elements. Put one of the possibilities into each new row on your diagram, then make as many deductions as you can in each of the scenarios.

If there are more than three scenarios or if none of them looks like it will yield many additional deductions, then don't bother with this step and go directly to trying out each of the answer choices.

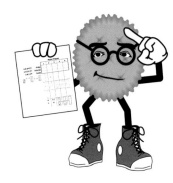

15.6.3 Use Your Previous Work

When your deductions aren't enough to answer a Universal question, put it off and come back to it after you have answered all the other questions. When you return, your diagram will contain a list of *some* of the legal configurations of the elements, and you can use that list to help you eliminate or choose answer choices.

When a question stem asks you to find the choice that *could be false*, then all the incorrect choices *must be true* (remember, those two phrases form a pair of opposites). However, just because you saw something to be true in all your previous work does not guarantee that it must be true all the time, because your previous work does not contain every legal configuration.

Your previous work can show you what is *possible* and what is *not required*. But it *__can't__* show you what is *required* in all configurations or *impossible* in all configurations, since your previous work does not show all configurations.

This leads to the following:

How To Use Your Previous Work			
If the question stem asks you to find the choice that:			
Must Be True	*Could Be False*	*Could Be True*	*Must Be False*
The correct choice is: Required	Not required	Possible	Impossible
The four incorrect choices are: Not required	Required	Impossible	Possible
If a choice was true in *all* your previous work: Then it's possible, and you should **hold on to it**.	Then it's possible, and you should **hold on to it**.	Then it's possible, and you should **pick it**.	Then it's possible, and you should **eliminate it**.
If a choice was *sometimes* true and *sometimes* false in your previous work: Then it's not required, and you should **eliminate it**.	Then it's not required, and you should **pick it**.	Then it's possible, and you should **pick it**.	Then it's possible, and you should **eliminate it**.
If the choice was false in *all* your previous work: Then it's not required, and you should **eliminate it**.	Then it's not required, and you should **pick it**.	Then it's not required, and you should **hold on to it**.	Then it's not required, and you should **hold on to it**.

15.6.4 Try Out the Answer Choices

Trying out the answer choices is your last resort, because it is so time consuming. However, on every LSAT, you will encounter questions on which your deductions and your previous work are not enough to get you to the correct answer, so you should know what to do in those cases.

Proving Something is Possible or Impossible

If you are faced with a question stem that asks you what *could be true* or what *must be false*, then your job is to discover which answer choices are possible and which are impossible. To do this, **put the answer choice, as it's written, into your diagram and see if any rules are broken**. This means trying to come up with a complete legal configuration in which the answer choice is *true*.

Proving Something is Required or Not Required

If you are faced with a question stem that asks you what *must be true* or what *could be false*, then your job is to discover which answer choices are required and which are not required. This can be more difficult. If you simply tried putting the answer choice into your diagram and seeing whether any rules were broken, you would not have completed the job—you would have proven that the choice is possible in at least one case, but that's not the same as proving it's required in all cases.

Instead, to prove something is required or not required, **use the diagram to try to disprove the answer choice**. This means trying to come up with a complete legal configuration in which the answer choice is *false*.

This leads to the following:

	How To Try Out The Answer Choices			
	If the question stem asks you to find the choice that:			
	Must Be True	*Could Be False*	*Could Be True*	*Must Be False*
The **correct choice** is:	Required	Not required	Possible	Impossible
The four **incorrect choices** are:	Not required	Required	Impossible	Possible
For each answer choice:	Try to come up with a complete configuration in which it's **false**.	Try to come up with a complete configuration in which it's **false**.	Try to come up with a complete configuration in which it's **true**.	Try to come up with a complete configuration in which it's **true**.
If you are **successful**:	Then it's not required, and you should **eliminate it**.	Then it's not required, and you should **pick it**.	Then it's possible, and you should **pick it**	Then it's possible, and you should **eliminate it**.
If you are **unsuccessful**:	Then it's required, and you should **pick it**.	Then it's required, and you should **eliminate it**.	Then it's impossible, and you should **eliminate it**.	Then it's impossible, and you should **pick it**.

15.7 A REVIEW OF EACH QUESTION TYPE

15.7.1 RULE TESTERS

Rule Testers are questions that ask you to find a configuration of the elements that doesn't break any of the rules.

Rule Testers all share the following characteristics:

- The question stem asks you to pick the answer choice that could be a valid configuration, often using the phrase *complete and accurate* or *acceptable*.

- Each answer choice contains a full configuration of the elements. For example, if you are working on an Ordering game with eight spots, each answer choice would contain all eight elements in order.

- Rule Testers, when they appear, are almost always the first question for a particular game.

Here are some examples of Rule Tester question stems.

> Which one of the following could be the order in which the inventors present their devices, from Monday through Saturday?

> Which one of the following could be a complete and accurate matching of children to toys?

> Which one of the following could be a complete and accurate list of the engineers who are selected to serve on the board?

One of the reasons that Rule Testers are easy is that they require absolutely no work on the diagram. In fact, you don't even need to have a diagram in order to get a Rule Tester correct. All of your work comes when you attack the answers.

Attacking the answers on Rule Testers is very straightforward:

1. Look at a rule.

2. Eliminate the answer choices in which it is broken.

That's it. Just repeat this for each rule until there is only one answer choice left.

15.7.2 Truth Questions

The majority of questions in the Analytical Reasoning section are **Truth** questions. The question stem of a Truth question does not ask where a particular element must be, or which element must fill a certain spot. Instead, the stem is much vaguer. It asks what must, could, or cannot be true, and you must react to each answer choice.

Every Truth question ends with one of the following phrases:

- must be true

- could be true

- cannot be true

- could be false

- must be false

The phrases above are related to each other in a very specific way: they form pairs made up of direct opposites.

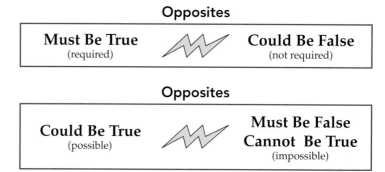

When a Truth question stem uses the word *EXCEPT*, it is really just asking you about the opposite. For example, if you see a question stem that says

Each of the following could be false EXCEPT:

you can simplify it by crossing out "could be false EXCEPT" and writing "must be true."

which one   must be true?
Each of the following ~~could be false EXCEPT:~~

which one   could be false?
Each of the following ~~must be true EXCEPT:~~

which one   could be true?
Each of the following ~~must be false EXCEPT:~~

which one   must be false?
Each of the following ~~could be true EXCEPT:~~

Work a Truth question just as you would any Local or Universal question. After each new deduction you make, check the answer choices to see if you have done enough to find the correct answer. It may help you to work more efficiently if you glance at the answer choices to see what they are concerned with.

15.7.3 SPOT & ELEMENT QUESTIONS

Spot questions are concerned with what happens in a particular spot. **Element** questions are concerned with what happens to a particular element. Their question stems always refer to a specific spot or element.

Here are some examples of Element question stems:

> If Bamforth's second appointment is with Ward, then Bamforth's appointment with Ovrahim must be the

> Which one of the following could be the bin holding apples?

Here are some examples of Spot question stems:

> If Omnicorp is included in the audit, which one of the following companies must also be included in the audit?

> Which one of the following advertisements CANNOT be the one featured on billboard 4?

Work these questions just as you would any Local or Universal question, but as you look at your diagram and the answer choices, pay particularly close attention to the spot or element with which the question stem is concerned.

15.7.4 LIST QUESTIONS

List questions ask you to make a list of all the elements that can (or cannot) be placed in a particular spot, or they ask you to make a list of all the spots into which a certain element can (or cannot) be placed.

List questions have the following characteristics:

- The question stem asks for a *complete and accurate* list of elements that could occupy a particular spot or a *complete and accurate* list of spots that could be occupied by a particular element.

- The question stem refers to either a specific element or a specific spot on the diagram.

- The answer choices are composed of either a list of elements or a list of spots.

Here are some examples of List questions:

> If Keri renovates the gymnasium, which one of the following is a complete and accurate list of buildings any one of which could be renovated by John?

> Which one of the following is a complete and accurate list of teams that CANNOT be ranked fifth?

> If the soybeans are planted third during the first cycle, which one of the following is a complete and accurate list of crops any one of which could be planted fourth during the second cycle?

Don't confuse List questions with Rule Tester questions. Although both question stems often use the phrase "complete and accurate," the two question types are very different. Since there could be many possible legal configurations of the elements, Rule Testers ask you which answer choice *could* be a complete configuration. But there is only one accurate list of all the spots in which a certain element can go, so List questions ask you which answer choice *is* the complete list of those spots. Compare:

Rule Tester: Which one of the following could be a complete and accurate list of the crops planted by the farmer, in order from first to seventh?

List question: Which one of the following is a complete and accurate list of the crops any one of which may be planted fifth?

The process of elimination is a powerful tool that you can use on List questions. You don't have to figure out the entire list all at once. You can figure out one thing at a time and let the answer choices guide you:

1. First, use your master diagram and previous work to discover an element or spot that must be **included** in the correct answer list. Then eliminate any answer choices that don't contain that element or spot. Keep repeating the process for every element or spot that you know for sure must be included in the correct answer.

2. Next, repeat the process for any elements or spots that must be **excluded** from the correct answer list and eliminate the answer choices that contain those elements or those spots.

3. Finally, look at the remaining answer choices and find the differences between them. The answer choices will generally be very similar with only one or two differences. Explore those differences and ignore any common features.

15.7.5 MINIMUM/MAXIMUM QUESTIONS

Minimum/Maximum questions are concerned with extreme possibilities.

In an Ordering or Grid game, a Min/Max question might ask the latest spot in the order that an element could occupy or the least number of spaces that could separate two elements. In a Binary or Grouping game, a Min/Max question might be concerned with the maximum number of elements that could occupy a certain group.

Min/Max questions have the following characteristics:

• The question stem asks for a *minimum* or *maximum* number of elements or spots or for the earliest or latest spot an element could occupy.

• Each answer choice is composed of a number or a spot in an ordinal sequence—such as fourth, Wednesday, five, etc.

Here are some examples of Min/Max question stems:

If the guitar solo is ranked fourth, then the highest ranking that the jazz ensemble could have is

What is the minimum number of people who could attend the ballet?

If the couch is not moved, what is the greatest possible number of furniture pieces that could be moved?

There could be at most how many days between the day the physics lecture is given and the day the neurology lecture is given?

If you can't directly figure out the answer to a Min/Max question, then work on the answer choices. There is a very specific way in which to attack the answer choices for this type of question. Your strategy is to try out each choice, starting with the **biggest** number on a Maximum question, or the **smallest** number on a Minimum question

For example, if you saw a question asking you to find the maximum number of people that could attend the conference, try putting all the people in the conference. If that doesn't work, try leaving out just one (and choose well—don't pick someone who will drag others out with him). Doesn't work? Try leaving two people out, and so on, until you find the highest number that will work.

For a question asking you to find the minimum number of days in between X and Y in an Ordering game, try putting X and Y immediately next to each other (you may have to try putting them in several different places). Doesn't work? Try putting them only one space apart (again, in several places). Keep going until you find the minimum.

15.7.6 COMPLETE CONFIGURATION QUESTIONS

Complete Configuration questions are concerned with broad conclusions you can reach about the entire configuration of the elements.

Complete Configuration questions can ask one of three things:

- How many elements can be definitely placed, or how many groups or spots are completely determined?

- How many different configurations are possible?

- What additional information would lead to only one possible configuration or no possible configurations?

Here are some examples of Complete Configuration question stems:

> Which one of the following, if known, would allow one to completely determine the order in which the movies were presented and identify the director of each?

> If Mike finishes the race before Katie, then exactly how many different orders are there in which the seven runners could finish the race?

> For how many cars is it possible to determine exactly when each was built?

> Which one of the following conditions, if added to the existing conditions, would result in a set of conditions to which no arrangement of pictures could conform?

Making deductions is always an important part of every game, but to answer Complete Configuration questions, you have to be especially thorough. You have to count *all* the possibilities, so you need to make sure you've explored *all* the possibilities.

In questions that ask you to determine what would lead to there being a single possible configuration or no possible configuration, you have to attack the answers by trying each one out in your diagram.

15.7.7 RULE CHANGERS

Rule Changers are questions that change the rules of the game. They may remove a rule, change a rule, or replace one rule with another rule.

Rule Changers have the following characteristics:

- The question stem *changes, replaces, removes,* or *suspends* one of the original rules of the game. The question stem usually explicitly tells you this, but sometimes it simply adds a new rule that contradicts one of the original rules of the game.

- The question stem tells you that all of the other rules remain in effect.

- When they appear, Rule Changers are always the last question in a particular game.

Here are some examples of Rule Changer question stems:

Assume that the condition is removed that prevents sequoias from being planted next to willows. If all other conditions remain the same, each of the following could be true EXCEPT:

If L is presented immediately before K but all the other conditions remain in effect, which one of the following could be an accurate list of presentations, listed in order from first through seventh?

If the condition that exactly three persons attend the festival is changed to require that exactly five persons attend the festival, but all other conditions remain the same, then which one of the following persons CANNOT attend the festival?

Suppose that the condition requiring that Reta speaks more languages than Silvia is replaced by a new condition requiring that Reta and Silvia speak exactly two of the same languages. If all of the other original conditions remain in effect, which one of the following must be true?

Sometimes a Local question is worded like a Rule Changer, but none of the original rules is changed or removed—the question simply adds a new rule. These questions can be approached in the same manner as any other Local question.

The best way to deal with a Rule Changer is to create a new diagram reflecting the information from the new rule. Since the new diagram applies only to the Rule Changer, you should answer any Rule Changer last so you won't be tempted to consult the new diagram to answer other questions.

To create the new diagram:

1. Copy the backbone used for the master diagram. Do not copy any of your original deductions.

2. Symbolize the new rule.

3. Determine which of the original rules are still valid and copy the symbols for them.

4. Make as many new deductions as you can with the new rule and the remaining original rules. (You can now copy any deductions that still apply.)

Then proceed just as you would on any other question.

STOP. THIS IS THE END OF LECTURE 8. DO NOT PROCEED TO THE CORRESPONDING EXAM UNTIL INSTRUCTED TO DO SO IN CLASS.

IN-CLASS EXAM ICE LECTURE 1

EXAMINATION

LECTURE 1 EXAM
Time—25 minutes
15 Questions

Directions: Each group of questions in this section is based on a set of conditions. In answering some of the questions, it may be useful to draw a rough diagram. Choose the response that most accurately and completely answers each question and circle it.

Questions 1–5

A hotel has exactly seven floors, which are numbered in order with the first floor at the bottom and the seventh floor at the top. The floors are each redecorated in exactly one of seven decorating styles—O, P, Q, R, S, T, and U. Each style is used to redecorate exactly one of the seven floors in accordance with the following conditions:

Style O is not used to redecorate the bottom floor or the top floor.

The floor redecorated in style T is higher than both the floor redecorated in style R and the floor redecorated in style P.

The floor redecorated in style U is directly below the floor redecorated in style P.

The fifth floor is redecorated in style S.

1. Which one of the following could be a complete and accurate list of the styles used to decorate each floor, listed in order from the first floor to the seventh floor?

   (A) Q, U, P, O, R, S, T
   (B) U, P, R, Q, S, O, T
   (C) R, O, P, U, S, T, Q
   (D) R, T, U, P, S, O, Q
   (E) R, U, P, T, S, Q, O

2. If T is the style used to redecorate the fourth floor, then which one of the following lists could accurately identify the styles used to redecorate each floor, listed in order from the first floor to the seventh floor?

   (A) U, R, P, T, S, O, Q
   (B) U, P, R, Q, S, O, T
   (C) O, U, P, T, S, R, Q
   (D) R, U, P, T, S, O, Q
   (E) R, U, P, T, Q, O, S

3. If the second floor is redecorated in style Q, then style R must be used to redecorate the

   (A) first floor
   (B) third floor
   (C) fourth floor
   (D) sixth floor
   (E) seventh floor

4. Which one of the following floors could be redecorated in style T?

   (A) the first floor
   (B) the second floor
   (C) the third floor
   (D) the fifth floor
   (E) the sixth floor

5. If R is the style used to redecorate the third floor, then which one of the following could be true?

   (A) The first floor is redecorated in style Q.
   (B) The second floor is redecorated in style O.
   (C) The fourth floor is redecorated in style P.
   (D) The sixth floor is redecorated in style T.
   (E) The sixth floor is redecorated in style U.

GO ON TO THE NEXT PAGE.

Questions 6–10

In a single day, a lawyer must schedule consecutive appointments with each of exactly six clients—Franny, Gretchen, Henry, Ingrid, Jacob, and Kirk. Each appointment, and a lunch break, must be scheduled for a separate one-hour block, starting at either 10:00, 11:00, 12:00, 1:00, 2:00, 3:00, or 4:00. The schedule must also conform to the following restrictions:

The lunch break must be scheduled to start no earlier than 12:00 and no later than 2:00.

The appointment with Ingrid must be scheduled for either 10:00 or 3:00.

The appointment with Gretchen cannot be scheduled immediately after the appointment with Henry.

The appointment with Jacob must be scheduled after lunch but before the appointment with Kirk.

The appointment with Franny must be scheduled before lunch.

6. Which one of the following could be an acceptable schedule of the lawyer's lunch and appointments, in order from 10:00 to 4:00?

   (A) Henry, Franny, Gretchen, lunch, Ingrid, Jacob, Kirk
   (B) Franny, Gretchen, Henry, lunch, Jacob, Ingrid, Kirk
   (C) Franny, lunch, Jacob, Henry, Kirk, Ingrid, Gretchen
   (D) Ingrid, Franny, lunch, Gretchen, Kirk, Jacob, Henry
   (E) Ingrid, Henry, Gretchen, Franny, lunch, Jacob, Kirk

7. If the appointment with Henry is scheduled before the appointment with Gretchen, which one of the following could be an acceptable schedule of the lawyer's lunch and appointments, in order from 10:00 to 4:00?

   (A) Ingrid, Franny, Jacob, lunch, Henry, Kirk, Gretchen
   (B) Franny, Gretchen, Henry, lunch, Jacob, Ingrid, Kirk
   (C) Ingrid, Franny, lunch, Jacob, Henry, Gretchen, Kirk
   (D) Henry, Franny, Gretchen, lunch, Jacob, Ingrid, Kirk
   (E) Ingrid, Henry, lunch, Gretchen, Franny, Jacob, Kirk

8. If the appointment with Henry is scheduled for 3:00, then which one of the following must be true?

   (A) The appointment with Gretchen is scheduled for 11:00.
   (B) The appointment with Kirk is scheduled for 4:00.
   (C) The appointment with Jacob is scheduled for 1:00.
   (D) The appointment with Franny is scheduled for some time before the appointment with Ingrid.
   (E) The appointment with Kirk is scheduled for some time before the appointment with Henry.

9. The appointment with Kirk could be scheduled for

   (A) 10:00
   (B) 11:00
   (C) 12:00
   (D) 1:00
   (E) 2:00

10. If the appointment with Jacob is scheduled immediately after the appointment with Gretchen, then the appointment with Henry CANNOT be scheduled for

   (A) 10:00
   (B) 11:00
   (C) 12:00
   (D) 1:00
   (E) 3:00

GO ON TO THE NEXT PAGE.

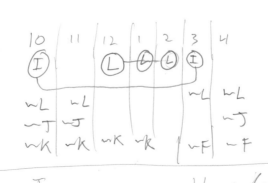

Lecture 1 Examination

Questions 11–15

A school conducts a student survey to decide between eight nicknames—Hustlers, Impalas, Juggernauts, Kingsmen, Lumberjacks, Marauders, Nighthawks, and Outlaws. As a result, the nicknames are ranked from first (most popular) to eighth (least popular), with no ties. The rankings are consistent with the following:

Hustlers is more popular than both Kingsmen and Lumberjacks.

Outlaws and Impalas are each less popular than Lumberjacks.

Nighthawks is more popular than Hustlers but less popular than Juggernauts.

Marauders is more popular than Impalas.

11. Which one of the following could be the order of the nicknames, ranked from most popular to least popular?

    (A) Marauders, Juggernauts, Hustlers, Kingsmen, Nighthawks, Lumberjacks, Outlaws, Impalas
    (B) Marauders, Juggernauts, Nighthawks, Hustlers, Lumberjacks, Outlaws, Kingsmen, Impalas
    (C) Juggernauts, Nighthawks, Hustlers, Lumberjacks, Impalas, Marauders, Kingsmen, Outlaws
    (D) Juggernauts, Nighthawks, Lumberjacks, Hustlers, Marauders, Impalas, Kingsmen, Outlaws
    (E) Juggernauts, Marauders, Nighthawks, Hustlers, Outlaws, Lumberjacks, Impalas, Kingsmen

12. If Marauders is more popular than Kingsmen, then which one of the following could be the order of the nicknames, ranked from most popular to least popular?

    (A) Marauders, Nighthawks, Juggernauts, Hustlers, Lumberjacks, Outlaws, Kingsmen, Impalas
    (B) Marauders, Juggernauts, Kingsmen, Nighthawks, Hustlers, Lumberjacks, Outlaws, Impalas
    (C) Juggernauts, Nighthawks, Marauders, Hustlers, Lumberjacks, Kingsmen, Impalas, Outlaws
    (D) Juggernauts, Marauders, Nighthawks, Hustlers, Impalas, Kingsmen, Lumberjacks, Outlaws
    (E) Juggernauts, Nighthawks, Hustlers, Lumberjacks, Kingsmen, Marauders, Outlaws, Impalas

13. If Marauders is the most popular nickname, then Hustlers must be ranked

    (A) second
    (B) third
    (C) fourth
    (D) fifth
    (E) sixth

14. If Impalas is more popular than Kingsmen, then Marauders CANNOT be ranked

    (A) third
    (B) fourth
    (C) fifth
    (D) sixth
    (E) seventh

15. Lumberjacks could be ranked

    (A) first
    (B) third
    (C) fifth
    (D) seventh
    (E) eighth

M – J – N – H – L – O – K I

STOP

IF YOU FINISH BEFORE TIME IS CALLED, YOU MAY CHECK YOUR WORK ON THIS EXAM ONLY.
DO NOT WORK ON ANY OTHER EXAM IN THE BOOK.

H I J K L M N O

1 2 3 4 5 6 7 8

Answers

1. B
2. D
3. A
4. E
5. D
6. B
7. D
8. B
9. E
10. D
11. B
12. C
13. C
14. E
15. C

IN-CLASS EXAM **ICE** LECTURE **2**

EXAMINATION

LECTURE 2 EXAM
Time—25 minutes
15 Questions

<u>Directions:</u> Each group of questions in this section is based on a set of conditions. In answering some of the questions, it may be useful to draw a rough diagram. Choose the response that most accurately and completely answers each question and circle it.

<u>Questions 1–5</u>

A company must choose at least one of its seven new products—T, U, V, W, X, Y, and Z—to promote. The selection is consistent with the following conditions:
  If X is promoted, then neither T nor V is promoted.
  Z is promoted only if X is also promoted.
  If U is promoted, then Y or Z is also promoted.
  V is promoted if W is not promoted.

1. Which one of the following could be a complete and accurate list of the products that are NOT promoted?

   (A) T, W, V, Y
   (B) T, W, X, Z
   (C) U, V, Y, Z
   (D) V, X, Y
   (E) X, Y, Z

2. If Z is promoted, which one of the following must be true?

   (A) U is not promoted.
   (B) Z is not promoted.
   (C) V is promoted.
   (D) W is promoted.
   (E) Y is promoted.

3. Which one of the following could be true?

   (A) U is the only product promoted.
   (B) V is the only product promoted.
   (C) X is the only product promoted.
   (D) Y is the only product promoted.
   (E) Z is the only product promoted.

4. If Y is not promoted, which one of the following must be false?

   (A) Both T and U are promoted.
   (B) Both T and V are promoted.
   (C) Both U and X are promoted
   (D) Both U and Z are promoted.
   (E) Both X and Z are promoted.

5. If X is promoted, which one of the following could be a complete and accurate list of all the products promoted?

   (A) U, W, X
   (B) U, W, Y, Z
   (C) U, X, Y, Z
   (D) V, W, X, Y
   (E) W, X, Y, Z

GO ON TO THE NEXT PAGE.

Lecture 2 Examination

Questions 6–10

Six people—Faye, George, Harvey, Joan, Kurt, and Nathan—will each give exactly one presentation at a two-day meeting. Each person will present on either Monday or Tuesday. The presentations must conform to the following conditions:

Faye presents on Monday unless Joan or Nathan presents on Monday.

George presents on Tuesday only if Kurt presents on Monday.

If Harvey presents on Monday, then Faye and Kurt present on Tuesday.

Nathan presents on Monday if Kurt presents on Monday.

6. Which one of the following could be a complete and accurate list of the people who present on Monday?

(A) Faye, Nathan
(B) Faye, George, Kurt
(C) Harvey, George
(D) Faye, Harvey, George
(E) George, Nathan

7. If Faye and George present on the same day, which one of the following must be true?

(A) George presents on Tuesday.
(B) Harvey presents on Tuesday.
(C) Joan presents on Monday.
(D) Kurt presents on Monday.
(E) Nathan Presents on Monday.

8. Each of the following could be true EXCEPT:

(A) Faye and Kurt both present on Monday.
(B) Harvey and George both present on Monday.
(C) George and Harvey both present on Tuesday.
(D) George and Nathan both present on Tuesday.
(E) Harvey and Joan both present on Tuesday.

9. If George presents on Tuesday, then which one of the following must be false?

(A) Faye presents on Tuesday.
(B) Harvey presents on Monday.
(C) Joan presents on Tuesday.
(D) Kurt presents on Monday.
(E) Nathan presents on Monday.

10. If Harvey presents on Monday, which one of the following could be a complete and accurate list of the people who present on Tuesday?

(A) Faye, George, Kurt, Nathan
(B) Faye, Joan, Kurt, Nathan
(C) Faye, Harvey, Kurt, Nathan
(D) Faye, Kurt, Nathan
(E) Kurt, Nathan

GO ON TO THE NEXT PAGE.

Copyright © 2007 Examkrackers, Inc.

Lecture 2 Examination

Questions 11–15

A florist arranges bouquets using one or more of exactly seven types of flowers—lilacs, marigolds, orchids, petunias, roses, tulips, and violets—in a manner consistent with the following conditions:

Orchids are not included in any bouquet that contains both lilacs and tulips.

Marigolds and roses are included in every bouquet that does not contain tulips.

Neither petunias nor roses are included in any bouquet that does not contain lilacs.

Petunias are included in every bouquet that does not contain violets.

Violets are not included in any bouquet that contains marigolds.

11. Which one of the following could be a complete and accurate list of the flowers included in a bouquet?

   (A)   lilacs, marigolds, orchids, roses
   (B)   lilacs, marigolds, orchids, petunias
   (C)   lilacs, roses, tulips, violets
   (D)   marigolds, orchids, tulips, violets
   (E)   orchids, roses, tulips, violets

12. Which one of the following must be false?

   (A)   A bouquet includes both orchids and marigolds.
   (B)   A bouquet includes both lilacs and violets.
   (C)   A bouquet includes neither orchids nor roses.
   (D)   A bouquet includes neither petunias nor tulips.
   (E)   A bouquet includes neither tulips nor violets.

13. If a bouquet includes marigolds, which one of the following must be true?

   (A)   The bouquet also includes lilacs.
   (B)   The bouquet also includes orchids.
   (C)   The bouquet also includes violets.
   (D)   The bouquet does not include roses.
   (E)   The bouquet does not include tulips.

14. If a bouquet includes neither roses nor violets, which one of the following could be false?

   (A)   The bouquet includes lilacs.
   (B)   The bouquet does not include marigolds.
   (C)   The bouquet does not include orchids.
   (D)   The bouquet includes petunias.
   (E)   The bouquet includes tulips.

15. If a bouquet contains orchids, each of the following could be true EXCEPT:

   (A)   The bouquet also includes both lilacs and roses.
   (B)   The bouquet also includes both lilacs and marigolds.
   (C)   The bouquet also includes both marigolds and petunias.
   (D)   The bouquet also includes both marigolds and tulips.
   (E)   The bouquet also includes both tulips and violets.

STOP

IF YOU FINISH BEFORE TIME IS CALLED, YOU MAY CHECK YOUR WORK ON THIS EXAM ONLY. DO NOT WORK ON ANY OTHER EXAM IN THE BOOK.

Answers

1. B
2. D
3. B
4. A
5. E
6. E
7. B
8. D
9. B
10. D
11. C
12. D
13. A
14. B
15. D

IN-CLASS EXAM ICE LECTURE 3

EXAMINATION

LECTURE 3 EXAM

Time—25 minutes

15 Questions

Directions: Each group of questions in this section is based on a set of conditions. In answering some of the questions, it may be useful to draw a rough diagram. Choose the response that most accurately and completely answers each question and circle it.

Questions 1–5

A technician is scheduled to visit six offices—K, L, M, N, O, and P. He will perform installations in three of the offices, and repairs in the other three. The order of the visits is subject to the following restrictions:

The technician does not perform two repairs in a row.
The technician visits O immediately before or after M.
The technician performs an installation on the fourth visit.
The visit immediately following the visit to M is an installation.
The technician performs a repair at L.

1. Which one of the following is an acceptable order of visits?

(A) K, P, N, O, M, L
(B) L, P, O, M, N, K
(C) M, O, P, L, N, K
(D) N, L, P, K, M, O
(E) P, O, L, M, K, N

2. If the technician performs installations at K, M, and P, then he could visit L

(A) second
(B) third
(C) fourth
(D) fifth
(E) sixth

3. Which one of the following must be false?

(A) The technician performs an installation in the first office he visits.
(B) The technician performs an installation in the second office he visits.
(C) The technician performs a repair in the third office he visits.
(D) The technician performs a repair in the fifth office he visits.
(E) The technician performs an installation in the sixth office he visits.

4. If the technician visits K fifth and N sixth, then at which one of the following offices must the technician perform an installation?

(A) K
(B) M
(C) N
(D) O
(E) P

5. If the technician visits L fifth, then which one of the following could be true?

(A) K receives an installation on the first visit.
(B) M receives an installation on the fourth visit.
(C) N receives a repair on the third visit.
(D) O receives a repair on the third visit.
(E) P receives a repair on the sixth visit.

GO ON TO THE NEXT PAGE.

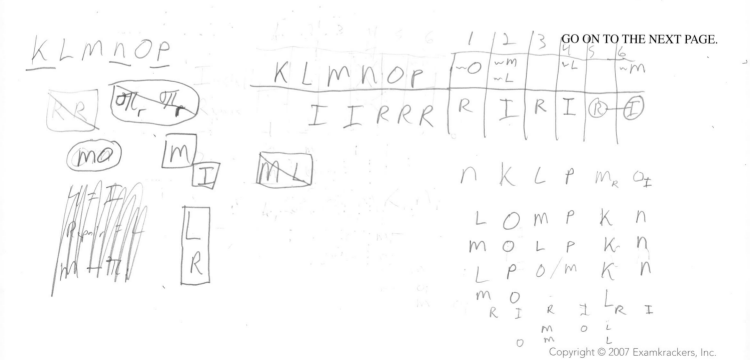

Lecture 3 Examination

Questions 6–10

Six airplanes—S, T, W, X, Y, and Z—will be launched from a runway, one at a time. Three of the airplanes are jet planes, and the other three are propeller planes. The order in which the planes are launched is subject to the following conditions:

The third plane launched is a propeller plane.
A jet launch is followed by another jet launch exactly once.
Y is a jet plane.
If W is a propeller plane, then Z is a jet plane.
T is launched directly before Y.

6.   If propeller planes are launched fourth and fifth, then which one of the following could be the order in which the planes are launched?

(A)   S, T, Y, W, X, Z
(B)   T, Y, Z, X, W, S
(C)   X, Z, S, W, T, Y
(D)   Y, Z, X, S, W, T
(E)   Z, S, W, T, Y, X

7.   If the order in which the planes are launched is T, Y, Z, S, X, W, then a propeller plane must be launched

(A)   first
(B)   second
(C)   fourth
(D)   fifth
(E)   sixth

8.   Each of the following could be true EXCEPT:

(A)   S and T are both jet planes.
(B)   S and T are both propeller planes.
(C)   W and X are both jet planes.
(D)   W and X are both propeller planes.
(E)   W and Z are both jet planes.

9.   If the plane launched immediately before T is a jet, then the fourth plane launched must be

(A)   T
(B)   W
(C)   X
(D)   Y
(E)   Z

10.   If Y is the last plane launched, then which one of the following must be true?

(A)   The first plane launched is a propeller plane.
(B)   The second plane launched is a jet plane.
(C)   The second plane launched is a propeller plane.
(D)   The fourth plane launched is a jet plane.
(E)   The fourth plane launched is a propeller plane.

GO ON TO THE NEXT PAGE.

Questions 11–15

The town of Smithville is holding a theater festival. During the festival, six plays will be performed, one each on Thursday and Friday evening, and both a matinee and evening show on Saturday and Sunday. The six plays are directed by Foley, Gomez, Hart, Jacoby, Kogan and Lowe, not necessarily in that order. Two of the plays were written by Miller, two by Nicholls, and two by O'Neill. The order in which the plays are performed is consistent with the following conditions:

    Both of the plays written by Miller must be performed on the same day.

    The play directed by Hart must be performed during a matinee.

    The play directed by Kogan was written by O'Neill, and must be performed before the play directed by Lowe, but after the play directed by Jacoby.

    Both plays written by Nicholls must be performed before either play written by Miller.

    Foley does not direct either play written by Miller.

    Gomez does not direct either play written by Nicholls.

11.   If both plays written by O'Neill are performed on Sunday, then which one of the following could direct the play performed on Friday?

    (A)   Foley
    (B)   Gomez
    (C)   Hart
    (D)   Kogan
    (E)   Lowe

12.   If Jacoby directs one of the Saturday plays, which of the following could be true?

    (A)   Lowe directs one of the O'Neill plays.
    (B)   Jacoby directs one of the O'Neill plays.
    (C)   The Thursday play is written by O'Neill.
    (D)   The play directed by Gomez is performed on Saturday.
    (E)   The play directed by Hart is performed on Saturday.

13.   Which one of the following statements must be false?

    (A)   The Sunday matinee is directed by Lowe.
    (B)   Both plays written by O'Neill are performed on Sunday.
    (C)   The play directed by Jacoby is performed on Saturday.
    (D)   The play directed by Jacoby is written by Miller.
    (E)   Both plays written by Nicholls are performed on Saturday.

14.   If one of the matinees is a play written by O'Neill and directed by Foley, then Gomez must direct the play at which one of the following times?

    (A)   Thursday
    (B)   Friday
    (C)   Saturday evening
    (D)   Sunday matinee
    (E)   Sunday evening

15.   If the play performed on Friday is directed by Kogan, then which one of the following could be true?

    (A)   Jacoby directs a play written by Miller.
    (B)   Lowe directs the Sunday matinee.
    (C)   Both plays written by Miller are performed on Saturday.
    (D)   The Sunday evening play is directed by Foley.
    (E)   Gomez directs the Thursday play.

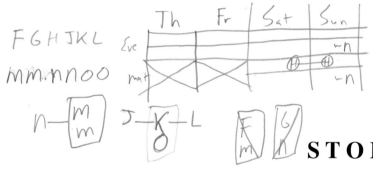

S T O P

IF YOU FINISH BEFORE TIME IS CALLED, YOU MAY CHECK YOUR WORK ON THIS EXAM ONLY. DO NOT WORK ON ANY OTHER EXAM IN THE BOOK.

J

G_O F_n J_n H_m

K_O L_m

H_m K_O

n n G_m K_O

J_m L_O

J_m L_O

H L

J

MM nn OO

J G F_O H_m J_n K_O F_O H_m

K_O L_m F_O H_m

G L_n G_m

J_n n H_m F_O n n H_m F_O

L_m K_O

m

J_n K_O H_O L_m

F_n G_m

Answers

1. B
2. E
3. A
4. E
5. C
6. C
7. C
8. A
9. D
10. E
11. A
12. C
13. D
14. E
15. B

IN-CLASS EXAM ICE LECTURE 4

EXAMINATION

LECTURE 4 EXAM
Time—25 minutes
15 Questions

Directions: Each group of questions in this section is based on a set of conditions. In answering some of the questions, it may be useful to draw a rough diagram. Choose the response that most accurately and completely answers each question and circle it.

Questions 1–5

An athletic meet features competition in three sports—gymnastics, swimming, and track. Four schools—H, I, K, and L—will each send two teams to the meet. Each team participates in one sport, and no two teams from the same school participate in the same sport.

    Three schools send swim teams.

    L and exactly two other schools send track teams.

    If I sends a swim team, then K sends a gymnastics team.

    H does not send both a track team and a gymnastics team.

1.   If K sends both a swim team and a track team, then which one of the following is a complete and accurate list of the sports teams that H could send?

    (A)   gymnastics
    (B)   gymnastics, swim
    (C)   gymnastics, track
    (D)   swim, track
    (E)   gymnastics, swim, track

2.   If H sends a gymnastics team, then which one of the following is a complete and accurate list of the other schools any one of which could also send a gymnastics team?

    (A)   K
    (B)   L
    (C)   I, K
    (D)   K, L
    (E)   I, K, L

3.   Which one of the following must be false?

    (A)   Both H and I send gymnastics teams.
    (B)   Both H and I send track teams.
    (C)   Both H and K send gymnastics teams.
    (D)   Both H and K send track teams.
    (E)   Both H and L send gymnastics teams.

4.   If I does not send a swim team, then which one of the following is a complete and accurate list of the schools any one of which could send a track team?

    (A)   H, L
    (B)   I, L
    (C)   H, I, K
    (D)   H, I, L
    (E)   H, I, K, L

5.   If both H and K send track teams, then which one of the following must be true?

    (A)   Both I and K send gymnastics teams.
    (B)   Both I and K send swim teams.
    (C)   Both I and L send gymnastics teams.
    (D)   Both K and L send swim teams.
    (E)   Both K and L send gymnastics teams.

GO ON TO THE NEXT PAGE.

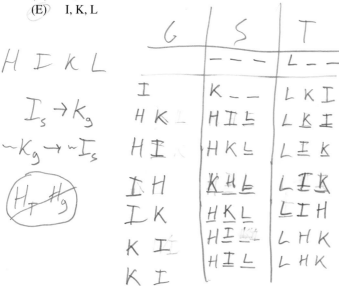

Questions 6–10

Each of three shops—Players, Renegade, and Sportstore—sells at least one of the following five products—fishing poles, golf clubs, hockey sticks, ice skates, and kayaks—and no other products. Each product is sold by at least one of the three shops. The following conditions apply:

Exactly two shops sell fishing poles.
Players sells hockey sticks but not kayaks.
Renegade sells exactly one product.
No shop sells both golf clubs and ice skates.
Any shop that sells kayaks also sells fishing poles.
Any shop that sells hockey sticks also sells ice skates.

6. Which one of the following is a complete and accurate list of the products that CANNOT be sold by Players?

(A) kayaks
(B) fishing poles, kayaks
(C) fishing poles, golf clubs
(D) golf clubs, kayaks
(E) fishing poles, golf clubs, kayaks

7. Which one of the following could be a complete and accurate list of the products sold by Sportstore?

(A) fishing poles, golf clubs
(B) fishing poles, kayaks
(C) hockey sticks, ice skates, kayaks
(D) fishing poles, golf clubs, ice skates, kayaks
(E) fishing poles, golf clubs, hockey sticks, ice skates, kayaks

8. If Sportstore sells exactly three products, then which one of the following is a complete and accurate list of the shops any one of which could sell hockey sticks?

(A) Players
(B) Sportstore
(C) Players, Renegade
(D) Players, Sportstore
(E) Players, Renegade, Sportstore

9. If the product sold by Renegade is also one of the products sold by Players, then each of the following must be true EXCEPT:

(A) Players sells fishing poles.
(B) Players sells ice skates.
(C) Sportstore sells golf clubs.
(D) Sportstore sells ice skates.
(E) Sportstore sells kayaks.

10. If Players sells exactly three products, then which one of the following is a complete and accurate list of the products any one of which could be the product sold by Renegade?

(A) fishing poles
(B) golf clubs
(C) fishing poles, ice skates
(D) golf clubs, ice skates
(E) fishing poles, golf clubs, ice skates

GO ON TO THE NEXT PAGE.

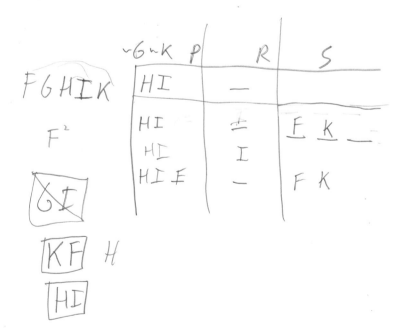

Lecture 4 Examination

Questions 11–15

A total of seven pieces of furniture are to be placed throughout three rooms in a house—two in the family room, two in the great room, and three in the living room. Two of the pieces of furniture—H and J—are ottomans. Two others—K and N— are recliners. The remaining three pieces—X, Y, and Z —are sofas. The placement of the pieces of furniture is consistent with the following:

H must be placed in the same room as a recliner.
N must be placed in the same room as J or a sofa.
Y must not be placed in any room with an ottoman.

11. Which one of the following could be a complete and accurate list of the contents of one room?

(A)   H, N
(B)   H, Z
(C)   J, Y
(D)   H, N, Z
(E)   K, X, Z

12. If each sofa is placed in a different room, then which one of the following is a complete and accurate list of the furniture pieces any one of which could be placed in the living room?

(A)   H, K, X, Z
(B)   K, N, X, Z
(C)   H, K, N, X, Z
(D)   H, J, K, N, X, Z
(E)   H, K, N, X, Y, Z

13. Which one of the following statements CANNOT be true?

(A)   Both ottomans are in the same room.
(B)   Both recliners are in the same room.
(C)   All three sofas are in the same room.
(D)   Each recliner is in a room with a sofa.
(E)   No room has two pieces of the same kind of furniture.

14. If both J and X are placed in the family room, then which one of the following is a complete and accurate list of the furniture pieces any one of which could be placed in the great room?

(A)   H, K, N
(B)   H, K, Y
(C)   K, N, Y
(D)   H, K, N, Y
(E)   H, K, N, Y, Z

15. If H and N are placed in the same room, then which one of the following is a complete and accurate list of the rooms any one of which could be the room in which K is placed?

(A)   great room
(B)   living room
(C)   family room, great room
(D)   great room, living room
(E)   family room, great room, living room

STOP

IF YOU FINISH BEFORE TIME IS CALLED, YOU MAY CHECK YOUR WORK ON THIS EXAM ONLY.
DO NOT WORK ON ANY OTHER EXAM IN THE BOOK.

Answers

1. B
2. C
3. E
4. E
5. A
6. D
7. B
8. A
9. D
10. D
11. D
12. C
13. B
14. D
15. C

IN-CLASS EXAM ICE LECTURE 5

EXAMINATION

LECTURE 5 EXAM

Time—25 minutes

15 Questions

Directions: Each group of questions in this section is based on a set of conditions. In answering some of the questions, it may be useful to draw a rough diagram. Choose the response that most accurately and completely answers each question and circle it.

Questions 1–5

A gallery's exhibit consists of a display of exactly six paintings—F, G, H, J, K, and L—each of which is located in either the main hall or the side hall. Each painting was produced in a different century from any other painting. The following constraints must be observed:

    K is in the side hall.

    H and L are not in the same hall.

    If G is in the main hall, then H and J are in the main hall, J being produced in a later century than H but in an earlier century than G.

    If G is in the side hall, then L is in the main hall and was produced in an earlier century than any other painting in the main hall.

    If J is in the side hall, then H is in the side hall, H being produced in a later century than K but in an earlier century than J.

1. Which one of the following could be a complete and accurate list of the paintings in the main hall, listed in production order from earliest century to latest century?

    (A)   L, F

    (B)   F, J, L

    (C)   H, G, J

    (D)   H, K, J, G

    (E)   H, L, J, F

2. Which one of the following paintings could be the only painting in its hall?

    (A)   F

    (B)   G

    (C)   J

    (D)   K

    (E)   L

3. If L is in the main hall, which one of the following statements must be true?

    (A)   F is in the main hall.

    (B)   G is in the side hall.

    (C)   H is in the main hall.

    (D)   J is in the main hall.

    (E)   J is in the side hall.

4. If H is in the main hall, which one of the following statements could be true?

    (A)   G and L are in the same hall, G being produced in an earlier century than L.

    (B)   G and K are in the same hall, G being produced in an earlier century than K.

    (C)   J and K are in the same hall, J being produced in an earlier century than K.

    (D)   J and L are in the same hall, J being produced in an earlier century than L.

    (E)   K and L are in the same hall, K being produced in an earlier century than L.

5. If the condition that H and L are not in the same hall is suspended but all other conditions remain in effect, which one of the following statements must be false?

    (A)   Exactly five paintings are in the side hall.

    (B)   Exactly five paintings are in the main hall.

    (C)   J and exactly two other paintings are in the side hall.

    (D)   F and exactly three other paintings are in the main hall.

    (E)   H and exactly two other paintings are in the main hall.

GO ON TO THE NEXT PAGE.

Questions 6–10

On each of five work days—Monday through Friday—a business orders lunch from a different one of seven restaurants—Mexellent, Orientalicious, Pizzastic, Ribulous, Subtacular, Thaimazing, or Vegificent—in a manner consistent with the following conditions:

>The business orders from Ribulous on Wednesday.
>If the business orders from both Pizzastic and Thaimazing, it orders from Thaimazing earlier in the week.
>The business does not order from Vegificent and Subtacular on consecutive days.
>If the business orders from Mexellent, then it orders from Thaimazing on either the day immediately before or the day immediately after it orders from Mexellent.
>If the business orders from Orientalicious, then it orders from Vegificent the next day.
>Thursday is the only day on which the business can order from Subtacular.

6. Which one of the following could be a complete and accurate list of the five restaurants from which the business orders, listed in order from Monday to Friday?

    (A) Orientalicious, Vegificent, Ribulous, Thaimazing, Mexellent
    (B) Mexellent, Subtacular, Ribulous, Orientalicious, Vegificent,
    (C) Orientalicious, Thaimazing, Ribulous, Pizzastic, Vegificent
    (D) Pizzastic, Vegificent, Ribulous, Mexellent, Thaimazing
    (E) Thaimazing, Pizzastic, Ribulous, Subtacular, Vegificent

7. Which one of the following is a complete and accurate list of the restaurants any one of which the business could order from on Tuesday?

    (A) Mexellent, Thaimazing, Vegificent
    (B) Mexellent, Orientalicious, Thaimazing, Vegificent
    (C) Mexellent, Pizzastic, Thaimazing, Vegificent
    (D) Mexellent, Subtacular, Thaimazing, Vegificent
    (E) Mexellent, Orientalicious, Pizzastic, Thaimazing, Vegificent

8. In any given week, the business must order from at least one restaurant in which one of the following pairs?

    (A) Mexellent, Orientalicious
    (B) Mexellent, Pizzastic
    (C) Orientalicious, Vegificent
    (D) Pizzastic, Subtacular
    (E) Subtacular, Thaimazing

9. Suppose the business orders from Pizzastic on the day immediately before it orders from Thaimazing, but all other conditions remain the same. The business CANNOT order from which one of the following restaurants?

    (A) Orientalicious
    (B) Pizzastic
    (C) Ribulous
    (D) Subtacular
    (E) Vegificent

10. Suppose the condition that the business orders from Ribulous on Wednesday is replaced with the condition that the business orders from Ribulous on Friday. If all the other conditions remain the same, then which one of the following must be false?

    (A) The business orders from Mexellent on Thursday.
    (B) The business orders from Orientalicious on Tuesday.
    (C) The business orders from Pizzastic on Monday.
    (D) The business orders from Thaimazing on Monday.
    (E) The business orders from Vegificent on Tuesday.

GO ON TO THE NEXT PAGE.

Questions 11–15

Each of a company's five products—N, O, P, Q, and R—is produced by exactly one of its five factories—V, W, X, Y, and Z. Each factory is overseen by exactly one of the company's three supervisors—Karl oversees two factories, Liz oversees two factories, and Ming oversees one factory, subject to the following conditions:

    No supervisor oversees the production of both N and P.
    Ming oversees factory X, which produces either Q or R.
    The same supervisor oversees factory Y and the production of O, regardless of whether factory Y produces O.

11. If Karl oversees the production of both P and Q, which one of the following must be true?

    (A)   Liz oversees factory Y.
    (B)   Liz oversees factory Z.
    (C)   Factory W produces N.
    (D)   Factory V produces O.
    (E)   Factory X produces Q.

12. Which one of the following must be true?

    (A)   If Karl oversees the production of N, then factory Y produces O.
    (B)   If Karl oversees the production of both N and R, then factory Y produces P.
    (C)   If Liz oversees the production of both P and Q, then Karl oversees factory Y.
    (D)   If Ming oversees the production of Q, then Karl oversees the production of R.
    (E)   If Ming oversees the production of R, then Karl oversees the production of O.

13. If Karl oversees factories W and Z, which one of the following could be true?

    (A)   Factory Z produces O.
    (B)   Factory Y produces Q.
    (C)   Factory V produces R.
    (D)   Karl oversees the production of N.
    (E)   Karl oversees the production of O.

14. If Liz oversees the production of O by factory Z, then any of the following could be true EXCEPT:

    (A)   Karl oversees the production of N.
    (B)   Liz oversees the production of N.
    (C)   Factory Y produces P.
    (D)   Factory X produces Q.
    (E)   Factory Y produces Q.

15. Suppose the same supervisor oversees the production of both N and P, but all other conditions remain in effect. If factory W produces R, which one of the following must be true?

    (A)   Either factory Y or factory Z produces N.
    (B)   Neither factory Y nor factory Z produces N.
    (C)   Either factory V or factory Z produces O.
    (D)   Neither factory Y nor factory V produces P.
    (E)   Either factory V or factory Z produces P.

STOP

IF YOU FINISH BEFORE TIME IS CALLED, YOU MAY CHECK YOUR WORK ON THIS EXAM ONLY. DO NOT WORK ON ANY OTHER EXAM IN THE BOOK.

Answers

1. A
2. E
3. B
4. E
5. C
6. A
7. C
8. E
9. D
10. C
11. A
12. C
13. D
14. E
15. E

EXAMINATION

LECTURE 6 EXAM

Time—25 minutes

15 Questions

Directions: Each group of questions in this section is based on a set of conditions. In answering some of the questions, it may be useful to draw a rough diagram. Choose the response that most accurately and completely answers each question and circle it.

Questions 1-5

A quadrangle on a university campus contains six buildings, which are numbered and arranged in straight rows as follows:

North Side: 1   2   3
South Side: 4   5   6

The only buildings that face each other are buildings 1 and 4, buildings 2 and 5, and buildings 3 and 6. The grounds department will connect all the buildings with a single continuous bicycle trail. The trail is composed of five straight legs, each of which directly connects exactly two of the buildings. The following conditions apply:

Each building is directly connected by a leg of the trail to another building.

No building is directly connected by legs of the trail to more than two other buildings.

No leg of the trail crosses any other leg.

One leg of the trail directly connects buildings 1 and 5, and another leg directly connects buildings 2 and 3.

1. Which one of the following statements could be true?

   (A)   One leg of the trail directly connects buildings 4 and 2.
   (B)   One leg of the trail directly connects buildings 4 and 3.
   (C)   One leg of the trail directly connects buildings 4 and 6.
   (D)   One leg of the trail directly connects buildings 1 and 2 and another leg directly connects buildings 2 and 4.
   (E)   One leg of the trail directly connects buildings 6 and 3 and another leg directly connects buildings 6 and 5.

2. If one leg of the trail directly connects buildings 2 and 5, then the two buildings in which one of the following pairs must be directly connected to each other by a leg?

   (A)   1 and 2
   (B)   2 and 6
   (C)   3 and 6
   (D)   4 and 5
   (E)   5 and 6

3. If one leg of the trail directly connects buildings 2 and 6, then which one of the following statements could be true?

   (A)   Building 1 is directly connected to building 4.
   (B)   Building 2 is directly connected to building 5.
   (C)   Building 3 is directly connected to building 6.
   (D)   Building 3 is directly connected to exactly two buildings.
   (E)   Building 6 is directly connected to exactly one building.

4. Which one of the following buildings cannot be directly connected by legs of the trail to exactly two other buildings?

   (A)   2
   (B)   3
   (C)   4
   (D)   5
   (E)   6

5. If no leg of the trail directly connects any building on the north side with the building on the south side that faces it, then each of the following statements must be true EXCEPT:

   (A)   A leg of the trail directly connects buildings 4 and 5.
   (B)   A leg of the trail directly connects buildings 5 and 6.
   (C)   Building 3 is directly connected to exactly one other building.
   (D)   Building 5 is directly connected to exactly two other buildings.
   (E)   Building 6 is directly connected to exactly two other buildings.

GO ON TO THE NEXT PAGE.

Lecture 6 Examination

Questions 6-10

Eight trade representatives from three countries meet to discuss relations between their nations. Three representatives—F, G, and H—are Korean, three representatives—M, N, and O—are Tunisian, and two representatives—R and S—are Jamaican. The representatives sit at a circular table, around which are placed eight chairs, numbered sequentially from 1 to 8. Any two of them are said to be sitting directly across from one another if and only if there are exactly three other people sitting between them, counting in either direction around the table. The following restrictions govern the seating arrangement:

   The Korean representatives sit next to each other.
   The Jamaican representatives sit directly across from each other.
   R sits in chair 4.
   F sits in chair 1.
   If R sits next to M, then R does not also sit next to H.

6. Which one of the following representatives could sit in chair 2?

   (A)   O
   (B)   N
   (C)   M
   (D)   R
   (E)   H

7. Each of the following statements must be true EXCEPT:

   (A)   The representative in chair 8 is Tunisian.
   (B)   The representative in chair 2 is Korean.
   (C)   The representative in chair 6 is Tunisian.
   (D)   The representative in chair 3 is Korean.
   (E)   The representative in chair 7 is Tunisian.

8. Which one of the following representatives must sit next to F?

   (A)   G
   (B)   H
   (C)   R
   (D)   S
   (E)   M

9. For which one of the following representatives are there two and no more than two chairs either one of which could be the chair in which the representative sits?

   (A)   G
   (B)   R
   (C)   M
   (D)   N
   (E)   O

10. If N sits in chair 7, then the two representatives in which one of the following pairs CANNOT both sit in even-numbered chairs?

   (A)   G and M
   (B)   G and O
   (C)   H and S
   (D)   H and M
   (E)   H and O

GO ON TO THE NEXT PAGE.

Questions 11-15

On each of three consecutive evenings—Friday, Saturday, and Sunday—the Oaklyn theater will show four movies—Gravity, Monolith, Sleepwalking, and Zanzibar—using its five screens, which are numbered 1 to 5. Each screen will be used to show exactly one movie on each night. The movies will be shown according to the following specifications:

  No movie is shown on the same screen on consecutive evenings.

  Neither Gravity nor Monolith is shown on any screen on which Sleepwalking was shown the previous evening.

  Neither Gravity nor Sleepwalking is shown on any screen on which Zanzibar was shown the previous evening.

  On any evening, Zanzibar is shown on only one screen.

11. Which one of the following could be the movies shown on screens 1 and 2 on Friday and Saturday?

  (A) Friday: Gravity on screen 1, Zanzibar on screen 2
       Saturday: Sleepwalking on screen 1, Monolith on screen 2
  (B) Friday: Monolith on screen 1, Sleepwalking on screen 2
       Saturday: Monolith on screen 1, Zanzibar on screen 2
  (C) Friday: Sleepwalking on screen 1, Gravity on screen 2
       Saturday: Zanzibar on screen 1, Zanzibar on screen 2
  (D) Friday: Sleepwalking on screen 1, Sleepwalking on screen 2
       Saturday: Monolith on screen 1, Zanzibar on screen 2
  (E) Friday: Zanzibar on screen 1, Monolith on screen 2
       Saturday: Gravity on screen 1, Gravity on screen 2

12. If on Friday, Gravity and Monolith are shown on screens 1 and 2, respectively, the movies that are shown on Saturday on screens 1 and 2, respectively, could be

  (A) Gravity and Monolith
  (B) Monolith and Gravity
  (C) Monolith and Zanzibar
  (D) Zanzibar and Monolith
  (E) Zanzibar and Zanzibar

13. Which one of the following must be true?

  (A) Sleepwalking is shown on exactly two of the screens on Friday.
  (B) Sleepwalking is shown on exactly one of the screens on Saturday.
  (C) Sleepwalking is shown on exactly two of the screens on Saturday.
  (D) Sleepwalking is shown on exactly one of the screens on Sunday.
  (E) Sleepwalking is shown on exactly two of the screens on Sunday.

14. If on Saturday, Zanzibar is shown on screen 1, which one of the following must be true?

  (A) Gravity is shown on exactly one of the screens on Sunday.
  (B) Monolith is shown on exactly one of the screens on Sunday.
  (C) Gravity is shown on screen 1 on Friday.
  (D) Monolith is shown on screen 1 on Friday.
  (E) Sleepwalking is shown on screen 1 on Friday.

15. If on Saturday, Gravity and Monolith are shown on screens 1 and 2, respectively, the movies that are shown on Friday on screens 1 and 2, respectively, could be

  (A) Monolith and Gravity
  (B) Monolith and Sleepwalking
  (C) Sleepwalking and Gravity
  (D) Sleepwalking and Zanzibar
  (E) Zanzibar and Gravity

STOP

IF YOU FINISH BEFORE TIME IS CALLED, YOU MAY CHECK YOUR WORK ON THIS EXAM ONLY. DO NOT WORK ON ANY OTHER EXAM IN THE BOOK.

Answers

1. E
2. C
3. A
4. C
5. B
6. E
7. A
8. D
9. A
10. B
11. A
12. B
13. B
14. E
15. A

IN-CLASS EXAM ICE LECTURE 7

EXAMINATION

LECTURE 7 EXAM
Time—25 minutes
15 Questions

Directions: Each group of questions in this section is based on a set of conditions. In answering some of the questions, it may be useful to draw a rough diagram. Choose the response that most accurately and completely answers each question and circle it.

Questions 1–5

A jeweler has ten items of three different types—necklaces H, I, J, K and M; rings P and Q; and watches X, Y, and Z. Each item is made entirely of a single metal—H, I, J, P, and X are gold; K, M, Q, Y, and Z are silver. In the store's display window, the jeweler places pairs of items consisting of one gold and one silver item of the same type. At most two pairs can be in the display window at a time. The remaining items must be distributed between an upper shelf and a lower shelf inside the store. The jeweler must observe the following restrictions:

Neither shelf can contain more than four items.
Any two items that are both of the same metal and of the same type as each other cannot be on a shelf together.
Whenever either Y or M is in the display window, J cannot be in the display window.

1. Which one of the following is a possible arrangement of the items?

	Display Window	Lower Shelf	Upper Shelf
(A)	H, I, K, M	J, Y, Z	P, Q, X
(B)	J, K, X, Y	I, M, Q	H, P, Z
(C)	P, Q, X, Y	I, K, M	H, J, Z
(D)	H, K	J, M, Q, Z	I, P, X, Y
(E)	H, K, M	J, Q, Z	I, M, P, X, Y

2. Which one of the following lists two pairs of items that the jeweler can place in the display window at the same time?

(A) I and M; X and Z
(B) J and K; X and Y
(C) J and M; P and Q
(D) P and Q; X and Y
(E) P and Q; X and Z

3. If H and I are among the items that are placed on the shelves, then it must be true that

(A) Q is in the display window.
(B) X is in the display window.
(C) Z is in the display window.
(D) K is on one of the shelves.
(E) Y is on one of the shelves.

4. If H and K are among the items placed on the shelves, which one of the following is a pair of items that must be in the display window?

(A) I and M
(B) J and M
(C) P and Q
(D) X and Y
(E) X and Z

5. Which one of the following CANNOT be true?

(A) One pair of necklaces are the only items in the display window together.
(B) One pair of watches and one pair of necklaces are in the display window together.
(C) One pair of watches and one pair of rings are in the display window together.
(D) One pair of rings and one pair of necklaces are in the display window together.
(E) Two pairs of necklaces are in the display window together.

GO ON TO THE NEXT PAGE.

Questions 6–10

The president of a nonprofit charity group will interview seven candidates for a job opening within the organization. The candidates—Franklin, Kratzer, Lippay, Putnam, Rivera, Wiechecki, and Ying—must be interviewed consecutively and one at a time. The president is constrained by the following conditions:

Franklin is interviewed either immediately before or immediately after Ying is interviewed.

Wiechecki is interviewed either immediately before or immediately after Putnam is interviewed.

Ying is interviewed at some time before Wiechecki is interviewed.

Putnam is interviewed at some time before Kratzer is interviewed.

Rivera is not interviewed first.

6. If Rivera is interviewed third, which one of the following could be true?

    (A)   Franklin is interviewed fourth.
    (B)   Kratzer is interviewed fifth.
    (C)   Kratzer is interviewed sixth.
    (D)   Lippay is interviewed fifth.
    (E)   Wiechecki is interviewed second.

7. The earliest that Kratzer could be interviewed is

    (A)   third
    (B)   fourth
    (C)   fifth
    (D)   sixth
    (E)   seventh

8. If Ying is interviewed fourth, which one of the following must be true?

    (A)   Franklin is interviewed fifth.
    (B)   Kratzer is interviewed sixth.
    (C)   Lippay is interviewed first.
    (D)   Rivera is interviewed third.
    (E)   Wiechecki is interviewed fifth.

9. If Kratzer is interviewed at some time before Lippay is interviewed, which one of the following must be false?

    (A)   Lippay is interviewed immediately before Rivera is interviewed.
    (B)   Rivera is interviewed immediately before Franklin is interviewed.
    (C)   Rivera is interviewed immediately before Kratzer is interviewed.
    (D)   Wiechecki is interviewed immediately before Kratzer is interviewed.
    (E)   Ying is interviewed immediately before Putnam is interviewed.

10. The order in which the candidates are interviewed is completely determined if which one of the following is true?

    (A)   Franklin is interviewed immediately before Rivera is interviewed, and Wiechecki is interviewed immediately before Putnam is interviewed.
    (B)   Franklin is interviewed immediately before Ying is interviewed, and Ying is interviewed immediately before Wiechecki is interviewed.
    (C)   Franklin is interviewed immediately before Putnam is interviewed, and Wiechecki is interviewed immediately before Kratzer is interviewed.
    (D)   Rivera is interviewed immediately before Franklin is interviewed, and Putnam is interviewed immediately before Kratzer is interviewed.
    (E)   Rivera is interviewed immediately before Wiechecki is interviewed, and Ying is interviewed immediately before Franklin is interviewed.

GO ON TO THE NEXT PAGE.

Questions 11–15

In a certain week, a tollbooth operator must staff the morning and evening shifts on each of exactly four days, Monday through Thursday. The operator must choose exactly one of five employees—Heather, Julia, Luke, Petra, and Robbie—to work each shift. The following conditions must apply:

No employee works both the morning shift and the evening shift on the same day.

No employee works the morning shift or the evening shift more than once during the week.

Heather, Julia, and Luke are the only employees available to work on Monday.

Heather, Luke, Petra, and Robbie are the only employees available to work on Tuesday.

Luke and Petra are the only employees available to work on Wednesday.

Heather, Luke, Petra, and Robbie are the only employees available to work on Thursday.

Luke works Tuesday morning.

11. Petra must work which one of the following shifts?

(A) Tuesday evening
(B) Wednesday morning
(C) Wednesday evening
(D) Thursday morning
(E) Thursday evening

12. Which one of the following employees must work in the evening?

(A) Petra
(B) Heather
(C) Robbie
(D) Luke
(E) Julia

13. If Robbie works twice in the week, then which one of the following statements could be true?

(A) Heather works Monday morning.
(B) Heather works Tuesday evening.
(C) Heather works Thursday morning.
(D) Petra works Tuesday evening.
(E) Robbie works Thursday evening.

14. If Robbie does not work in the morning, then which one of the following statements could be true?

(A) Heather works Monday morning.
(B) Heather works Tuesday evening.
(C) Julia works Monday evening.
(D) Petra works Tuesday evening.
(E) Petra works Thursday morning.

15. If Julia works Monday morning, then which one of the following statements CANNOT be true?

(A) Heather works Tuesday evening.
(B) Heather works Thursday morning.
(C) Petra works Tuesday evening.
(D) Robbie works Thursday morning.
(E) Robbie works Thursday evening.

STOP

IF YOU FINISH BEFORE TIME IS CALLED, YOU MAY CHECK YOUR WORK ON THIS EXAM ONLY.
DO NOT WORK ON ANY OTHER EXAM IN THE BOOK.

Answers

1. D
2. A
3. E
4. A
5. C
6. C
7. C
8. C
9. B
10. D
11. B
12. D
13. A
14. D
15. A

IN-CLASS EXAM   ICE   LECTURE   8

EXAMINATION

LECTURE 8 EXAM
Time—25 minutes
15 Questions

Directions: Each group of questions in this section is based on a set of conditions. In answering some of the questions, it may be useful to draw a rough diagram. Choose the response that most accurately and completely answers each question and circle it.

Questions 1–5

Exactly eight people—H, J, K, L, M, N, O, and P—will take part in a trivia contest. The contestants will be divided into three teams, each named for a color. Two people will be on the red team, while the blue team and the yellow team will each have three people. The following conditions apply:

    H cannot be on the same team as M.
    If N is on the blue team, H must also be on the blue team.
    Neither O nor L is on the same team as J.
    O is on the red team.
    P is on the blue team.

1. Which one of the following is an acceptable assignment of contestants to the three teams?

  (A)   Red team: H, O; blue team: J, N, P; yellow team: K, L, M
  (B)   Red team: K, L; blue team: H, N, P; yellow team: J, M, O
  (C)   Red team: N, O; blue team: K, L, P; yellow team: H, J, M
  (D)   Red team: L, O; blue team: H, K, P; yellow team: J, M, N
  (E)   Red team: N, O; blue team: H, K, P; yellow team: J, L, M

2. Which one of the following is a complete and accurate list of teams any one of which could be the team on which M competes?

  (A)   the red team
  (B)   the blue team
  (C)   the red team, the blue team
  (D)   the red team, the yellow team
  (E)   the red team, the blue team, the yellow team

3. If K is on the blue team, which one of the following is a contestant who must be on the yellow team?

  (A)   H
  (B)   J
  (C)   L
  (D)   M
  (E)   N

4. If K is on the red team, each of the following is a pair of contestants who could be on the blue team EXCEPT:

  (A)   J and H
  (B)   L and H
  (C)   M and J
  (D)   M and L
  (E)   N and H

5. Which one of the following must be true?

  (A)   If H and J are on the yellow team, K is on the yellow team.
  (B)   If L and M are on the blue team, N is on the red team.
  (C)   If L and M are on the blue team, H is on the red team.
  (D)   If K and M are on the blue team, L is on the red team.
  (E)   If K and N are on the yellow team, M is on the red team.

GO ON TO THE NEXT PAGE.

Questions 6–10

In a dealer's lot, six cars are parked next to each other in a rectangle. The cars are numbered as shown:

1   3   5

2   4   6

Each car was made by exactly one of two manufacturers—Vigoride or Welmayde.

Each car is exactly one of two types—a hatchback or a sedan.

Each car is parked directly adjacent to another car made by the same manufacturer.

Each car is parked directly adjacent to another car of the same type.

Car 3 is a sedan.

Car 4 is a hatchback.

Car 5 is a Welmayde.

6. If all of the sedans are Vigorides, which one of the following must be true?

(A) Car 1 is a Welmayde.
(B) Car 2 is a Vigoride.
(C) Car 4 is a Welmayde.
(D) Car 5 is a sedan.
(E) Car 6 is a hatchback.

7. It is possible that the only two Vigorides among the six cars are

(A) cars 1 and 4
(B) cars 1 and 6
(C) cars 2 and 3
(D) cars 2 and 4
(E) cars 2 and 6

8. If there are exactly three Welmaydes and three Vigorides, which one of the following cars must be a Vigoride?

(A) car 1
(B) car 2
(C) car 3
(D) car 4
(E) car 6

9. If exactly two cars are Welmaydes and exactly two cars are sedans, which one of the following must be false?

(A) Car 1 is a sedan, and car 6 is a Welmayde.
(B) Cars 1 and 3 are both sedans.
(C) Car 2 is a sedan, and car 3 is a Welmayde.
(D) Car 3 is both a sedan and a Welmayde.
(E) Car 5 is a sedan.

10. Which one of the following could be true?

(A) Cars 1 and 2 are two of exactly three hatchbacks.
(B) Cars 1 and 6 are two of exactly three hatchbacks.
(C) Cars 1 and 6 are two of exactly three sedans.
(D) Cars 2 and 6 are two of exactly three sedans.
(E) Cars 2 and 5 are two of exactly three sedans.

GO ON TO THE NEXT PAGE.

Questions 11–15

A theater must determine its upcoming schedule of events. Eight events—musicals J, K, and L; plays Q and R; and workshops X, Y, and Z—must be ordered from first through eighth, in accordance with the following restrictions:

The first event cannot be a workshop.

X must immediately follow Q.

Z must be scheduled for some time before Y, but Z cannot immediately precede Y.

J must be scheduled for some time after K.

J and K must be separated by the same number of events as separate Y and Z.

11. Which one of the following is an acceptable ordering of the events from first to eighth?

   (A)   Z, K, Y, J, Q, X, L, R
   (B)   L, X, Q, Z, K, Y, J, R
   (C)   L, Q, X, Z, Y, R, K, J
   (D)   K, Q, X, J, Z, R, L, Y
   (E)   Q, X, Z, L, Y, K, J, R

12. The largest possible number of events that can separate Q from Z is

   (A)   two
   (B)   three
   (C)   four
   (D)   five
   (E)   six

13. If each of the three workshops is immediately followed by a musical, which one of the following events must be a play?

   (A)   the first
   (B)   the second
   (C)   the third
   (D)   the fourth
   (E)   the fifth

14. The largest possible number of events that can separate J from K is

   (A)   three
   (B)   four
   (C)   five
   (D)   six
   (E)   seven

15. If Q is scheduled as the fifth event, then which one of the following is a complete and accurate list of the positions in the schedule any one of which could be Z's position?

   (A)   first, third, fourth
   (B)   first, second, third
   (C)   second, third, fourth
   (D)   second, third, fourth, sixth
   (E)   third, fourth, sixth, seventh

STOP

IF YOU FINISH BEFORE TIME IS CALLED, YOU MAY CHECK YOUR WORK ON THIS EXAM ONLY.
DO NOT WORK ON ANY OTHER EXAM IN THE BOOK.

Answers

1. D
2. E
3. E
4. E
5. D
6. E
7. D
8. B
9. C
10. A
11. D
12. C
13. A
14. C
15. C

EXPLANATIONS

QUESTIONS 1–5

Identify

You can identify this as an Ordering game because the situation asks you to put the styles in an order, 1–7, and all the elements fit into a single order—there are no elements left out of the order, there is no ordering within two separate groups, and there is no more than one order to be determined.

Set Up

First, decide on a diagram. In this case, use the natural order of the floors. There is no problem with making the diagram vertical, since floors in a building are vertical. However, because you will be using horizontal diagrams for nearly every game, you may wish to just use a horizontal diagram here as well to keep things familiar.

Next, take stock of the elements. In this case, they are already just letters (not names), so write these letters next to your diagram.

O P Q R S T U

1	2	3	4	5	6	7

Finally, symbolize the rules.

> **Rule 1** says O is not first or seventh. Symbolize this directly on the diagram as a pair of forbidden spots for O.

> **Rule 2** is a relative order rule. Symbolize it as

Rule 3 is a block rule. Symbolize it as $\boxed{\text{UP}}$

Rule 4 is an exact spot rule. Put **S** directly on the diagram in the fifth floor.

At this point, your diagram looks like this.

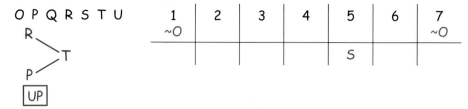

Deduce

Finally, make as many deductions as you can. One thing you should notice right away is that **P** is involved in both the relative order rule and the block rule. You can combine those two symbols into one larger symbol:

Using this combined symbol, you can now make some endpoint deductions. **T** cannot be first, second, or third since there must be at least three other elements before it. **R** can't be seventh because it must precede **T**.

The block of **U** and **P** is even more restricted because **S** in the fifth spot gets in the way. The latest that block could fit is third and fourth, which allows you to deduce that **P** can't be sixth or seventh, and **U** can't be fourth, sixth, or seventh. **P** is also forbidden to be first since it must follow **U**. At this point your diagram should look like this:

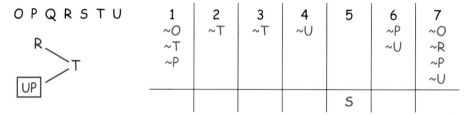

There's one final deduction you can make. Look at the seventh spot. Four elements are forbidden there, and **S** is already determined in the fifth spot, so there are only two possible elements left that could be seventh: **T** or **Q**. This is worth writing on your master diagram as an either/or spot.

MASTER DIAGRAM

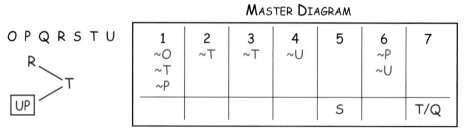

Question 1

1. Which one of the following could be a complete and accurate list of the styles used to decorate each floor, listed in order from the first floor to the seventh floor?

   (A) Q, U, P, O, R, S, T
   (B) U, P, R, Q, S, O, T
   (C) R, O, P, U, S, T, Q
   (D) R, T, U, P, S, O, Q
   (E) R, U, P, T, S, Q, O

This is a Rule Tester question. You can tell because it asks you to pick the answer choice that could be a valid configuration, and each answer choice contains a full configuration of the elements.

To attack the answer choices, look at each rule and eliminate the choice in which it is broken. Rule 1 is broken in choice (E), which has O seventh. Rule 2 is broken in choice (D), which has P on a higher floor than T. Rule 3 is broken in choice (C), which puts P before U. Rule 4 is broken in choice (A), which has S sixth.

Choice (B) is the correct answer.

Question 2

2. If T is the style used to redecorate the fourth floor, then which one of the following lists could accurately identify the styles used to redecorate each floor, listed in order from the first floor to the seventh floor?

   (A) U, R, P, T, S, O, Q
   (B) U, P, R, Q, S, O, T
   (C) O, U, P, T, S, R, Q
   (D) R, U, P, T, S, O, Q
   (E) R, U, P, T, Q, O, S

This is another Rule Tester question. It's also a Local question because it gives you a new rule to follow in the question stem when it tells you T must be fourth.

Again, look at each rule (including the new one in the question stem) and eliminate any choice in which it is broken. The new rule is broken in choice (B), which has T seventh. Rule 1 is broken in choice (C), where O is first. Rule 2 is also broken in choice (C). Rule 3 is broken in choice (A), since U and P are not consecutive. Rule 4 is broken in choice (E), which puts S seventh.

Choice (D) is the correct answer.

Question 3

3. If the second floor is redecorated in style Q, then style R must be used to redecorate the

   (A) first floor
   (B) third floor
   (C) fourth floor
   (D) sixth floor
   (E) seventh floor

This is a Local question because it gives you a new rule to follow in the question stem. Give yourself a new row in your diagram, put the new rule in, and see what happens.

MASTER DIAGRAM

O P Q R S T U

R
 \
  > T
UP /

1	2	3	4	5	6	7
~O	~T	~T	~U		~P	
~T					~U	
~P						
				S		T/Q
R	Q	U	P	S	O	T	#3

A lot of things happen when you put **Q** second. First, the only place you have room to put **U** and **P** is third and fourth. Next, you know the seventh spot has to be filled by **T** because **Q** is already somewhere else. Now, there are only two spots left, and **O** can't be first, so it must be sixth. That leaves **R** to take the final remaining spot, which is the first.

Choice (A) is the correct answer.

Question 4

4. Which one of the following floors could be redecorated in style T?

(A) the first floor
(B) the second floor
(C) the third floor
(D) the fifth floor
(E) the sixth floor

This is a Universal question because it doesn't give you any new rules. Check your master diagram. You deduced that **T** can't be first, second, or third, and **S** is already taking up the fifth spot. That gets rid of choices (A), (B), (C), and (D). Only choice (E) remains, so it must be correct.

Choice (E) is the correct answer.

Question 5

5. If R is the style used to redecorate the third floor, then which one of the following could be true?

(A) The first floor is redecorated in style Q.
(B) The second floor is redecorated in style O.
(C) The fourth floor is redecorated in style P.
(D) The sixth floor is redecorated in style T.
(E) The sixth floor is redecorated in style U.

This is a Local question. Put the new rule on your diagram and figure out as much as you can.

MASTER DIAGRAM

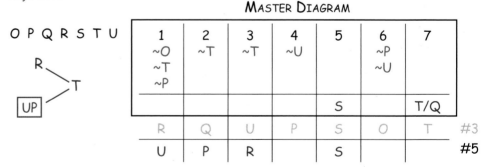

O P Q R S T U

R
 \
  > T
UP /

1	2	3	4	5	6	7
~O	~T	~T	~U		~P	
~T					~U	
~P						
				S		T/Q
R	Q	U	P	S	O	T	#3
U	P	R		S			#5

You can figure out just one more thing in this case. The only place where **U** and **P** can fit is first and second. The remaining elements, **O**, **Q**, and **T**, can go in any of the remaining spots, as long as **O** isn't seventh. Now look at the answer choices. According to the diagram, only choice (D) could be true.

Choice (D) is the correct answer.

QUESTIONS 6–10

Identify

You can identify this as an Ordering game because the situation asks you to put the appointments in order from 10–4, and all the elements fit into a single order.

Set Up

For the diagram, use the natural order of the times, from 10:00–4:00.

Next, take stock of the elements. You can abbreviate the clients using their first initials. Also, notice that there are six people but seven time slots. One of the spots will be filled with a lunch break. The best way to deal with this is to create an additional element, L, to denote lunch. Then you can treat the lunch break just like any other element to be placed.

F G H I J K L	10	11	12	1	2	3	4

Next, symbolize the rules.

> **Rule 1** can be symbolized on the diagram by showing the forbidden spots for L.
>
> **Rule 2** is a barbell rule for I. Put this on the diagram.
>
> **Rule 3** is an antiblock rule. Symbolize it as
>
> **Rule 4** is a relative order rule involving three elements. Symbolize it as L—J—K.
>
> **Rule 5** is another relative order rule symbolize it as F—L.

Your diagram should look like this:

F G H I J K L	10	11	12	1	2	3	4
L—J—K	~L	~L				~L	~L
F—L 	I					○	

Deduce

Finally, make as many deductions as you can. Since they both contain L, you can combine the two relative order rules into one long chain. Then using that chain, you can make some endpoint deductions. For example, F can't be in 2, 3, or 4 because at least three other elements must follow it. L is not restricted any further. Now look at J. You may be tempted to say J can't be in 10 or 11, and that is true, but it's not the whole story. If you tried to put J in 12, you would run into a problem since L must precede J, but L can't be before 12. Thus the earliest J can be is 1, and the earliest K can be is 2 (not 1 as you might expect).

That leaves you with this:

MASTER DIAGRAM

F G H I J K L	10	11	12	1	2	3	4
F—L—J—K	~L ~J	~L ~J	~J ~K	~K	~F	~L ~F	~L ~F
	~K	~K					
	I					○	

Lecture 1 Explanations

The Rules

The lunch break must be scheduled to start no earlier than 12:00 and no later than 2:00.

The appointment with Ingrid must be scheduled for either 10:00 or 3:00.

The appointment with Gretchen cannot be scheduled immediately after the appointment with Henry.

The appointment with Jacob must be scheduled after lunch but before the appointment with Kirk.

The appointment with Franny must be scheduled before lunch.

Question 6

6. Which one of the following could be an acceptable schedule of the lawyer's lunch and appointments, in order from 10:00 to 4:00?

    (A) Henry, Franny, Gretchen, lunch, Ingrid, Jacob, Kirk
    (B) Franny, Gretchen, Henry, lunch, Jacob, Ingrid, Kirk
    (C) Franny, lunch, Jacob, Henry, Kirk, Ingrid, Gretchen
    (D) Ingrid, Franny, lunch, Gretchen, Kirk, Jacob, Henry
    (E) Ingrid, Henry, Gretchen, Franny, lunch, Jacob, Kirk

This is a Rule Tester question. Look at each rule and eliminate the choices in which it is broken.

Rule 1 is broken in choice (C), which has L in 11. Rule 2 is broken in choice (A), which puts I in 2. Rule 3 is broken in choice (E), which has G immediately after H. Rule 4 is broken in choice (D), which put J after K. Since there is now only one choice left, you don't have to bother with Rule 5.

Choice (B) is the correct answer.

Question 7

7. If the appointment with Henry is scheduled before the appointment with Gretchen, which one of the following could be an acceptable schedule of the lawyer's lunch and appointments, in order from 10:00 to 4:00?

    (A) Ingrid, Franny, Jacob, lunch, Henry, Kirk, Gretchen
    (B) Franny, Gretchen, Henry, lunch, Jacob, Ingrid, Kirk
    (C) Ingrid, Franny, lunch, Jacob, Henry, Gretchen, Kirk
    (D) Henry, Franny, Gretchen, lunch, Jacob, Ingrid, Kirk
    (E) Ingrid, Henry, lunch, Gretchen, Franny, Jacob, Kirk

This is another Rule Tester, with the additional feature of a new rule in the question stem. As always, look at each rule and eliminate the choices in which it is broken.

The new rule in the question stem is broken in choice (B), which has H after G. Rule 1 is not broken in any answer choice, nor is Rule 2. Rule 3 is broken in choice (C), since G immediately follows H. Rule 4 is broken in choice (A), where J is before L. Rule 5 is broken in choice (E), since F is after L.

Choice (D) is the correct answer.

Question 8

8. If the appointment with Henry is scheduled for 3:00, then which one of the following must be true?

    (A) The appointment with Gretchen is scheduled for 11:00.
    (B) The appointment with Kirk is scheduled for 4:00.
    (C) The appointment with Jacob is scheduled for 1:00.
    (D) The appointment with Franny is scheduled for some time before the appointment with Ingrid.
    (E) The appointment with Kirk is scheduled for some time before the appointment with Henry.

This is a Local question. Create a new row on your diagram, put the new rule in, and see what else you can figure out.

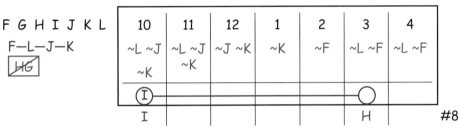

The first obvious deduction is that **I** has to be in 10, because of the barbell. Can you figure anything else out? Because of the antiblock, **G** can't be in 4. That means **G** will be somewhere between 11–2. There are only four spots between 11–2, and **G** takes up one of them, so you won't be able to fit all four of the remaining elements (the relative order chain) there. That means **K** has to be in 4.

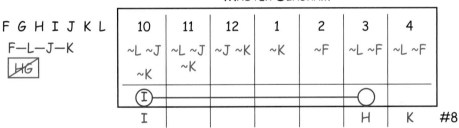

The remaining elements have to fit into the spots between 11–2, but there could be lots of different orders. No problem. You have already done enough to see that choice (B) must be true.

Choice (B) is the correct answer.

Question 9

9. The appointment with Kirk could be scheduled for

    (A) 10:00
    (B) 11:00
    (C) 12:00
    (D) 1:00
    (E) 2:00

This is a Universal question. Check your master diagram. You deduced that **K** can't be in 10, 11, 12, or 1. That gets rid of choices (A), (B), (C), and (D). Only choice (E) remains, so it must be correct.

Choice (E) is the correct answer.

Lecture 1 Explanations

Question 10

10. If the appointment with Jacob is scheduled immediately after the appointment with Gretchen, then the appointment with Henry CANNOT be scheduled for

   (A)   10:00
   (B)   11:00
   (C)   12:00
   (D)   1:00
   (E)   3:00

This is a Local question. You want to put the new rule into a new row on the diagram, but the question stem isn't specific enough to tell you exactly where to put J and G. Your approach in this case is to symbolize the new rule *to the right* of the diagram, next to a new row. You can incorporate the new block rule right into your existing relative order chain to create the symbol for the new rule.

MASTER DIAGRAM

F G H I J K L

F—L—J—K

HG (crossed out)

	10	11	12	1	2	3	4
	~L ~J	~L ~J	~J	~K	~F	~L ~F	~L ~F
	~K	~K	~K				
	I					O	
	I					H	K	#8

#10
F—L— GJ —K

Things look pretty nebulous at this point. It seems like there could be lots of different ways to fit this chain into the diagram. If you can't see where to proceed from here, then start attacking the answer choices. One of the spots listed in the answer choices is impossible for H, so try them out and see which ones work and which one doesn't.

MASTER DIAGRAM

F G H I J K L

F—L—J—K

HG (crossed out)

	10	11	12	1	2	3	4
	~L ~J	~L ~J	~J	~K	~F	~L ~F	~L ~F
	~K	~K	~K				
	I					O	
	I					H	K	#8
(A)	H	F	L	G	J	I	K
(B)	I	H	F	L	G	J	K
(C)	I	F	H	L	G	J	K
(D)				H			

#10
F—L— GJ —K

Choices (A), (B), and (C) work, but when you try to put H in 1, there's a problem. The earliest L can be is 12, which means you'd have to put G, J, and K in 2, 3, and 4, respectively. But that would put G immediately after H, which is not allowed. H cannot be scheduled for 1:00, so choice (D) is correct.

Choice (D) is the correct answer.

QUESTIONS 11–15

Identify

You can identify this as an Ordering game because the situation asks you to put the nicknames in order from first to eighth, and all the elements fit into a single order.

Set Up

For the diagram, use the natural order of the ranking, from first to eighth. It's also helpful to note on your diagram which end is most popular and which end is least popular. This will ensure that you don't get mixed up when the game refers to a nickname being "more" popular than another.

For your stock, abbreviate the nicknames using their first initials.

```
              most pop.                          least pop.
H I J K L M N O    1 | 2 | 3 | 4 | 5 | 6 | 7 | 8
```

Now symbolize the rules.

Rule 1 is a relative order rule with three elements:

$$H < \begin{array}{c} K \\ L \end{array}$$

Rule 2 is another relative order rule with three elements:

$$L < \begin{array}{c} O \\ I \end{array}$$

Rule 3 is another relative order rule with three elements: J—N—H

Rule 4 is a final relative order rule: M—I

Deduce

Finally, make as many deductions as you can. This is an interesting game because all the rules are relative order rules. Furthermore, every element is involved in at least one of the rules, and lots of linking is possible. In fact, you can combine every single symbol into a large super-symbol:

```
              K   O
             /   /
J—N—H—L—I
             /
          M
```

When an LSAT game allows you to create something like this, there are a few things you should do. First, notice that there is a central "spine" of elements (J through I) that is relatively stable—these elements will always appear in that order. There are two elements (K and O) that are more fluid. For example, you know that O must have at least four elements before it (J through L) but it could show up anywhere in the second half of the order—even before K. The last element, M, is the most fluid of all. As long as it precedes I, it can fall anywhere in the order, from first all the way down to seventh.

When you have relative order rules, you usually make endpoint deductions showing where certain elements are forbidden to go. However, when you have all the elements together in one huge symbol, doing so would be time consuming and not particularly helpful. Instead, you should just get a general sense of where elements will be. J will certainly be near the beginning of the order—first or second. L will be somewhere in the middle. I will be near the end—sixth, seventh, or eighth. That's about all you need to do in terms of deductions.

The Rules

Hustlers is more popular than both Kingsmen and Lumberjacks.
Outlaws and Impalas are each less popular than Lumberjacks.
Nighthawks is more popular than Hustlers but less popular than Juggernauts.
Marauders is more popular than Impalas.

MASTER DIAGRAM

most pop.							least pop.
1	2	3	4	5	6	7	8

H I J K L M N O

```
        K   O
        /   /
J—N—H—L—I
        \
         M
```

Question 11

11. Which one of the following could be the order of the nicknames, ranked from most popular to least popular?

(A) Marauders, Juggernauts, Hustlers, Kingsmen, Night-hawks, Lumberjacks, Outlaws, Impalas

(B) Marauders, Juggernauts, Nighthawks, Hustlers, Lumberjacks, Outlaws, Kingsmen, Impalas

(C) Juggernauts, Nighthawks, Hustlers, Lumberjacks, Impalas, Marauders, Kingsmen, Outlaws

(D) Juggernauts, Nighthawks, Lumberjacks, Hustlers, Marauders, Impalas, Kingsmen, Outlaws

(E) Juggernauts, Marauders, Nighthawks, Hustlers, Outlaws, Lumberjacks, Impalas, Kingsmen

This is a Rule Tester question. Look at each rule and eliminate the choices in which it is broken.

Rule 1 is broken in choice (D), where L precedes H. Rule 2 is broken in choice (E), where O is before L. Rule 3 is broken in choice (A), where H precedes N. Rule 4 is broken in (C), since M follows I.

Choice (B) is the correct answer.

Question 12

12. If Marauders is more popular than Kingsmen, then which one of the following could be the order of the nicknames, ranked from most popular to least popular?

(A) Marauders, Nighthawks, Juggernauts, Hustlers, Lumberjacks, Outlaws, Kingsmen, Impalas

(B) Marauders, Juggernauts, Kingsmen, Nighthawks, Hustlers, Lumberjacks, Outlaws, Impalas

(C) Juggernauts, Nighthawks, Marauders, Hustlers, Lumberjacks, Kingsmen, Impalas, Outlaws

(D) Juggernauts, Marauders, Nighthawks, Hustlers, Impalas, Kingsmen, Lumberjacks, Outlaws

(E) Juggernauts, Nighthawks, Hustlers, Lumberjacks, Kingsmen, Marauders, Outlaws, Impalas

This is another Rule Tester question, with a new rule in the question stem. Use the normal approach.

The new rule in the question stem is broken in choice (E), since K precedes M. Rule 1 is broken in choice (B), where K is before H. Rule 2 is broken in choice (D), because I comes before L. Rule 3 is broken in choice (A), since J follows N. Only choice (C) remains.

Choice (C) is the correct answer.

Question 13

13. If Marauders is the most popular nickname, then Hustlers must be ranked

   (A) second
   (B) third
   (C) fourth
   (D) fifth
   (E) sixth

This is a Local question. Give yourself a new row on the diagram and put the new information in.

MASTER DIAGRAM

	most pop.							least pop.	
HIJKLMNO	1	2	3	4	5	6	7	8	
	M	J	N	H					#13

K O
/ /
J—N—H—L—I
/
M

When **M** is placed first, all the rest of the relative order rules flow left-to-right, which means you can definitely say that **J**, **N**, and **H** are in spots 2–4. After that, the order is not completely nailed down, but that doesn't matter. You have done enough to answer the question. **H** must be fourth.

Choice (C) is the correct answer.

Question 14

14. If Impalas is more popular than Kingsmen, then which one of the following could be true?

   (A) Outlaws is ranked fourth.
   (B) Impalas is ranked fifth.
   (C) Lumberjacks is ranked sixth.
   (D) Marauders is ranked seventh.
   (E) Kingsmen is ranked seventh.

This is another Local question. Give yourself a new row on the diagram. Unfortunately, the new rule is not specific enough for you to be able to definitively place anything on the diagram. However, you can still symbolize the new rule to the right of the diagram. If **K** is later than **I**, then you can move **K** further down the line in the super-chain. You still preserve the requirement that **K** is later than **H**, but your symbol becomes more specific and incorporates the new rule when you redraw it like this:

O
/
J—N—H—L—I—K
/
M

You still can't determine precisely where anything is, but take a look at the answer choices and compare them to your new symbol.

Choice (A) is impossible because at least four elements (**J–L**) must precede **O**. Choice (B) is impossible since at least five elements (**J–L** and **M**) must precede **I**. Choice (C) is impossible since at least three elements (**O**, **I**, and **K**) must follow **L**. Choice (D) is impossible because at least two elements (**I** and **K**) must follow **M**. Choice (E) is the only one left, and the symbol shows it's possible.

Choice (E) is the correct answer.

Question 15

15. Lumberjacks could be ranked

(A) first
(B) third
(C) fifth
(D) seventh
(E) eighth

This is a Universal question. Look at your master diagram to see the possibilities for L. You can see that J, N, and H must precede L, so it can't be ranked 1–3. That gets rid of choices (A) and (B). O and I must follow L, so it can't be ranked 7 or 8. That gets rid of choices (D) and (E).

Choice (C) is the correct answer.

EXPLANATIONS

QUESTIONS 1–5

IDENTIFY

You can identify this as a Binary game because the situation asks you to put the products into two groups—Promoted and Not Promoted—and because there is no mention of any order.

SET UP

First, decide on a diagram. You want every Binary diagram to revolve around *yes* and *no*, and in this case, the game is already set up that way. The two groups are Promoted and Not Promoted. The situation tells you there is at least one product promoted, so underline one space in the Promoted group to remind you that it can't be empty.

Next, take stock of the elements. In this case, they are already just letters (not names), so write these letters next to your diagram.

T U V W X Y Z	Promoted	Not Promoted
	$\underline{}$	

Finally, symbolize the rules.

Rule 1 has NEITHER T NOR V. That means the same as ~T AND ~V.

$$X \longrightarrow \text{~}T \text{ AND } \text{~}V$$
$$T \text{ OR } V \longrightarrow \text{~}X$$

Rule 2: turn the *only if* into an arrow.

$$Z \longrightarrow X$$
$$\text{~}X \longrightarrow \text{~}Z$$

Rule 3: remember to switch the OR into an AND in the contrapositive.

$$U \longrightarrow Y \text{ or } Z$$
$$\sim Y \text{ and } \sim Z \longrightarrow \sim U$$

Rule 4:

$$\sim W \longrightarrow V$$
$$\sim V \longrightarrow W$$

DEDUCE

Finally, make as many deductions as you can. In games with all conditional rules, you will almost never be able to definitively place any of the elements. However, one thing you can look for is linkable chains. There are some possible links to be made here. For example, the X in rules 1 and 2 can be linked. There is also some linking possible between the V's and the Z's that appear in multiple rules. It's up to you how much of this you want to write out. Many people don't like to bother with linking when it comes to ANDs and ORs, since you can still complete the game without doing it. Here, we'll just make the first link.

Since you can't place anything, here's the master diagram:

T U V W X Y Z	Promoted	Not Promoted
$Z \longrightarrow X \longrightarrow \sim T$ and $\sim V$	—	
T or $V \longrightarrow \sim X \longrightarrow \sim Z$		
$U \longrightarrow Y$ or Z		
$\sim Y$ and $\sim Z \longrightarrow \sim U$		
$\sim W \longrightarrow V$		
$\sim V \longrightarrow W$		

The Rules

If X is promoted, then neither T nor V is promoted.
Z is promoted only if X is also promoted.
If U is promoted, then Y or Z is also promoted.
V is promoted if W is not promoted.

Question 1

1. Which one of the following could be a complete and accurate list of the products that are NOT promoted?

    (A) T, W, V, Y
    (B) T, W, X, Z
    (C) U, V, Y, Z
    (D) V, X, Y
    (E) X, Y, Z

This is a Rule Tester question. Each choice gives you a complete list of the elements *not* promoted, which also implicitly tells you which ones *are*. Thus, each choice really gives you a complete configuration.

Rule 1 is broken in choice (C) since X is promoted (it's not on the Not Promoted list) but so is T (it's also missing). Rule 2 is broken in choice (D) since X is not promoted but Z is. Rule 3 is broken in choice (E) since U should also not be promoted. Rule 4 is broken in choice (A) since both V and W are not promoted.

Now that you know choice (B) is a possible configuration, put it on your diagram so you can use it as part of your previous work.

Choice (B) is the correct answer.

Question 2

2. If Z is promoted, which one of the following must be true?

    (A)   U is not promoted.
    (B)   Z is not promoted.
    (C)   V is promoted.
    (D)   W is promoted.
    (E)   Y is promoted.

This is a Truth question because it ends with the phrase *must be true*. It's also a Local question. Put the new rule on the diagram and see what happens.

TUVWXYZ

$Z \rightarrow X \rightarrow \sim T$ AND $\sim V$

T OR $V \rightarrow \sim X \rightarrow \sim Z$

$U \rightarrow Y$ OR Z

$\sim Y$ AND $\sim Z \rightarrow \sim U$

$\sim W \rightarrow V$

$\sim V \rightarrow W$

Promoted	Not Promoted	
U V Y	T W X Z	#1
Z X W	T V	#2

In this case, the first chain makes X promoted and both T and V not. That in turn means W is promoted. That's all you can determine, but that's enough to be able to pick choice (D).

Choice (D) is the correct answer.

Question 3

3. Which one of the following could be true?

    (A)   U is the only product promoted.
    (B)   V is the only product promoted.
    (C)   X is the only product promoted.
    (D)   Y is the only product promoted.
    (E)   Z is the only product promoted.

This is a Truth question since it ends with the phrase *could be true*. It's also a Universal question since there is no new rule. A quick glance at the answer choices shows you that each one is concerned with what could be the only product promoted. When there is only one product promoted, the other six must be not promoted. Take a look at your master diagram. There is one rule that should draw your attention—from rule 4, you can see that if you try to make either V or W not promoted, then the other one jumps into the Promoted group. Thus there's no way you could have both of them not promoted. One of them must always be promoted, so if there is going to be only one product promoted, it must be either V or W. Looking at the answer choices, you'll see that choice (B) is the only one that is a possibility.

If you hadn't seen this deduction, then your approach would be first to save the question for later and see if your previous work helps, then to try out each answer choice by trying to make it true. For example, try to make U promoted and everything else not promoted and see if any rules are broken. Keep repeating this process until you find an answer choice that is possible.

Choice (B) is the correct answer.

Lecture 2 Explanations

Question 4

4. If Y is not promoted, which one of the following must be false?

(A) Both T and U are promoted.
(B) Both T and V are promoted.
(C) Both U and X are promoted.
(D) Both U and Z are promoted.
(E) Both X and Z are promoted.

This is a Truth question, since it ends with the phrase *must be false*. It's also a Local question. Put Y in Not Promoted.

T U V W X Y Z	Promoted	Not Promoted	
Z → X → ~T AND ~V	U V Y	T W X Z	#1
T OR V → ~X → ~Z	Z X W	T V	#2
U → Y OR Z	V	T U W X Y Z	#3
~Y AND ~Z → ~U		Y	**#4**
~W → V			
~V → W			

Unfortunately, nothing happens! Having Y alone in Not Promoted is not enough to trigger any conditionals. Time to look at the master diagram. Since this question stem is looking for something that's impossible, pay attention to what would create a contradiction to what you already know, which is that Y is not promoted. If U were promoted and Z were not, then Y would have to be promoted, which would be impossible.

No answer choice offers U promoted and Z not, but some other things can end up causing Z to not be promoted, such as X not being promoted or T or V being promoted. Sure enough, choice (A) offers T and U both promoted, which leads to this impossibility:

T U V W X Y Z	Promoted	Not Promoted	
Z → X → ~T AND ~V	U V Y	T W X Z	#1
T OR V → ~X → ~Z	Z X W	T V	#2
U → Y OR Z	V	T U W X Y Z	#3
~Y AND ~Z → ~U		Y	**#4**
~W → V	~~T U Y~~	~~Y X Z~~	
~V → W			

Cross out this line in your diagram so you don't mistakenly use it later.

If you had not seen these deductions, you would have had to attack each answer choice by trying to prove it to be possible.

Choice (A) is the correct answer.

Question 5

5. If X is promoted, which one of the following could be a complete and accurate list of all the products promoted?

(A) U, W, X
(B) U, W, Y, Z
(C) U, X, Y, Z
(D) V, W, X, Y
(E) W, X, Y, Z

This is a Local Rule Tester question. If you put X in the Promoted group, a few things happen:

T U V W X Y Z

Z → X → ~T AND ~V

T OR V → ~X → ~Z

U → Y OR Z

~Y AND ~Z → ~U

~W → V

~V → W

Promoted	Not Promoted	
U V Y	T W X Z	#1
Z X W	T V	#2
V	T U W X Y Z	#3
	Y	#4
~~T U Y~~	~~Y X Z~~	
X W	T V	#5

So you can eliminate choice (B), which is missing X, choice (C), which is missing W, and choice (D), which features V as a promoted element. Finally, look at the overall rules of the game. Rule 3 is broken in choice (A), which has U but lacks Y or Z.

Choice (E) is the correct answer.

QUESTIONS 6–10

IDENTIFY

You can identify this as a Binary game because the situation asks you to sort the people into two groups—Monday and Tuesday. Don't be distracted by the fact that the two groups happen to be two consecutive days of the week—a glance at the rules and questions reveals that there is no mention of before and after or consecutive elements. Order is not important in this game, only whether a person is in the Monday group or the Tuesday group.

SET UP

First, decide on a diagram. You want every Binary diagram to revolve around *yes* and *no*, so in this case, reorient the way you think about the groups and designate one of them *Monday* and one of them *Not Monday* (a.k.a. Tuesday).

Next, symbolize the stock of elements by writing the initial of each person to the left of the diagram.

Now symbolize the rules. As you might expect, they are all conditionals.

> **Rule 1:** Turn the *unless* into *if not*. Since the *not* applies to the OR, make sure to change it into AND.
>
> ~J AND ~N → F
> ~F → J OR N

Rule 2: The rule says, "George presents on Tuesday…" but in your reoriented thinking, this means, "George does not present on Monday…" So the symbol for this is ~G.

$$\sim G \longrightarrow K$$
$$\sim K \longrightarrow G$$

Rule 3:

$$H \longrightarrow \sim F \text{ AND } \sim K$$
$$F \text{ OR } K \longrightarrow \sim H$$

Rule 4:

$$K \longrightarrow N$$
$$\sim N \longrightarrow \sim K$$

Deduce

Again, lots of linking is possible. On this master diagram, we'll link rules 2 and 3 and leave the more complex rules unlinked. You can choose to do more or less depending on your comfort level with conditionals.

F G H J K N

Monday	Not Monday (Tuesday)

$$\sim J \text{ AND } \sim N \longrightarrow F$$
$$\sim F \longrightarrow J \text{ OR } N$$

$$\sim G \longrightarrow K \longrightarrow N$$
$$\sim N \longrightarrow \sim K \longrightarrow G$$

$$H \longrightarrow \sim F \text{ AND } \sim K$$
$$F \text{ OR } K \longrightarrow \sim H$$

The Rules

Faye presents on Monday unless Joan or Nathan presents on Monday.

George presents on Tuesday only if Kurt presents on Monday.

If Harvey presents on Monday, then Faye and Kurt present on Tuesday.

Nathan presents on Monday if Kurt presents on Monday.

Question 6

6. Which one of the following could be a complete and accurate list of the people who present on Monday?

   (A) Faye, Nathan
   (B) Faye, George, Kurt
   (C) Harvey, George
   (D) Faye, Harvey, George
   (E) George, Nathan

This is a Rule Tester question. Rule 1 is broken in choice (C), which is missing **F**. Rule 2 is broken in choice (A), which is missing **G**. Rule 3 is broken in choice (D), since **F** should not be on Monday. Rule 4 is broken in choice (B), which is missing **N**. Since choice (E) shows a legal configuration, put it on your diagram so you can refer back to it if you need it.

Choice (E) is the correct answer.

Question 7

7. If Faye and George present on the same day, which one of the following must be true?

   (A) George presents on Tuesday.
   (B) Harvey presents on Tuesday.
   (C) Joan presents on Monday.
   (D) Kurt presents on Monday.
   (E) Nathan Presents on Monday.

This is a Local Truth question. You want to put the new rule on the diagram and see what happens, but the new rule is a little vague because it doesn't tell you *which* day to put **F** and **G** on. You can work around this by giving yourself *two* new rows in the diagram and trying out both scenarios.

F G H J K N

~J AND ~N → F
~F → J OR N

~G → K → N
~N → ~K → G

H → ~F AND ~K
F OR K → ~H

	Monday	Not Monday (Tuesday)	
	G N	F H J K	#6
	F G	H	**#7**
	K N	F G H	

In the first scenario, the only result is that H is on Tuesday. In the second, G being on Tuesday forces K and N to be on Monday, which in turn puts H on Tuesday. The question stem asks for something that *must be true*, and you can see that H is on Tuesday in every possible scenario. Sure enough, that matches choice (B).

Choice (B) is the correct answer.

Question 8

This is a Universal Truth question. Since there is no new rule, check your master diagram. Unfortunately, the master diagram in this case is of very little help since it's empty. Your next strategy is to postpone this question until you have a large collection of previous work to look back upon for help. Move on to question 9.

Question 9

9. If George presents on Tuesday, then which one of the following must be false?

   (A) Faye presents on Tuesday.
   (B) Harvey presents on Monday.
   (C) Joan presents on Tuesday.
   (D) Kurt presents on Monday.
   (E) Nathan presents on Monday.

This is a Local Truth question. Put G on Tuesday and see what happens.

F G H J K N

~J AND ~N → F
~F → J OR N

~G → K → N
~N → ~K → G

H → ~F AND ~K
F OR K → ~H

	Monday	Not Monday (Tuesday)	
	G N	F H J K	#6
	F G	H	#7
	K N	F G H	
	K N	G H	**#9**

K and N get put on Monday, which puts H on Tuesday. You're looking for something impossible, and choice (B) contradicts the diagram, which makes it the answer you're looking for.

Choice (B) is the correct answer.

Question 10

10. If Harvey presents on Monday, which one of the following could be a complete and accurate list of the people who present on Tuesday?

    (A) Faye, George, Kurt, Nathan
    (B) Faye, Joan, Kurt, Nathan
    (C) Faye, Harvey, Kurt, Nathan,
    (D) Faye, Kurt, Nathan
    (E) Kurt, Nathan

This is a Local Rule Tester question. Put H on Monday and see what happens.

F G H J K N

~J AND ~N → F
~F → J OR N

~G → K → N
~N → ~K → G

H → ~F AND ~K
F OR K → ~H

	Monday	Not Monday (Tuesday)	
	G N	F H J K	#6
	F G	H	#7
	K N	F G H	
	K N	G H	#9
	H G J/N	F K	#10

F and K have to be on Tuesday, and G has to be on Monday. F being on Tuesday means *either* J or N has to be on Monday, but you don't know which one. Reserve a spot on Monday for one of those two, and symbolize with a dotted line that the other can go on either day. This means that the correct answer, which is a possible configuration of the elements on Tuesday, must have both F and K, and could have either J or N but not both. Only choice (D) shows a legal possibility.

Choice (D) is the correct answer.

Question 8

8.   Each of the following could be true EXCEPT:

   (A)   Faye and Kurt both present on Monday.
   (B)   Harvey and George both present on Monday.
   (C)   George and Harvey both present on Tuesday.
   (D)   George and Nathan both present on Tuesday.
   (E)   Harvey and Joan both present on Tuesday.

Now you can return to question 8. The question stem can be simplified to say, "Which one of the following must be false?" Look back at your previous work and eliminate any answer choice that you proved possible.

Choice (A): This did not appear in any of your previous work. *Hold on to it.*

Choice (B): This was true in question 10. *Eliminate it.*

Choice (C): This was true in question 9. *Eliminate it.*

Choice (D): This did not appear in any of your previous work. *Hold on to it.*

Choice (E): This was true in question 6. *Eliminate it.*

Now you are down to just two choices. To test out each one in your diagram, try to make a complete configuration with the choice as it's written, and see if any rules are broken. Here's choice (A):

F G H J K N

~J AND ~N → F
~F → J OR N

~G → K → N
~N → ~K → G

H → ~F AND ~K
F OR K → ~H

	Monday	Not Monday (Tuesday)	
	G N	F H J K	#6
	F G	H	#7
	K N	F G H	
	K N	G H	#9
	H G J/N	F K	#10
	F K N	H G J	#8

Since choice (A) works, you can eliminate it. Only choice (D) is left, so it must be correct. If you're not sure, try it out in your diagram, and you'll see that it leads to a broken rule, which means it must be false. That's what you're looking for.

Choice (D) is the correct answer.

QUESTIONS 11–15

Identify

You can identify this as a Binary game because the situation asks you to put the flowers into two groups—Included and Not Included.

Set Up

Use the standard Binary diagram. The two groups are already defined in terms of *yes* and *no*, so you don't have to change anything.

Next, symbolize the stock of elements by writing the initial of each flower to the left of the diagram.

Now symbolize the rules. As you might expect, they are all conditionals. They are relatively straightforward once you recognize that the words *any* and *every* work just like the word *if*.

Deduce

Some linking is possible. In this master diagram, we've linked the last two rules but left the ones containing AND and OR unlinked.

L M O P R T V | Included | Not Included

L AND T → ~O
O → ~L OR ~T

~T → M AND R
~M OR ~R → T

~L → ~P AND ~R
R OR P → L

M → ~V → P
~P → V → ~M

Question 11

11. Which one of the following could be a complete and accurate list of the flowers included in a bouquet?

(A) lilacs, marigolds, orchids, roses
(B) lilacs, marigolds, orchids, petunias
(C) lilacs, roses, tulips, violets
(D) marigolds, orchids, tulips, violets
(E) orchids, roses, tulips, violets

The Rules

Orchids are not included in any bouquet that contains both lilacs and tulips.

Marigolds and roses are included in every bouquet that does not contain tulips.

Neither petunias nor roses are included in any bouquet that does not contain lilacs.

Petunias are included in every bouquet that does not contain violets.

Violets are not included in any bouquet that contains marigolds.

This is a Rule Tester question. Rule 1 is not broken in any choice. Rule 2 is broken in choice (B), which is missing **R**. Rule 3 is broken in choice (E) since it shouldn't include **R**. Rule 4 is broken in choice (A), which lacks both **P** and **V**. Rule 5 is broken in choice (D), which has both **M** and **V**. Fill in the correct answer, (C), as a possible configuration in your diagram.

Choice (C) is the correct answer.

Question 12

This is a Universal Truth question. As there is no new rule, check your master diagram. Unfortunately, the master diagram in this case is of very little help since it's empty. Your next strategy is to postpone this question until you have a large collection of previous work to look back upon for help. Move on to question 13.

Question 13

13. If a bouquet includes marigolds, which one of the following must be true?

    (A) The bouquet also includes lilacs.
    (B) The bouquet also includes orchids.
    (C) The bouquet also includes violets.
    (D) The bouquet does not include roses.
    (E) The bouquet does not include tulips.

This is a Local Truth question. Put the new rule on your diagram.

L M O P R T V

L AND T → ~O
O → ~L OR ~T

~T → M AND R
~M OR ~R → T

~L → ~P AND ~R
R OR P → L

M → ~V → P
~P → V → ~M

	Included	Not Included	
	L R T V	M O P	#11
	M P L	V	#13

From the rules, you can tell that the bouquet also includes P and L, and does not include V. Choice (A) matches the diagram.

Choice (A) is the correct answer.

Question 14

14. If a bouquet includes neither roses nor violets, which one of the following could be false?

    (A) The bouquet includes lilacs.
    (B) The bouquet does not include marigolds.
    (C) The bouquet does not include orchids.
    (D) The bouquet includes petunias.
    (E) The bouquet includes tulips.

This is another Local Truth question, so put the new rule on your diagram. A number of consequences occur:

L M O P R T V

L AND T → ~O
O → ~L OR ~T

~T → M AND R
~M OR ~R → T

~L → ~P AND ~R
R OR P → L

M → ~V → P
~P → V → ~M

	Included	Not Included	
	L R T V	M O P	#11
	M P L	V	#13
	T P L	R V O	#14

Since the question stem asks for the thing that *could be false* (is not required), eliminate any answer choice that *must be true* (is required). Only choice (B) does not have to be true.

Choice (B) is the correct answer.

Lecture 2 Explanations

Question 15

15. If a bouquet contains orchids, each of the following could be true EXCEPT:

(A) The bouquet also includes both lilacs and roses.
(B) The bouquet also includes both lilacs and marigolds.
(C) The bouquet also includes both marigolds and petunias.
(D) The bouquet also includes both marigolds and tulips.
(E) The bouquet also includes both tulips and violets.

This is another Local Truth question, so put the new rule on your diagram. When you include O, rule 1 tells you that either L or T must be excluded, but how do you know which one? The best way to deal with this is to explore both scenarios. Give yourself two new lines in the diagram. In one of them, make L not included, and in the other, make T not included. Then explore what happens in each scenario.

L M O P R T V	Included	Not Included	
L AND T → ~O	L R T V	M O P	#11
O → ~L OR ~T	M P L	V	#13
~T → M AND R	T P L	R V O	#14
~M OR ~R → T	O V T	L P R M	#15
~L → ~P AND ~R	O M R L P	T V	
R OR P → L			
M → ~V → P			
~P → V → ~M			

In each scenario, all the elements are completely determined. The question stem in effect asks you to find the choice that must be false, so you can eliminate anything that was true in *either* scenario. Only choice (D) was never true, so that's the one you're looking for.

Choice (D) is the correct answer.

Question 12

12. Which one of the following must be false?

(A) A bouquet includes both orchids and marigolds.
(B) A bouquet includes both lilacs and violets.
(C) A bouquet includes neither orchids nor roses.
(D) A bouquet includes neither petunias nor tulips.
(E) A bouquet includes neither tulips nor violets.

Now you can return to question 12. The question stem asks you what *must be false*. You can look back at your full collection of previous work and eliminate any choice that *could be true* in any question.

Choice (A): This was true in question 15. *Eliminate it.*

Choice (B): This was true in question 11. *Eliminate it.*

Choice (C): This was true in question 14. *Eliminate it.*

Choice (D): This did not appear in any of your previous work. *Hold on to it.*

Choice (E): This was true in question 15. *Eliminate it.*

Good news: there is only one choice left. You can pick choice (D) with confidence.

Choice (D) is the correct answer.

EXPLANATIONS

QUESTIONS 1–5

IDENTIFY

You can identify this as a Grid game because there are more than two factors to figure out. There is an order (first through sixth), and for each visit you have to figure out: 1) the office, 2) the type of job, and 3) the place in the order.

SET UP

Begin by choosing an appropriate diagram. You know you need a grid since this is a Grid game. When there is a natural order, it's best to use that as the columns, so use 1–6 as the columns in this case. Then give yourself two rows, one for the offices and one for the job types.

To symbolize the stock, notice how the elements will fit into your diagram. Since all the offices go into one row, put the elements K–P next to the first row. Since all the job types will go into a separate row, put the elements R and I next to the second row, and put three of each since you know exactly how many of each he will perform.

Now symbolize the rules.

> **Rule 1:** You can use an antiblock:

> **Rule 2:** Use a soft block for this:

> **Rule 3:** You can put an I directly on the diagram in the fourth spot in the second row.

Lecture 3 Explanations

Rule 4: This looks like a block rule, but since **M** and **I** occupy different rows on your diagram, you have to modify your block symbol to show that they must be in consecutive columns *and* different rows:

Rule 5: This is a block rule, and since the rule refers to two elements that must be together in the *same* visit, use a vertical block:

So far, the diagram looks like this:

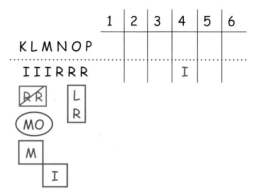

Deduce

There are a number of deductions to be made here. First, since you have to keep the **R**'s separated, two of them must precede the **I** in spot 4 and one of them must follow it. The two before spot 4 can't be next to each other, so spots 1 and 3 must have **R**'s, and spot 2 must have an **I**. Spots 5 and 6 must have the remaining **I** and **R**, but they could come in either order.

Next, think about the awkward-looking block with **M** and **I**. You know you can't put **M** sixth because it needs to precede an **I**. You also can't put **M** second because of the **R** you deduced to be third. You also know that **O** can't be first since that would force **M** to be second, which is not allowed.

Finally, since **L** must be a repair, it can't be second or fourth, and it can't immediately follow **M**. You can symbolize this last deduction as a new antiblock.

Also notice that **K**, **N**, and **P** are not restricted by any rules, so they are free agents. Underline them in the stock.

Your master diagram now looks like this:

Master Diagram

	1	2	3	4	5	6
K L M N O P	~O	~L ~M		~L		~M
I I I R R R	R	I	R	I	R	I

Question 1

1. Which one of the following is an acceptable order of visits?

(A) K, P, N, O, M, L
(B) L, P, O, M, N, K
(C) M, O, P, L, N, K
(D) N, L, P, K, M, O
(E) P, O, L, M, K, N

The Rules

The technician does not perform two repairs in a row.
The technician visits O immediately before or after M.
The technician performs an installation on the fourth visit.
The visit immediately following the visit to M is an installation.
The technician performs a repair at L.

This is a Rule Tester question, but it's a little different from Rule Testers you have seen before because it only gives you *one* of the rows in the grid, not the complete configuration of all the elements.

You can still approach this by looking at each rule and eliminating each choice in which it is broken. The difference is that you won't be able to directly use every rule as it is written, and you will instead need to look at some of your deductions. First start with the symbols that relate to the top row. You can eliminate choice (E) since M and O are not consecutive, and you can eliminate choice (A) since L immediately follows M, which violates the antiblock you deduced.

Now look at the forbidden spot symbols in the first row of the diagram. You can get rid of choice (D) because L is second, and choice (C) because L is fourth. Only choice (B) is left, and it's correct. You can fill it in as a possible configuration in your diagram.

Choice (B) is the correct answer.

Question 2

2. If the technician performs installations at K, M, and P, then he could visit L

(A) second
(B) third
(C) fourth
(D) fifth
(E) sixth

This is an Element question because it specifically asks you about L. It's also a Local question since it gives you a new rule. You want to put the new rule on the diagram, but where? Four different spots could have an I, and where do the different offices go? To try to make this vague rule more specific, consider the most constrained element, which in this case is M. If M must *be* an installation, and since M must also immediately *precede* an installation, then there have to be two I's in a row. The only place this can happen is in spots 4 and 5:

Master Diagram

K L M N O P	1	2	3	4	5	6
	~O	~L ~M		~L		~M
I I I R R R	R	I	R	I	(R) (I)	

		L	P	O	M	N	K	#1
R R	L R	R	I	R	I	I	R	
MO			(K)	O	M	(P)		#2
M	M L							
I		R	I	R	I	I	R	

K and P have to be in spots 2 and 5, since those are the other two installation spots after M goes in 4. That means O must be in 3 in order to be next to M. The two remaining elements, L and N, can go in 1 and 6 in either order. Since the question stem asks you about L, you know the answer must be either first or sixth, so pick choice (E).

Choice (E) is the correct answer.

Question 3

3. Which one of the following must be false?

(A) The technician performs an installation in the first office he visits.

(B) The technician performs an installation in the second office he visits.

(C) The technician performs a repair in the third office he visits.

(D) The technician performs a repair in the fifth office he visits.

(E) The technician performs an installation in the sixth office he visits.

This is a Universal Truth question. Before postponing it, check your master diagram to see if you can already answer the question. Sure enough, choice (A) contradicts the master diagram, and since you're looking for something that must be false, this is it. Hooray for deductions!

Choice (A) is the correct answer.

Question 4

4. If the technician visits K fifth and N sixth, then at which one of the following offices must the technician perform an installation?

(A) K
(B) M
(C) N
(D) O
(E) P

This is a Local question and it's kind of a cross between a Spot and an Element question. Approach it like any other Local question, but pay particular attention to the **I**'s and what must be paired with them. Start by putting the new rule on the diagram:

It looks like the **I** and **R** in 5 and 6 can still go either way, so neither **K** nor **N** *must* be an installation. Get rid of choices (A) and (C). In spots 1–4, you have to fit **L** (in spot 1 or 3), **P**, and the consecutive soft block of **M** and **O**. The one thing you can't allow is for spots 1 and 3 to *both* be occupied before you place the block, since that would prevent you from being able to put **M** and **O** next to each other. That means **P** can't be in spot 1 or 3—and thus **P** must be an installation.

Choice (E) is the correct answer.

Question 5

5. If the technician visits L fifth, then which one of the following could be true?

(A) K receives an installation on the first visit.
(B) M receives an installation on the fourth visit.
(C) N receives a repair on the third visit.
(D) O receives a repair on the third visit.
(E) P receives a repair on the sixth visit.

This is a Local Truth question. Put **L** fifth and see what happens.

Master Diagram

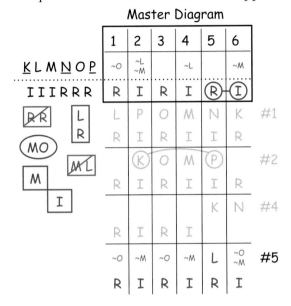

Putting **L** fifth means **R** is also fifth. This has a lot of implications for **M** and **O**, as shown. As you look at the answers, each of them has some problem that makes it impossible, except for choice (C).

Choice (C) is the correct answer.

QUESTIONS 6–10

IDENTIFY

You can identify this as a Grid game because there are three factors to figure out: 1) the plane, 2) the type, and 3) the place in the order.

SET UP

There is again a natural order involved (1–6), so use that to form the columns of your diagram. Create one row to contain the planes and a second row to contain the types.

To form the stock, write the planes next to the first row, and write three **J**'s and three **P**'s next to the second row to indicate how many of each you have to use.

Now symbolize the rules.

Rule 1: Put this directly on the diagram as a **P** in the third spot.

Rule 2: This one is a little strange, but it basically means that you need a block of two **J**'s, but you are forbidden to have all three **J**'s in a row. You can represent this with two symbols:

Rule 3: This is a vertical block:

Rule 4: This is a conditional statement, and you can symbolize it using vertical blocks on the left and right sides of the arrow:

$$\boxed{\begin{array}{c}W\\P\end{array}} \rightarrow \boxed{\begin{array}{c}Z\\J\end{array}}$$

$$\boxed{\begin{array}{c}Z\\P\end{array}} \rightarrow \boxed{\begin{array}{c}W\\J\end{array}}$$

This is correct, but it's a little bit ugly and awkward. Is there a simpler way to symbolize this rule? If you think about it, this rule is basically saying that they can't both be prop planes—either W or Z must be a jet. (It's also possible that they're both jets.) A simpler symbol for that would be:

$$\boxed{\begin{array}{c}W/Z\\J\end{array}}$$

Rule 5: You can symbolize this as a block:

$$\boxed{T\ Y}$$

At this point your diagram should look like this:

	1	2	3	4	5	6
S T W X Y Z						
J J J P P P			P			

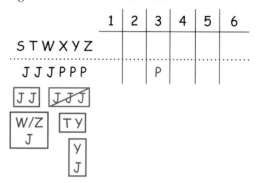

Deduce

There are a number of deductions to be made. First, notice that Y is involved in two of the blocks. You can combine them to make one larger block:

$$\boxed{\begin{array}{cc}T&Y\\&\boxed{J}\end{array}}$$

Using the larger block, you can make some endpoint deductions, and you can also see that Y can't be third and T can't be second.

The other rule that warrants some examination is rule 1. You must have two consecutive jets, but you cannot have three consecutive jets. This means you will have a block of two J's somewhere and a single J somewhere else. A quick glance at the diagram reveals that these two pieces have to be separated by the P in spot 3: either the block is before spot 3 and the single J after, or the single J is before spot 3 and the block after. There are too many possibilities to be able to mark anything definitively on the diagram, but understanding beforehand how the elements work together with the diagram is vital to being able to get through the game quickly.

Finally, S and X are free agents, so underline them.

Master Diagram

	1	2	3	4	5	6
S T W X Y Z	~Y	~T	~Y			~T
J J J P P P			P			

JJ   J̶J̶J̶

W/Z   T Y
  J   J

Question 6

6. If propeller planes are launched fourth and fifth, then which one of the following could be the order in which the planes are launched?

   (A)   S, T, Y, W, X, Z
   (B)   T, Y, Z, X, W, S
   (C)   X, Z, S, W, T, Y
   (D)   Y, Z, X, S, W, T
   (E)   Z, S, W, T, Y, X

The Rules

The third plane launched is a propeller plane.
A jet launch is followed by another jet launch exactly once.
Y is a jet plane.
If W is a propeller plane, then Z is a jet plane.
T is launched directly before Y.

This is a Rule Tester question, but again it's a little different since it only gives you one of the rows, not the entire diagram. It's also Local. Put the new rule on the diagram.

Master Diagram

	1	2	3	4	5	6
S T W X Y Z	~Y	~T	~Y			~T
J J J P P P			P			

JJ   J̶J̶J̶

W/Z   T Y
  J   J

#6

J	J	P	P	P	J

Now look at the rules. To be efficient, look at the most constrained elements first. For example, the L-shaped block with T and Y can only fit across spots 1–2 or 5–6. This eliminates choices (A), (D), and (E). Next, either W or Z must be a jet, so get rid of choice (B), which has them both as prop planes. Only choice (C) is left, so put it into your diagram as a possible configuration.

Choice (C) is the correct answer.

Question 7

7. If the order in which the planes are launched is T, Y, Z, S, X, W, then a propeller plane must be launched

   (A)   first
   (B)   second
   (C)   fourth
   (D)   fifth
   (E)   sixth

This is an Element question since it asks you where P must go. It's also Local. Put the new information on the diagram and figure out more.

Master Diagram

	1	2	3	4	5	6
S T W X Y Z	~Y	~T	~Y			~T
J J J P P P			P			

X	Z	S	W	T	Y	#6
J	J	P	P	P	J	
T	Y	Z	S	X	W	#7
	J	P	P		J	

With the order of the planes given, there are some obvious deductions. First, there must be a J in 2 because of Y. Next, since Z is a prop plane, W must be a jet. Finally, think about where you must put the other J. Since you have to have a block of two in a row, the final J must be next to one of the J's already placed—in either spot 1 or spot 5. That means spot 4 is definitely a P.

Choice (C) is the correct answer.

Question 8

It's best to postpone this Universal Truth question until later.

Question 9

9. If the plane launched immediately before T is a jet, then the fourth plane launched must be

   (A)   T
   (B)   W
   (C)   X
   (D)   Y
   (E)   Z

This is a Spot question since it asks you about spot 4. It's also Local, but the new rule is vague—it doesn't tell you where to put anything on the diagram. First try symbolizing the new rule to the right of the diagram as a big block containing all the information.

	T	Y
J		J

Now think about where this big block could fit. The two J's have to avoid any odd-numbered spots because the P in 3 won't allow that. Putting the J's in spots 2 and 4 seems to work, but putting them in spots 4 and 6 is impossible since there would then be no way to have two—but not three—consecutive J's. Thus, the big block has to fit into spots 2–4.

Master Diagram

	1	2	3	4	5	6	
S T W X Y Z	~y	~T	~y			~T	
J J J P P P			P				
	X	Z	S	W	T	Y	#6
	J	J	P	P	P	J	
	T	Y	Z	S	X	W	#7
		J	P	P		J	
			T	Y			#9
		J	P	J			

(left-side boxes: [J J] [~~J J J~~] [W/Z | T Y] J ... J)

(#9 box: T Y / J ... J)

You could figure out more, but since the stem asks you about spot 4, you have already done enough to pick the correct answer.

Choice (D) is the correct answer.

Question 10

10. If Y is the last plane launched, then which one of the following must be true?

(A) The first plane launched is a propeller plane.
(B) The second plane launched is a jet plane.
(C) The second plane launched is a propeller plane.
(D) The fourth plane launched is a jet plane.
(E) The fourth plane launched is a propeller plane.

This is a Local Truth question. Put the new information on the diagram and see what happens.

Master Diagram

	1	2	3	4	5	6	
S T W X Y Z	~y	~T	~y			~T	
J J J P P P			P				
	X	Z	S	W	T	Y	#6
	J	J	P	P	P	J	
	T	Y	Z	S	X	W	#7
		J	P	P		J	
			T	Y			#9
		J	P	J			
					T	Y	#10
		P	P			J	

(left-side boxes: [J J] [~~J J J~~] [W/Z | T Y] J ... J)

(#9 box: T Y / J ... J)

Again, think about the most constrained elements. You need to have a block of two J's, and you need to have a single J, and these two pieces have to be separated by the P in 3. Thus, with the J in 6 there's no way the J's can reach to spot 4. Spot 4 has to have a P.

Choice (E) is the correct answer.

Question 8

8. Each of the following could be true EXCEPT:

 (A) S and T are both jet planes.
 (B) S and T are both propeller planes.
 (C) W and X are both jet planes.
 (D) W and X are both propeller planes.
 (E) W and Z are both jet planes.

Now you can return to question 8. Because you're looking for something that must be false, you can eliminate anything you saw to be possible in your previous work. Choice (B) was true in question 6, and choice (C) was possible in question 7. With some imagination, you can see that both (D) and (E) are possible in question 10.

Only choice (A) is left, and it's correct. It also makes sense if you think about it. You know Y is a jet, and either W or Z has to be the second jet. If, as choice (A) suggests, S and T were both jets, then you would have four jets, which is impossible.

Choice (A) is the correct answer.

QUESTIONS 11–15

IDENTIFY

This game is a Grid game as you have three factors to associate with each other: the time slot, the director, and the playwright.

SET UP

Because they are consecutive, use the time slots as the columns. Then set aside one row each for the directors and the playwrights. The situation tells you how many of each element there is, so write the stock for each row next to that row.

Next, symbolize the rules.

Rule 1: Both M's are on the same day. This must be Saturday or Sunday. Put this directly on the diagram as a barbell.

Rule 2: H must do a matinee. Again, put this directly on the diagram.

Rule 3 combines a vertical block and some relative order rules:

$$J - \boxed{\begin{matrix} K \\ O \end{matrix}} - L$$

Rule 4 is also a relative order rule, and you know from rule 1 that the M's are consecutive.

$$N - N - \boxed{MM}$$

Rules 5 and 6 are antiblocks:

DEDUCE

You can use the chains in rules 3 and 4 to make some simple endpoint deductions. Otherwise, it seems like there are a lot of different possibilities and considerations. It would probably take too long to try to map them all out, so just get started on the questions.

Master Diagram

	Thu	Fri	Sat mat	Sat eve	Sun mat	Sun eve
F G H J K L	~K ~L	~L	(H) ───	─── ○	~J	~J ~K
M M N N O O			M M ───	─── □ □	~N	~N

J— |K| —L
   |O|

N—N— |MM|

Question 11

11. If both plays written by O'Neill are performed on Sunday, then which one of the following could direct the play performed on Friday?

(A) Foley
(B) Gomez
(C) Hart
(D) Kogan
(E) Lowe

This is a Local Spot question since it asks about a particular spot (Friday). Put the new information on the diagram and see what else happens.

Master Diagram

	Thu	Fri	Sat mat	Sat eve	Sun mat	Sun eve	
F G H J K L	~K ~L	~L	(H) ───	─── ○	~J	~J ~K	
M M N N O O			M M ───	─── □ □	~N	~N	
J— |K| —L |O|	(F)───(J)		H	G	K	L	#11
	N	N	M	M	O	O	

N—N— |MM|

The O's on Sunday kick the M's onto Saturday, leaving the N's to go on Thursday and Friday. Since K cannot be last but still needs an O, it will be a Sunday matinee, followed by L. There is now only one matinee left for H, on Saturday. G, which needs to avoid being with N, must be on Saturday evening. Thus, Friday must have one of the two remaining elements, F or J.

Choice (A) is the correct answer.

Question 12

12. If Jacoby directs one of the Saturday plays, which of the following could be true?

(A) Lowe directs one of the O'Neill plays.
(B) Jacoby directs one of the O'Neill plays.
(C) The Thursday play is written by O'Neill.
(D) The play directed by Gomez is performed on Satur-day.
(E) The play directed by Hart is performed on Saturday.

This is a Local Truth question. It tells you that **J** goes on Saturday, but you don't know at which time. The best approach is to try each scenario. Set aside two new grids. In one, put **J** in Saturday evening, and in the other put J in the Saturday matinee. Then figure out as much as you can in both cases.

Master Diagram

The first scenario is impossible. By putting **J** on Saturday evening, **K** and **L** must go on Sunday, which puts the **M**'s on Saturday. That in turn puts the **N**'s on Thursday and Friday. With **H** taking the last weekend spot, **G** is left with no option other than going with **N**, which would break rule 6. Cross this configuration out so you don't mistakenly use it later.

The second scenario must be true. **H** takes the other matinee spot, putting **K** and **L** on the weekend evenings. With an **O** on Saturday, the **Ms** must go on Sunday. **G** needs a writer other than **N**, so it takes the last remaining **O**, leaving **F** and **J** with the **N**'s. **F** and **G** could go on either Thursday or Friday. This leaves choice (C) as the only possibility.

Choice (C) is the correct answer.

Question 13

The best approach for this Universal Truth question is to postpone it until you have more work on your diagram to look back on.

Question 14

14. If one of the matinees is a play written by O'Neill and directed by Foley, then Gomez must direct the play at which one of the following times?

(A) Thursday
(B) Friday
(C) Saturday evening
(D) Sunday matinee
(E) Sunday evening

This is a Local Element question because it asks you about a specific element (G). It says one of the matinees has F and O, but once again you don't know which. Again, it's best to explore each scenario.

Master Diagram

	Thu	Fri	Sat mat	Sat eve	Sun mat	Sun eve
F G H J K L	~K ~L	~L	(H)	O	~J	~J ~K
M M N N O O			M M		~N	~N

J— K —L
O

N—N—MM

F/M   G/N

F	J	H	G	K	L	#11
N	N	M	M	O	O	
H	J	M	M	K	L	#12
N	N	M	M	O	O	
F	G	J	K	H	L	
N	O	N	O	M	M	
J	K	F	L	H	G	#14
N	O	O	N	M	M	
H		M	M	F	O	

In the first scenario, the M's go on Sunday and H takes the other matinee. Since F is using one O and K will use another, G will have to go with M, and thus must be on Sunday evening. J, K and L take the remaining three spots, and the N's have to go with J and L. You have a complete setup.

In the second scenario, you run into a problem. The M's are kicked to Saturday and H takes the Saturday matinee. K, which cannot be last, will have to go on Thursday or Friday, but you also need to put both N's there to satisfy Rule 4. This scenario is impossible. Cross it out so you don't mistakenly use it later.

Choice (E) is the correct answer.

Question 15

15. If the play performed on Friday is directed by Kogan, then which one of the following could be true?

(A) Jacoby directs a play written by Miller.
(B) Lowe directs the Sunday matinee.
(C) Both plays written by Miller are performed on Saturday.
(D) The Sunday evening play is directed by Foley.
(E) Gomez directs the Thursday play.

This is a Local Truth question. Put the new rule on the diagram and deduce more.

Master Diagram

	Thu	Fri	Sat mat	Sat eve	Sun mat	Sun eve	
F G H J K L	~K ~L	~L	(H)—	—○	~J	~J ~K	
M M N N O O			M M	——	~N	~N	
J—[K/O]—L	(F)—	—(J)	H	G	K	L	#11
	N	N	M	M	O	O	
N—N—[MM]	H		H	J	K	L	#12
	N	N	M	M	O	O	
[F/M] [G/N]	F	G	J	K	H	L	
	N	O	N	O	M	M	
	J	K	F	L	H	G	#14
	N	O	O	N	M	M	
			H		F		
			M	M	O		
	J	K			~F	~F	#15
		O			M	M	

Think about the most constrained element. It's probably the block of **M**'s. That block cannot go on Saturday because you need room to fit two **N**'s before it. Therefore, it must be on Sunday. Now, because of rule 5, you know **F** cannot be on Sunday—it must be on Saturday. There are quite a few possibilities for the remaining letters, but as long as **G** and **N** are not together, it looks like anything else is permissible.

Choice (E) is the only one that mentions something possible with this configuration.

Choice (B) is the correct answer.

Question 13

13. Which one of the following statements must be false?

    (A)   The Sunday matinee is directed by Lowe.
    (B)   Both plays written by O'Neill are performed on
          Sunday.
    (C)   The play directed by Jacoby is performed on Satur-
          day.
    (D)   The play directed by Jacoby is written by Miller.
    (E)   Both plays written by Nicholls are performed on
          Saturday.

Now you can return to question 13. This one is looking for something impossible, so you can quickly eliminate any answer choice that contains something that you saw to be possible in your previous work.

Choice (A): You saw this as a possibility in question 15. *Eliminate it.*

Choice (B): You saw this happen in question 11. *Eliminate it.*

Choice (C): You saw this happen in question 12. *Eliminate it.*

Choice (D): You have never seen this happen. *Hold on to it.*

Choice (E): You saw this as a possibility in question 15. *Eliminate it.*

Good news! Only one choice remains. Pick (D).

Choice (D) is the correct answer.

Lecture 3 Explanations

EXPLANATIONS

QUESTIONS 1–5

IDENTIFY

You can identify this as a Grouping game because there is no mention of any order or consecutive elements, and there are more than two groups.

SET UP

In this case, a glance at the rules and questions shows that the best way to construct your diagram is to use the sports teams as the groups and the schools as the elements. That's because the answer choices for questions 2–5 will be easy to read if you can look at each sports team and see which schools are sending one.

Since the schools are the elements, and since the situation tells you that each school sends exactly two teams, the stock is composed of eight letters—each school name written twice. Put this to the left of your diagram.

Now symbolize the rules.

> **Rule 1:** This tells you how many spots you have in the Swim group. Put three underlined spaces there to show you the size of the group.

> **Rule 2:** This tells you there are three spots in the Track group, and it also tells you one of the schools there. Put three underlined spaces there, and put L in one of them.

> **Rule 3:** This is a conditional rule. Unlike in a Binary game, elements are not limited to the *yes/no* feature of just two groups. You have to use subscripts to indicate the different groups.

$$I_S \longrightarrow K_G$$
$$\sim K_G \longrightarrow \sim I_S$$

Rule 4: You could try to construct some kind of antiblock, but it always pays to think about the simplest way to symbolize every rule. In this case, since there are two H's and only three groups, the fact that H can't be in both Track and Gym means that there must be an H in Swim. Now you can symbolize that directly on the diagram.

DEDUCE

There is one small deduction to be made. Since you have eight elements, and since you know Swim and Track each have three, then Gym must have two. That's about it. Here's the master diagram:

Master Diagram

H H I I K K L L

$I_s \rightarrow K_G$

$\sim K_G \rightarrow \sim I_s$

Gymnastics	Swim	Track
__ __	H __ __	L __ __

Question 1

1. If K sends both a swim team and a track team, then which one of the following is a complete and accurate list of the sports teams that H could send?

   (A) gymnastics
   (B) gymnastics, swim
   (C) gymnastics, track
   (D) swim, track
   (E) gymnastics, swim, track

This is a List question because it asks you to determine what *is* the complete list of the places where H *could* go. It's also Local, so put the new information on your diagram.

Master Diagram

H H I I K K L L

$I_s \rightarrow K_G$

$\sim K_G \rightarrow \sim I_s$

Gymnastics	Swim	Track
__ __	H __ __	L __ __
I H	H K L	L K I

#1

Since K is not sending a gym team, the contrapositive is triggered, and I can't send a swim team—it must be in Gym and Track. Now Track is full, and the two H's must be in Gym and Swim (and L takes the final empty spot in Swim). That's enough to answer the question.

Choice (B) is the correct answer.

Question 2

2. If H sends a gymnastics team, then which one of the following is a complete and accurate list of the other schools any one of which could also send a gymnastics team?

   (A) K
   (B) L
   (C) I, K
   (D) K, L
   (E) I, K, L

This is another Local List question. See what happens when you put H in Gym.

Master Diagram

HHIIKKLL

$I_s \rightarrow K_G$

$\sim K_G \rightarrow \sim I_s$

Gymnastics	Swim	Track	
__ __	H __ __	L __ __	
I H	H K L	L K I	#1
H __	H __ __	L __ __	#2

Unfortunately, not much happens. That's okay—you have a few techniques you can use. First, notice that your previous work for question 1 had H in Gym, along with I. That means that I must be on the list of schools that could send a gym team when H is there. You can eliminate the choices that are missing I, so that gets rid of choices (A), (B), and (D). Now that you are down to only two choices, focus on the differences between them. Both contain K, so don't pay attention to that element. Instead, focus on L, which is present in choice (E) but not choice (C). Can L send a gym team? Try it out in your diagram:

Master Diagram

HHIIKKLL

$I_s \rightarrow K_G$

$\sim K_G \rightarrow \sim I_s$

Gymnastics	Swim	Track	
__ __	H __ __	L __ __	
I H	H K L	L K I	#1
~~H L~~	~~H I__~~	~~L I__~~	#2

No. If you put L in Gym, then Gym is full, and you have to put the two I's in Swim and Track. However, putting I in Swim means you need a K in Gym, which is impossible.

L is not allowed to send a gym team, so eliminate any choice that features L. Only choice (C) is left. Remember to cross out this line in your diagram so you don't accidentally use it later.

Choice (C) is the correct answer.

Question 3

This Universal Truth question is a good one to postpone until later.

Question 4

4. If I does not send a swim team, which one of the following is a complete and accurate list of the schools any one of which could send a track team?

(A) H, L
(B) I, L
(C) H, I, K
(D) H, I, L
(E) H, I, K, L

This is another Local List question. See what happens when you put the two I's in Gym and Track.

Master Diagram

HHIIKKLL

$I_s \rightarrow K_G$

$\sim K_G \rightarrow \sim I_s$

Gymnastics	Swim	Track	
__ __	H __ __	L __ __	
I H	H K L	L K I	#1
~~H L~~	~~H I__~~	~~L I__~~	#2
I (K)	H K L	L I (H)	#4

The three spots in Swim have to be filled by the other three schools. The remaining two spots are filled by H and K, in either order. Thus, any school could potentially send a track team, so the complete list contains every school.

Choice (E) is the correct answer.

Question 5

5. If both H and K send track teams, then which one of the following must be true?

    (A)   Both I and K send gymnastics teams.
    (B)   Both I and K send swim teams.
    (C)   Both I and L send gymnastics teams.
    (D)   Both K and L send swim teams.
    (E)   Both K and L send gymnastics teams.

This is a Local Truth question. See what happens on the diagram.

Master Diagram

HHIIKKLL

$I_S \rightarrow K_G$

$\sim K_G \rightarrow \sim I_S$

Gymnastics	Swim	Track	
__ __	H __ __	L __ __	
I H	H K L	L K I	#1
H L	H I __	L I __	#2
I Ⓚ	H K L	L I Ⓗ	#4
I K	H I L	L H K	**#5**

With Track full, the two **I**'s must be in Gym and Swim, which in turn forces the second **K** into Gym. **L** takes the last spot, in Swim. Choice (A) matches the diagram.

Choice (A) is the correct answer.

Question 3

3. Which one of the following must be false?

    (A)   Both H and I send gymnastics teams.
    (B)   Both H and I send track teams.
    (C)   Both H and K send gymnastics teams.
    (D)   Both H and K send track teams.
    (E)   Both H and L send gymnastics teams.

Now you can return to question 3. Since this question is asking you to find something impossible, you can eliminate any choice that you saw to be possible in your previous work.

Choice (A): You saw this happen in question 1. *Eliminate it.*

Choice (B): You saw this happen in question 4. *Eliminate it.*

Choice (C): You have never seen this happen. *Hold on to it.*

Choice (D): You saw this happen in question 5. *Eliminate it.*

Choice (E): You have never seen this happen. *Hold on to it.*

Now you're down to two choices. It's time to start trying them out in the diagram. Try to prove choice (C) possible:

Master Diagram

H H I I K K L L

$I_S \rightarrow K_G$

$\sim K_G \rightarrow \sim I_S$

Gymnastics	Swim	Track	
__ __	H __ __	L __ __	
I H	H K L	L K I	#1
H̶ L̶	H̶ I̶	L̶ I̶	#2
I Ⓚ	H K L	L I Ⓗ	#4
I K	H I L	L H K	#5
H K	H I L	L I K	**#3**

Yes, choice (C) is possible, so you can eliminate it. Choice (E) is the only one left, so it must be correct.

Choice (E) is the correct answer.

QUESTIONS 6–10

IDENTIFY

You can identify this as a Grouping game because there is no mention of any order or consecutive elements, and there are more than two groups.

SET UP

It's usually better to have fewer groups and more elements, and this game is no exception. Use the stores as the groups and the products as the elements.

There are five elements, but you don't know how many times each one will be used. Write the stock as the initials of the five elements to the left of the diagram.

Now symbolize the rules.

> **Rule 1:** This rule gives you more information about how many **F**'s you have. You can symbolize this by writing a $^{(2)}$ next to the **F** in the stock.
>
> **Rule 2:** You can symbolize this directly on the diagram in Players.
>
> **Rule 3:** Write a single underlined space in Renegade to show that only one element will go there.
>
> **Rule 4:** This can be symbolized with an antiblock:

> **Rules 5 and 6:** These are best symbolized as conditionals. For example, if a group has **K**, then it must also have **F**. You don't need subscripts in this case because the conditional symbols apply to each group equally.

$$K \rightarrow F$$
$$\sim F \rightarrow \sim K$$
$$H \rightarrow I$$
$$\sim I \rightarrow \sim H$$

Lecture 4 Explanations

At this point your diagram looks like this:

DEDUCE

There are a number of deductions you can make here. First, Players also needs an **I** because it has an **H**, and the presence of the **I** means **G** is forbidden in that group. Next, you know that Renegade can't have a **K** or an **H** because it only has room for one element, but those two elements can't travel alone. At this point, **K** is forbidden from both Players and Renegade, so it must be in Sportstore because every product is sold at least once. When **K** appears in Sportstore, it brings **F** along because of the conditional. Finally, you know you need exactly one more **F**, so you can put a barbell across the Players and Renegade.

Master Diagram

Question 6

6. Which one of the following is a complete and accurate list of the products that CANNOT be sold by Players?

(A) kayaks
(B) fishing poles, kayaks
(C) fishing poles, golf clubs
(D) golf clubs, kayaks
(E) fishing poles, golf clubs, kayaks

This is a Universal List question, so check your master diagram. You deduced that **K** and **G** are forbidden, and that everything else is allowed. That's enough to answer the question.

Choice (D) is the correct answer.

Question 7

7. Which one of the following could be a complete and accurate list of the products sold by Sportstore?

(A) fishing poles, golf clubs
(B) fishing poles, kayaks
(C) hockey sticks, ice skates, kayaks
(D) fishing poles, golf clubs, ice skates, kayaks
(E) fishing poles, golf clubs, hockey sticks, ice skates, kayaks

After seeing so many List questions, did you mistake this one for a List question too? It's not. It's a Rule Tester because it asks you what *could be* one permissible configuration of elements in Sportstore. Like many Rule Testers in Grouping games, it only gives you an incomplete configuration—it looks only at one group instead of the entire diagram. But you have to consider whether each choice would allow a valid full configuration.

First, look at your master diagram. You know Sportstore must always have **K** and **F**, so get rid of choices (A) and (C). Now look at the other rules. Rules 2 and 3 don't seem so useful, but rule 4 allows you to eliminate any choice with both **G** and **I**. That gets rid of choices (D) and (E). Choice (B) is correct, and you can put it into your diagram as a possible configuration.

Choice (B) is the correct answer.

The Rules

Exactly two shops sell fishing poles.
Players sells hockey sticks but not kayaks.
Renegade sells exactly one product.
No shop sells both golf clubs and ice skates.
Any shop that sells kayaks also sells fishing poles.
Any shop that sells hockey sticks also sells ice skates.

Question 8

8.   If Sportstore sells exactly three products, then which one of the following is a complete and accurate list of the shops any one of which could sell hockey sticks?

(A)   Players
(B)   Sportstore
(C)   Players, Renegade
(D)   Players, Sportstore
(E)   Players, Renegade, Sportstore

Back to the List questions. This one is Local, so put the new rule on the diagram.

Master Diagram

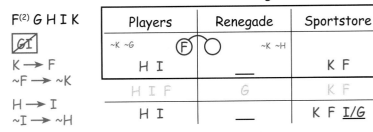

You know about two of the elements in Sportstore, so what's the third? It can't be **H** because **H** would bring **I** along with it and increase the total to four. But either **G** or **I** alone could be the third. You don't need to figure out any more because the question stem is about **H**. **H** is forbidden from Renegade and Sportstore, so choice (A) is correct.

Choice (A) is the correct answer.

Question 9

9.   If the product sold by Renegade is also one of the products sold by Players, then each of the following must be true EXCEPT:

(A)   Players sells fishing poles.
(B)   Players sells ice skates.
(C)   Sportstore sells golf clubs.
(D)   Sportstore sells ice skates.
(E)   Sportstore sells kayaks.

This is a Local Truth question, but its new rule is a little vague. *What* is the product they have in common? It can't be **K** or **G** since they are forbidden from Players. It can't be **H** since it is forbidden from Renegade. And it can't be **F** since you only have one **F** between the two groups. The common element must be **I**, and the **F** goes into Players.

Master Diagram

F$^{(2)}$ G H I K

~~G1~~

K → F
~F → ~K

H → I
~I → ~H

Players	Renegade	Sportstore	
~K ~G ⌒ (F)◯ ~K ~H			
H I	___	K F	
H I F	G	K F	#7
H I	___	K F I/G	#8
H I F	I	K F G	#9

Once you figure that out, you can also deduce that **G**, which must be sold somewhere, has to be in Sportstore. Nothing else can go there because of the antiblock, so this configuration is now complete. Choice (D) is the only one not required.

Choice (D) is the correct answer.

Question 10

10. If Players sells exactly three products, then which one of the following is a complete and accurate list of the products any one of which could be the product sold by Renegade?

   (A)   fishing poles
   (B)   golf clubs
   (C)   fishing poles, ice skates
   (D)   golf clubs, ice skates
   (E)   fishing poles, golf clubs, ice skates

This is a Local List question. *Which* three products does Players sell? Since K and G are forbidden, it must be H, I, and F.

Master Diagram

F$^{(2)}$ G H I K

~~G1~~

K → F
~F → ~K

H → I
~I → ~H

Players	Renegade	Sportstore	
~K ~G (F)⌒◯ ~K ~H			
H I	___	K F	
H I F	G	K F	#7
H I	___	K F I/G	#8
H I F	I	K F G	#9
H I F	I/G	K F	#10

Since you already have two F's at this point, Renegade can't have F, but it could have either I or G. That's enough to answer the question.

Choice (D) is the correct answer.

QUESTIONS 11–15

IDENTIFY

You can identify this as a Grouping game because there is no mention of any order or consecutive elements, and there are more than two groups.

SET UP

Since the pieces of furniture fit into different categories, you definitely want to use them as your elements, and the rooms as the groups.

The stock for this game is more complicated than most because of the categories. Write the elements to the left of your diagram, and differentiate between the categories by using uppercase for the ottomans, lowercase for the recliners, and script for the sofas.

Now symbolize the rules:

Rule 1: Since there are only two recliners, you can use two blocks:

$$\boxed{\text{H k}} \quad \text{OR} \quad \boxed{\text{H n}}$$

Rule 2: This one is a little more complicated. You can again use two blocks, but in one of them you have to use a generic space with a subscript to denote a sofa:

$$\boxed{\text{n J}} \quad \text{OR} \quad \boxed{\text{n } \underline{\quad}_{\text{\tiny s}}}$$

Rule 3: Since there are only two ottomans, it's easy enough to use two antiblocks:

DEDUCE

Next, examine your symbols for any deductions. First, none of the rules mentions any of the groups by name, so in many cases the elements in the family room and those in the great room will be interchangeable because those groups are the same size. Second, notice that **n** is the most constrained element, as it appears in two rules. If **H** is to ever appear in the same group as **n**, it must be in the group with three spaces (the living room), since having **H** and **n** alone together would not satisfy rule 2. Finally, *x* and *z* are not exactly free agents, but they are interchangeable.

Unfortunately, none of these observations allows you to place any elements definitively, so just go on and attend to the questions.

Here's the master diagram:

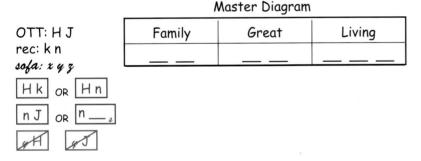

Master Diagram

	Family	Great	Living
	__ __	__ __	__ __ __

OTT: H J
rec: k n
sofa: x y z

Question 11

This is not a List question. It's more like a Rule Tester that gives you only one room instead of a complete diagram. It would probably be easier with more previous work to look back at.

Question 12

12. If each sofa is placed in a different room, then which one of the following is a complete and accurate list of the furniture pieces any one of which could be placed in the living room?

    (A) H, K, X, Z
    (B) K, N, X, Z
    (C) H, K, N, X, Z
    (D) H, J, K, N, X, Z
    (E) H, K, N, X, Y, Z

This is a Local List question. Putting the new rule on the diagram is a little tricky since it only talks about the *category* of sofas, not specific elements. You can start by reserving a spot in each group for a sofa, using subscripts.

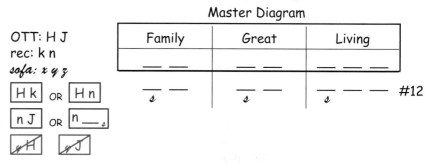

Now what? Look at the most constrained elements. You don't have to worry about n because it's guaranteed to be with a sofa no matter what. H needs to be involved in a block with a recliner, so it has to go in the living room. You have to keep *y* away from H (out of the living room), and also away from J, but there's no difference between the family and great rooms, and the other elements can go anywhere.

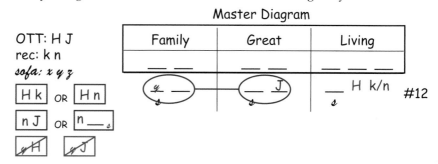

Thus, J and *y* can't go in the living room, but any other element can. This corresponds to choice (C).

Choice (C) is the correct answer.

Question 13

This Universal Truth question is another good one to postpone.

Question 14

14. If both J and X are placed in the family room, then which one of the following is a complete and accurate list of the furniture pieces any one of which could be placed in the great room?

(A) H, K, N
(B) H, K, Y
(C) K, N, Y
(D) H, K, N, Y
(E) H, K, N, Y, Z

This is a Local List question. Put J and *x* in the family room. Now what? There are a lot of possibilities. Start exploring some of them, centering your thinking on the most constrained elements, and use the process of elimination. First, try H in the great room.

Master Diagram

OTT: H J
rec: k n
sofa: x y z

	Family	Great	Living	
H k OR H n	y	J	__ H k/n	#12
n J OR n __	J x	H k	y n z	#14
H J				

This is possible, and **H** would have to be joined by **k**. Now you know that the correct answer, which is a list of every element allowed in the great room, has to include **H** and **k**, so you can eliminate choice (C), which lacks **H**. Next, try **H** in the living room.

Master Diagram

OTT: H J
rec: k n
sofa: x y z

	Family	Great	Living	
H k OR H n	y	J	__ H k/n	#12
n J OR n __	J x	H k	y n z	#14
H J	J x	y (n)	H (k) z	

You have to put *y* in the great room to keep it away from **H**. You can't put *z* in the great room because then **n** would be unhappy, so *z* has to be in the living room. The recliners could be in either room. Now you've shown that *y*, **n**, and **k** can also be in the great room, so you can eliminate choices (A) and (B), which are missing one of those elements. The only difference between the remaining choices is *z*, and since you explored every scenario, and *z* was never in the great room, you can eliminate choice (E) since *z* is not allowed there. Choice (D) is correct.

Choice (D) is the correct answer.

Question 15

15. If H and N are placed in the same room, then which one of the following is a complete and accurate list of the rooms any one of which could be the room in which K is placed?

(A) great room
(B) living room
(C) family room, great room
(D) great room, living room
(E) family room, great room, living room

This is another Local List question that focuses on **k**. The new rule is slightly vague—*which* room are they together in? But you should recall from the Deduce step that **H** and **n** can only be together in the living room. There are lots of possibilities once you do that, so start exploring a few and use the process of elimination. For example, if you put **J** in the living room too, then all the picky elements are happy:

Master Diagram

OTT: H J
rec: k n
sofa: x y z

| Hk | OR | Hn |

| nJ | OR | n___ |

| H̶ | | J̶ |

	Family	Great	Living	
	y/z	J	___ H k/n	#12
	J x	H k	y n z	#14
	J x	y (n)	H (k) z	
	x y	z k	H n J	#15

This shows that **k** could be in either the family room or the great room, so you can get rid of choices (A), (B), and (D), which are all missing one of those. If you're not sure about the living room, try it:

Master Diagram

OTT: H J
rec: k n
sofa: x y z

| Hk | OR | Hn |

| nJ | OR | n___ |

| H̶ | | J̶ |

	Family	Great	Living	
	y/z	J	___ H k/n	#12
	J x	H k	y n z	#14
	J x	y (n)	H (k) z	
	x y	z k	H n J	#15
			H n k	

This doesn't work since **n** is not satisfied. Get rid of choice (E) and pick choice (C).

Choice (C) is the correct answer.

Question 11

11. Which one of the following could be a complete and accurate list of the contents of one room?

 (A) H, N
 (B) H, Z
 (C) J, Y
 (D) H, N, Z
 (E) K, X, Z

Now return to the Universal questions. You can pick a choice here if you ever saw a room exactly those contents. Looking back at your previous work, choice (D) matches one of the possibilities in question 14. That's all you need to know—choice (D) is correct.

Choice (D) is the correct answer.

Question 13

13. Which one of the following statements CANNOT be true?

    (A)   Both ottomans are in the same room.
    (B)   Both recliners are in the same room.
    (C)   All three sofas are in the same room.
    (D)   Each recliner is in a room with a sofa.
    (E)   No room has two pieces of the same kind of
          furniture.

On this question, you can eliminate anything you previously saw to be possible.

Choice (A): You saw this happen in question 15. *Eliminate it.*

Choice (B): You have never seen this happen. *Hold on to it.*

Choice (C): You have never seen this happen. *Hold on to it.*

Choice (D): You saw this happen in questions 12 and 14. *Eliminate it.*

Choice (E): You saw this happen in question 12. *Eliminate it.*

Now you just have to decide between choices (B) and (C). Consider choice (B). Actually, your previous work can help here too. In question 15 you tried to put n and k together but found out this was impossible. Since you're looking for something impossible, choice (B) is your answer.

Choice (B) is the correct answer.

EXPLANATIONS

QUESTIONS 1–5

IDENTIFY

In this game, you are asked to sort the elements into two groups—the main hall and the side hall—so it initially looks like a Binary game. However, within each group there is also ordering, since each painting comes from an earlier or later century than the others. Because there are both grouping and ordering features, this is a Hybrid game.

SET UP

In this case, the ordering feature is a little vague. You don't know which centuries there are, only relatively earlier or later ones. Furthermore, you have no idea how many paintings occupy each order. Thus, it would be very difficult to organize your diagram around the ordering feature.

Instead, organize your diagram around the grouping feature. Start with a standard Binary diagram and label the groups Main and Not Main (Side). Then think about how you will handle the ordering feature. Since there are no specific centuries mentioned, the best way is to make everything look like relative order symbols: when you place an element into a group, use the "—" symbol to show whether it's earlier or later than another, if you know that information. You need to specify which direction is earlier, and since question 1 writes the answer choices with earliest on the left, you should do the same.

Now symbolize the rules.

> **Rule 1:** Put K on the diagram in the side hall.

> **Rule 2:** This can be symbolized with an antiblock:

Rule 3: This is a conditional rule. On the right side of the arrow, you should use a symbol that fully captures the information in the rule. You can use what looks like a relative order symbol:

$$G \longrightarrow H{-}J{-}G$$

When you make the contrapositive, think about what makes the most sense. Negating a relative order symbol seems complicated and weird, but you can still create a useful contrapositive by considering just the grouping aspect. The original rule resulted in H and J in the main hall; the contrapositive should tell you what to do when either of them is in the side hall:

$$\sim\!H \text{ OR } \sim\!J \longrightarrow \sim\!G$$

Rule 4: This is a conditional rule similar to rule 3. To show that L is the earliest, you can use a relative order symbol that puts L to the left of all other elements. To make the contrapositive, you can consider both the grouping aspect (L is in the side hall) and the ordering aspect (if any element—use the generic X—is earlier than L):

$$\sim\!G \longrightarrow L{-}all$$
$$\sim\!L \text{ OR } X{-}L \longrightarrow G$$

Rule 5: This is just like rule 3. The only difference is that you might want to use subscripts to show that the specified order takes place in the side hall. If you used ~'s, you might mistakenly think the symbol is telling you to *avoid* the order shown.

In the contrapositive, you don't have to bother with mentioning K in the main hall since rule 1 tells you that's impossible:

$$\sim\!J \longrightarrow K_s{-}H_s{-}J_s$$
$$H \longrightarrow J$$

DEDUCE

Because the conditional symbols are so complicated, it's probably best not to get involved with any linking. One useful deduction is possible, though: since the antiblock separates H and L, then you know there must be one spot reserved in each group for one element from that pair.

You should also notice that F is a free agent—it's not mentioned in any of the rules, so it can freely occupy either group. Underline F in the stock to remind you of this.

Here's the master diagram:

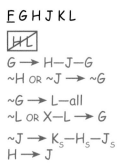

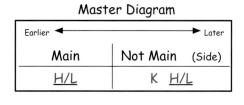

Question 1

1. Which one of the following could be a complete and accurate list of the paintings in the main hall, listed in production order from earliest century to latest century?

    (A)   L, F
    (B)   F, J, L
    (C)   H, G, J
    (D)   H, K, J, G
    (E)   H, L, J, F

This is a Rule Tester question. Look at each rule and eliminate the choices in which it is broken. Rule 1 is broken in choice (D), which has K in the main hall. Rule 2 is broken in choice (E) since H and L are together. Rule 3 is broken in choice (C), which ranks J later than G. Rule 4 is broken in choice (B), which ranks L later than other paintings even though G is in the side hall. Only choice (A) remains.

Choice (A) is the correct answer.

The Rules

K is in the side hall.

H and L are not in the same hall.

If G is in the main hall, then H and J are in the main hall, J being produced in a later century than H but in an earlier century than G.

If G is in the side hall, then L is in the main hall and was produced in an earlier century than any other painting in the main hall.

If J is in the side hall, then H is in the side hall, H being produced in a later century than K but in an earlier century than J.

Question 2

2. Which one of the following paintings could be the only painting in its hall?

    (A)   F
    (B)   G
    (C)   J
    (D)   K
    (E)   L

This is a Universal question. Look at your master diagram to see if you have already done enough to answer this question. You deduced that each hall must always have either H or L, so if a painting is going to be alone in a hall, that painting must be either H or L. Only choice (E) offers one of those two, so it must be correct.

Choice (E) is the correct answer.

Question 3

3. If L is in the main hall, which one of the following statements must be true?

    (A)   F is in the main hall.
    (B)   G is in the side hall.
    (C)   H is in the main hall.
    (D)   J is in the main hall.
    (E)   J is in the side hall.

This is a Local Truth question. Put L in the main hall and see what happens.

Because of the antiblock, H must be in the side hall, which then triggers the first conditional and tells you that G is in the side hall. That in turn tells you that L must be the earliest painting in the main hall. This is enough to answer the question.

Choice (B) is the correct answer.

Question 4

4. If H is in the main hall, which one of the following statements could be true?

    (A) G and L are in the same hall, G being produced in an earlier century than L.
    (B) G and K are in the same hall, G being produced in an earlier century than K.
    (C) J and K are in the same hall, J being produced in an earlier century than K.
    (D) J and L are in the same hall, J being produced in an earlier century than L.
    (E) K and L are in the same hall, K being produced in an earlier century than L.

This is another Local Truth question. Put H in the main hall and see what happens.

F G H J K L

H L

G → H–J–G
~H OR ~J → ~G

~G → L–all
~L OR X–L → G

~J → K_s–H_s–J_s
H → J

Master Diagram

Earlier ←	→ Later	
Main	**Not Main**	**(Side)**
H/L	K H/L	
L–F	K–H–J G	#1
L–	K H G	#3
H–J–G	K L	**#4**

Because of the antiblock, L must be in the side hall. This triggers the second conditional and puts G in the main hall. That in turn tells you that H, J, and G have to appear in that order in the main hall. You don't know the order of K and L in the side hall, and F is still a free agent. If you take a look at the answer choices, you'll see that only choice (E) could be true.

Choice (E) is the correct answer.

Question 5

5. If the condition that H and L are not in the same hall is suspended but all other conditions remain in effect, which one of the following statements must be false?

    (A) Exactly five paintings are in the side hall.
    (B) Exactly five paintings are in the main hall.
    (C) J and exactly two other paintings are in the side hall.
    (D) F and exactly three other paintings are in the main hall.
    (E) H and exactly two other paintings are in the main hall.

This is a Rule Changer question. It removes the antiblock, which in turn removes the deduction you made using the antiblock—the reserved spots in each group. This is actually not too hard to deal with. All you have to do is remember that H and L can now be together.

Now you can treat this like a Universal Truth question and eliminate any choice you previously saw to be true. Your previous work for question 4 shows that, with appropriate placement of F, both choices (D) and (E) could be true. Now try the remaining choices in your diagram. Here are some configurations proving choices (A) and (B) possible:

F G H J K L

H/L

G ⟶ H–J–G
~H OR ~J ⟶ ~G

~G ⟶ L–all
~L OR X–L ⟶ G

~J ⟶ K$_s$–H$_s$–J$_s$
H ⟶ J

Master Diagram

Earlier ◄─────────────────► Later		
Main	**Not Main**	**(Side)**
H/L	K	H/L
L–F	K–H–J G	#1
L–	K H G	#3
H–J–G	K L	#4
L	K H J G F	**#5**
L H J G F	K	
	~~K–H–J–G~~	

When you try choice (C), you run into a problem. Putting J in the side triggers the third conditional and puts K and H there too. But having H in the side hall triggers the first conditional and puts G in the side as well. Now you've violated the answer choice by having more that two paintings besides J in the side hall. This choice is impossible, which is what you're looking for.

Choice (C) is the correct answer.

QUESTIONS 6–10

IDENTIFY

This game closely resembles an Ordering game, with one important difference. There are only five places in the order (Monday–Friday), but there are seven elements. Thus, some of the elements must be left out of the order, and you should keep track of them with an "Out" group. This combination of ordering and grouping makes this a Hybrid game.

SET UP

Since there is a well-defined order of five days, your diagram should be based on this. The only difference between this diagram and a normal Ordering diagram is that you should also include an Out column to the right. Since you know exactly two of the elements must be left out, you can put two underlined spaces in the Out group.

Put the stock of elements to the left of the diagram, using the initials of the seven restaurants.

Now symbolize the rules.

> **Rule 1:** You can put R directly on the diagram in Wednesday.

> **Rule 2:** This looks like a conditional rule, and you might be tempted to write

$$P \text{ AND } T \longrightarrow T–P$$
$$P–T \longrightarrow \text{~}P \text{ OR } \text{~}T$$

This is correct, but it's a bit complicated, and the contrapositive is somewhat nonsensical. You can come up with a better symbol by thinking about what is *not* allowed. The one thing that can't happen is for both P and T to be in the order *and* for P to be earlier than T. You can show that with an anti–relative order symbol, like this:

P̶–̶T̶

Rule 3: This is a soft antiblock:

$$\widehat{SV}$$

Rule 4: This combines a conditional and a soft block. To make the contrapositive, forget about the ordering feature and just use the grouping:

$$M \longrightarrow \boxed{MT}$$
$$\sim T \longrightarrow \sim M$$

Rule 5: This calls for a regular block but is otherwise just like rule 4:

$$O \longrightarrow \boxed{O\ V}$$
$$\sim V \longrightarrow \sim O$$

Rule 6: A clearer way to express this rule is to say that **S** is either on Thursday or out. Then you can symbolize it directly on the diagram with a barbell.

DEDUCE

You already made some deductions when you came up with the symbols. You have some relative order and block symbols, which usually lead to automatic endpoint deductions in Ordering games, but things are a little more complicated here because of the Out group. For example, you may be tempted to say that **P** can't be on Monday since it can't precede **T** in the order. However, that's not correct—**P** could be on Monday if **T** were out.

Pretty much the only thing you can deduce is that **O** can't be on Tuesday or Friday because you wouldn't be able to place **V**. Here's the master diagram:

Master Diagram

M O P R S T V

P–T

$\widehat{SV}$

M	T	W	Th	F	Out
	~O	R	Ⓢ	~O	◯ ___

$$M \longrightarrow \boxed{MT}$$
$$\sim T \longrightarrow \sim M$$

$$O \longrightarrow \boxed{O\ V}$$
$$\sim V \longrightarrow \sim O$$

Question 6

6. Which one of the following could be a complete and accurate list of the five restaurants from which the business orders, listed in order from Monday to Friday?

(A) Orientalicious, Vegificent, Ribulous, Thaimazing, Mexellent

(B) Mexellent, Subtacular, Ribulous, Orientalicious, Vegificent,

(C) Orientalicious, Thaimazing, Ribulous, Pizzastic, Vegificent

(D) Pizzastic, Vegificent, Ribulous, Mexellent, Thaimazing

(E) Thaimazing, Pizzastic, Ribulous, Subtacular, Vegificent

This is a Rule Tester. Look at each rule and eliminate the choices in which it is broken. Rule 1 is not broken in any choice. Rule 2 is broken in choice (D) because **P** is earlier in the week than **T**. Rule 3 is broken in choice (E) because **S** and **V** are consecutive.

Rule 4 is broken in choice (B) because **T** is not next to **M**. Rule 5 is broken in choice (C) because **V** doesn't immediately follow **O**.

Choice (A) is the correct answer.

Question 7

7. Which one of the following is a complete and accurate list of the restaurants any one of which the business could order from on Tuesday?

   (A)   Mexellent, Thaimazing, Vegificent
   (B)   Mexellent, Orientalicious, Thaimazing, Vegificent
   (C)   Mexellent, Pizzastic, Thaimazing, Vegificent
   (D)   Mexellent, Subtacular, Thaimazing, Vegificent
   (E)   Mexellent, Orientalicious, Pizzastic, Thaimazing, Vegificent

This is a List question, so use the process of elimination. First, you deduced that **O** cannot be on Tuesday, so eliminate any choice that includes **O** on the list. That gets rid of choices (B) and (E). Next, you can see from the barbell that **S** can't be on Tuesday, so get rid of choice (D). Now you have only choices (A) and (C) left, so focus on the differences. The only difference is **P**. Can **P** be on Tuesday? Try it out:

Master Diagram

M O P R S T V

M → (MT)

~T → ~M

O → [O V]

~V → ~O

M	T	W	Th	F		Out		
	~O	R	S	~O		O		
O	V	R	T	M		S	P	#6
T	P	R	O	V		S	M	#7

This diagram shows one possible configuration with **P** on Tuesday, so you know it should be on the list. Get rid of choice (A) and pick choice (C).

Choice (C) is the correct answer.

Question 8

8. In any given week, the business must order from at least one restaurant in which one of the following pairs?

   (A)   Mexellent, Orientalicious
   (B)   Mexellent, Pizzastic
   (C)   Orientalicious, Vegificent
   (D)   Pizzastic, Subtacular
   (E)   Subtacular, Thaimazing

This Universal question might initially look challenging, but think about what it's really asking. The correct choice will feature a pair of restaurants, *both of which cannot be out*. Thus, the four incorrect choices will have pairs of restaurants that could both be out at the same time. So this question is a little like a Rule Tester, except you want to pick the choice that *does* break a rule when both of the restaurants are out.

Since you're thinking about the question in terms of the Out group, look at the symbols that have something to do with that group. For example, ~**T** → ~**M**. Do you see any choices that break this rule? Yes. Choice (E) puts **T** out but is missing the **M** out. Thus, choice (E) is correct.

What if you didn't see these deductions? The long way to do this question, since it is asking for something that must be true, is to try to *disprove* each answer choice in the diagram. For example, try to disprove choice (A) by coming up with a complete configuration in which the business orders from *neither* M nor O. If you're successful (which you would be) then you can eliminate choice (A) and move on to try to try to disprove choice (B). Only when you got to choice (E) would you be unable to disprove the choice, so you'd know that one was correct.

Choice (E) is the correct answer.

Question 9

9. Suppose the business orders from Pizzastic on the day immediately before it orders from Thaimazing, but all other conditions remain the same. The business CANNOT order from which one of the following restaurants?

(A) Orientalicious
(B) Pizzastic
(C) Ribulous
(D) Subtacular
(E) Vegificent

This is a Rule Changer. It takes away rule 2, so you have to reexamine your deductions to see if any of them are affected. In this case, they are not, so you don't have to worry about that.

This is also a Local question that tells you to put P immediately before T. But where? There are several possibilities, so start exploring them. First, try putting P and T on Monday and Tuesday.

Master Diagram

M O P R S T V

P T

S̶V̶

M → MT

~T → ~M

O → O V

	M	T	W	Th	F	Out		
		~O	R	S	~O	O		
	O	V	R	T	M	S	P	#6
	T	P	R	O	V	S	M	#7
	P	T	R	O	V		S	M	#9

When you do this, there is no way to have M next to T, so M must be out. What else is out? If you try to put O out, then S would be on Thursday and V would be next to it on Friday, which is forbidden. Thus, O must be in and on Thursday, with V on Friday.

This is not the only possible configuration with P immediately before T, but it does prove that O, P, R and V can be in, so you can eliminate choices (A), (B), (C), and (E), meaning choice (D) must be correct.

Choice (D) is the correct answer.

Question 10

10. Suppose the condition that the business orders from Ribulous on Wednesday is replaced with the condition that the business orders from Ribulous on Friday. If all the other conditions remain the same, then which one of the following must be false?

    (A)   The business orders from Mexellent on Thursday.
    (B)   The business orders from Orientalicious on Tuesday.
    (C)   The business orders from Pizzastic on Monday.
    (D)   The business orders from Thaimazing on Monday.
    (E)   The business orders from Vegificent on Tuesday.

This is a Rule Changer. It changes rule 1, so you have to reexamine your deductions again. In this case, the only thing that changes is that O is forbidden on Thursday instead of Tuesday.

Put R on Friday. Now what? You can't definitively place anything else, and your previous work is of no use as none of it featured R on Friday. You have to start trying out the answer choices. Put each one in the diagram and try to prove it possible. If you can, then eliminate the choice.

Master Diagram

M O P R S T V

P T

S̶V̶

M → MT

~T → ~M

O → O V

~V → ~O

	M	T	W	Th	F	Out		
		~o	R	S	~o	O _		
	O	V	R	T	M	S	P	#6
	T	P	R	O	V	S	M	#7
	P	T	R	O	V	S	M	#9
(A)	O	V	T	M	R	S	P	#10
(B)	T	O	V	P	R	S	M	
(C)	P̶	O̶	V	S̶	R̶	T̶	M̶	

Choices (A) and (B) are possible, as shown, but (C) is impossible. If you try to put P on Monday, the only way to avoid having P before T is to put T out. That means M is out and S has to be on Thursday. The only place left for O and V is Tuesday and Wednesday, but that breaks rule 3 by putting S and V next to each other. Choice (C) is impossible, and thus correct.

Choice (C) is the correct answer.

QUESTIONS 11–15

IDENTIFY

This game certainly has a grouping feature because there is no mention of order and the rules reference elements being in the same or different groups. However, there are *three* factors to figure out: 1) the supervisor, 2) the product, and 3) the factory. Thus, one row won't be enough to hold all the elements; you need a grid. Since this game has both grid and grouping features, it's a Hybrid game.

SET UP

You need some sort of grid, but since there is no order, how do you know which thing to use as the backbone? Think about regular Grouping games: it's usually better to have fewer groups and more elements. There are only three supervisors, but five of everything else, so use the supervisors as the backbone/groups. The situation tells you the size of each group, so put two underlined spots under Karl and Liz, and only one under Ming.

In each group, give yourself two rows: one for the products and one for the factories. Next to each row, put the stock of elements that will fit into that row. Think about how the elements will fit into the diagram: within a group, the factory that is directly below a product is the factory that actually produces that product.

Now symbolize the rules.

Rule 1: This is an antiblock. N and P can't be in the same group:

Rule 2: You can put X directly in the second row of the Ming group, and an either/or spot for Q or R in the first row.

Rule 3: This is like a soft block that spans two rows. O and Y have to be in the same group, but they don't necessarily have to be directly above and below each other. That is, Y doesn't have to produce O, but it could:

Deduce

There's not a whole lot to deduce here, but you should be able to see that Karl and Liz must oversee N and P, in either order. You can symbolize this as a barbell. Here's the master diagram:

Master Diagram

	Karl	Liz	Ming
Product: N O P Q R	___ Ⓝ—Ⓟ ___		Q/R
Factory: V W X Y Z			X

Question 11

11. If Karl oversees the production of both P and Q, which one of the following must be true?

(A) Liz oversees factory Y.
(B) Liz oversees factory Z.
(C) Factory W produces N.
(D) Factory V produces O.
(E) Factory X produces Q.

This is a Local Truth question. Put the new rule on the diagram and see what happens.

Master Diagram

	Karl		Liz		Ming	
Product: N O P Q R	___ Ⓝ—Ⓟ ___				Q/R	
Factory: V W X Y Z					X	
	P	Q	N	O	R	#11
			Ⓨ—◯		X	

With Q in Karl, Ming has to have R. That leaves N and O to fill out Liz, and O brings Y along with it, although you don't know which product Y is associated with. However, this is enough to answer the question.

Lecture 5 Explanations

Choice (A) is the correct answer.

Question 12

12. Which one of the following must be true?

    (A) If Karl oversees the production of N, then factory Y produces O.
    (B) If Karl oversees the production of both N and R, then factory Y produces P.
    (C) If Liz oversees the production of both P and Q, then Karl oversees factory Y.
    (D) If Ming oversees the production of Q, then Karl oversees the production of R.
    (E) If Ming oversees the production of R, then Karl oversees the production of O.

This is a Universal Truth question, but a glance at the answer choices shows that it's unusual. Each choice is a conditional! When this happens, your master diagram and previous work are unlikely to be helpful and, unfortunately, the best strategy is to plug in each answer choice and work through it. This is very time consuming, so try to choose the order in which you approach the choices wisely.

Choices (A) and (B) both propose that factory Y must produce a certain product, but nothing in any of the rules has anything to do with a certain factory producing a certain product, except for X. That's not to say choices (A) and (B) are guaranteed to be wrong, just that they are less likely to be right. Choice (C) seems more promising because it's a little less stringent. Try it out in the diagram. To do so, make the first part of the conditional true, and see if the second part must follow.

Yes. In fact, this is just the reverse of question 11. It has to be true, so choice (C) is correct.

Choice (C) is the correct answer.

Question 13

13. If Karl oversees factories W and Z, which one of the following could be true?

    (A) Factory Z produces O.
    (B) Factory Y produces Q.
    (C) Factory V produces R.
    (D) Karl oversees the production of N.
    (E) Karl oversees the production of O.

This is a Local Truth question. Try it out in the diagram.

Master Diagram

With W and Z in Karl, V and Y must go to Liz. That means O goes to Liz as well. Because of the antiblock, the other product for Liz must be N or P, and Karl must have an N or P as well, although in each case you don't know which product goes with which factory. Karl's final product is the one that Ming doesn't get, either Q or R. A lot is uncertain here, but only one answer choice could be true—choice (D).

Choice (D) is the correct answer.

Question 14

14. If Liz oversees the production of O by factory Z, then any of the following could be true EXCEPT:

(A) Karl oversees the production of N.
(B) Liz oversees the production of N.
(C) Factory Y produces P.
(D) Factory X produces Q.
(E) Factory Y produces Q.

This is another Local Truth question. Try it out in the diagram.

Master Diagram

Since Liz has O she must also have Y. That leaves factories V and W for Karl. Liz's other product is one from the N/P pair, and Karl's products are one from the Q/R pair and one from the N/P pair. Choice (E) is the impossible one.

Choice (E) is the correct answer.

Question 15

15.   Suppose the same supervisor oversees the production of both N and P, but all other conditions remain in effect. If factory W produces R, which one of the following must be true?

(A)   Either factory Y or factory Z produces N.
(B)   Neither factory Y nor factory Z produces N.
(C)   Either factory V or factory Z produces O.
(D)   Neither factory Y nor factory V produces P.
(E)   Either factory V or factory Z produces P.

This is a Rule Changer question. It replaces the N/P barbell across the two groups with a block that puts them in the same group. The question also gives you a new rule you can put on the diagram:

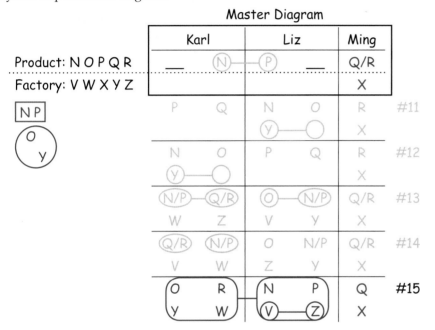

The Karl and Liz groups are completely interchangeable, so you can draw a giant barbell between them encompassing everything in each group. If R is in one group, then the N/P block has to be in the other, and O, along with Y, has to be with R and W. Q must go in Ming's group, and V and Z take the remaining spots, although you don't know which of them goes with N and which with P. According to the diagram, choice (E) is the only one that must be true.

Choice (E) is the correct answer.

EXPLANATIONS

QUESTIONS 1–5

IDENTIFY

You can identify this as a Map game because the situation gives you a map, and the "elements" you have to manipulate are the spatial connections between the fixed building locations. There is no ordering or grouping.

SET UP

Since the situation gives you a simple map of where the buildings are, use it. Your task in each question will be to draw the legs of the path on the map. You don't need to take stock of any elements other than to recognize that there must be five legs of the path, as the situation tells you.

When it comes to symbolizing the rules, the first thing you'll notice is that the rules are specifically tailored to this Map game, so they don't match very well with the symbols you are used to in other games. They're also not that complicated, so perhaps the best way to deal with them is to just write a few simple notes next to your diagram. The last rule is like an exact spot rule—you can draw those definite connections on your diagram.

Here's the diagram so far:

Five legs

Each bldg. connected
to 1 or 2 others

No crossing

1, 2 — 3
4 5 6

DEDUCE

There's not much to deduce here in terms of definite connections. Building 4 is a little unique because it's "cornered" by the connection between 1 and 5. It will have to connect to either 1 or 5, but not both. If it connected to both, then it would form a triangle between buildings 1, 4, and 5, and none of them would be able to connect to any other building because they'd all have two connections. It would thus be impossible to connect all the buildings with a single continuous path, as the situation requires. However, most of the rest of the diagram is wide open. Move on to the questions.

Question 1

1. Which one of the following statements could be true?
   - (A) One leg of the trail directly connects buildings 4 and 2.
   - (B) One leg of the trail directly connects buildings 4 and 3.
   - (C) One leg of the trail directly connects buildings 4 and 6.
   - (D) One leg of the trail directly connects buildings 1 and 2 and another leg directly connects buildings 2 and 4.
   - (E) One leg of the trail directly connects buildings 6 and 3 and another leg directly connects buildings 6 and 5.

This is a Universal Truth question. Check your master diagram. Choice (A) is impossible since the leg would cross the 1–5 leg. Choice (B) is impossible for the same reason. Choice (C) is impossible since the leg wouldn't be a straight line—it would have to curve around building 5. Choice (D) is impossible since building 1 would then have three legs connected to it. Choice (E) is possible and correct, as shown by this complete configuration:

Five legs

Each bldg. connected to 1 or 2 others

No crossing

Choice (E) is the correct answer.

Question 2

2. If one leg of the trail directly connects buildings 2 and 5, then the two buildings in which one of the following pairs must be directly connected to each other by a leg?
   - (A) 1 and 2
   - (B) 2 and 6
   - (C) 3 and 6
   - (D) 4 and 5
   - (E) 5 and 6

This is a Local question. Put the new rule on your diagram and see what happens.

Five legs

Each bldg. connected to 1 or 2 others

No crossing

Since building 5 now has two connections, building 4 has to be connected to building 1. Building 6 has to connect to building 3 since buildings 2 and 5 already have two connections. Choice (C) matches the diagram.

Choice (C) is the correct answer.

Question 3

3. If one leg of the trail directly connects buildings 2 and 6, then which one of the following statements could be true?

    (A)   Building 1 is directly connected to building 4.
    (B)   Building 2 is directly connected to building 5.
    (C)   Building 3 is directly connected to building 6.
    (D)   Building 3 is directly connected to exactly two buildings.
    (E)   Building 6 is directly connected to exactly one building.

This is a Local question. Put the new rule on your diagram and see what happens.

Five legs

Each bldg. connected to 1 or 2 others

 OR

No crossing

Building 2 has its two connections, and building 3 can't make any more connections without crossing an existing leg or forming a triangle. Thus, you have to use building 6 to connect to the rest of the buildings. It could be connected with building 5 or building 1 as shown, which in each case would determine what building 4 is connected to. Only choice (A) is possible according to the diagram.

Choice (A) is the correct answer.

Question 4

4. Which one of the following buildings cannot be directly connected by legs of the trail to exactly two other buildings?

    (A)   2
    (B)   3
    (C)   4
    (D)   5
    (E)   6

In the initial deductions, you saw that building 4 can only connect to one other building, so as to avoid forming a triangle. Your previous work also shows that every other building could potentially connect to two.

Choice (C) is the correct answer.

Question 5

5. If no leg of the trail directly connects any building on the north side with the building on the south side that faces it, then each of the following statements must be true EXCEPT:

    (A)   A leg of the trail directly connects buildings 4 and 5.
    (B)   A leg of the trail directly connects buildings 5 and 6.
    (C)   Building 3 is directly connected to exactly one other building.
    (D)   Building 5 is directly connected to exactly two other buildings.
    (E)   Building 6 is directly connected to exactly two other buildings.

This Local question gives you a new rule, but you have to make some deductions to see exactly how it works. Since building 4 can't connect to 1, it must connect to 5. If

Lecture 6 Explanations

you tried to connect building 1 to building 2, that would force a connection between 3 and 6, which is forbidden. Thus, building 1 has to connect to building 6, and the path is completed by a connection between buildings 2 and 6.

Five legs

Each bldg. connected to 1 or 2 others

No crossing

Only choice (B) is not required.

Choice (B) is the correct answer.

QUESTIONS 6–10

IDENTIFY

You can identify this as a Circular game because you have to arrange the elements around a circular table.

SET UP

As there are eight seats at the table your diagram should be an eight-pointed asterisk. Label the seats 1–8.

The elements in this game belong to three categories. As you write the stock, use uppercase, lowercase, and script to differentiate between the different categories.

Now symbolize the rules. It's easiest to start with the most specific rules and move on to the vaguer ones later.

> **Rules 3 and 4:** These are exact spot rules. Put the elements directly on the diagram in the places specified.
>
> **Rule 2:** Since r is in chair 4, s must be in chair 8. Put this directly on the diagram.
>
> **Rule 1:** If the Koreans are to be all together, then G and H must be in chairs 2 and 3, although you don't know in which order. Put this on the diagram as a barbell.
>
> **Rule 5:** You can symbolize this as a conditional. You have to use subscripts to denote the different chairs. Instead of "$\sim H_2$," you can write "H_3," since that's the only other place H can sit:
>
> $$m_5 \rightarrow H_2$$
> $$H_3 \rightarrow \sim m_5$$

DEDUCE

Because the situation and rules gave you so much information there's not much left to deduce. You can see that the Tunisians will also sit next to each other, in chairs 5–7. Here's the master diagram:

Master Diagram

KOR: F G H
tun: m n o
jam: r s

$$m_5 \rightarrow H_2$$
$$H_3 \rightarrow \sim m_5$$

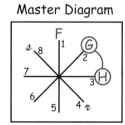

Question 6

6. Which one of the following representatives could sit in chair 2?

   (A) O
   (B) N
   (C) M
   (D) R
   (E) H

This is a Universal Spot question. According to your master diagram, either G or H could be in chair 2. Pick choice (E).

Choice (E) is the correct answer.

Question 7

7. Each of the following statements must be true EXCEPT:

   (A) The representative in chair 8 is Tunisian.
   (B) The representative in chair 2 is Korean.
   (C) The representative in chair 6 is Tunisian.
   (D) The representative in chair 3 is Korean.
   (E) The representative in chair 7 is Tunisian.

This is a Universal Truth question. According to your master diagram, choice (A) cannot be true since *l*, a Jamaican, is in chair 8.

Choice (A) is the correct answer.

Question 8

8. Which one of the following representatives must sit next to F?

   (A) G
   (B) H
   (C) R
   (D) S
   (E) M

This is a Universal Spot question. According to your master diagram, you're not sure whether G or H is next to F, but *l* is required to be next to F.

Choice (D) is the correct answer.

Question 9

9. For which one of the following representatives are there two and no more than two chairs either one of which could be the chair in which the representative sits?

   (A) G
   (B) R
   (C) M
   (D) N
   (E) O

This Universal question is concerned with how many choices each representative has for seating. Representatives F, *z*, and *l* each have only one choice since they are fixed in a certain seat. Representatives m, n, and o each have three choices: seat 5, 6, or 7. Thus, only G and H have exactly two choices. Pick choice (A).

Choice (A) is the correct answer.

Question 10

10. If N sits in chair 7, then the two representatives in which one of the following pairs CANNOT both sit in even-numbered chairs?

   (A) G and M
   (B) G and O
   (C) H and S
   (D) H and M
   (E) H and O

This is a local question. Put n in chair 7 and see what happens.

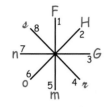 OR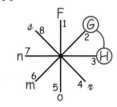

KOR: F G H
tun: m n o
jam: r s

$m_5 \rightarrow H_2$
$H_3 \rightarrow \sim m_5$

The only thing you really have to pay attention to is the conditional rule. There are two scenarios, depending on where m is. If m is in chair 5, then H has to be in 2, G in 3, and o in 6. If m is in chair 6, then o is in chair 5, but G and H could still be in either order. Thus, there's no way to have both G and o in even-numbered chairs.

Choice (B) is the correct answer.

QUESTIONS 11–15

IDENTIFY

This is a Grid game, as you can tell from the fact that you have three factors to figure out: 1) the screen, 2) the night, and 3) the movie. More specifically, it's also a Pattern game because you have to arrange the same four elements each night, and the arrangement on one night affects what happens on subsequent nights.

SET UP

You need a grid diagram. You could use either the screens or the nights as the columns, since they both have a natural order. We'll use the screens here since it produces a more horizontal diagram, which is what you're used to seeing.

That means the nights are the rows. For the stock, you can use the initials of the four movies. One of them will have to be repeated each night as there are more screens than movies. Put the same stock next to each row.

Now symbolize the rules.

   Rule 1: Symbolize this with a generic antiblock:

   Rule 2: Symbolize this with two vertical antiblocks:

   Rule 3: Again, use two vertical antiblocks:

Rule 4: You can symbolize this by putting a [1] next to Z in the stock for each row.

At this point your diagram looks like this:

		1	2	3	4	5
G M S Z[1]	Friday					
G M S Z[1]	Saturday					
G M S Z[1]	Sunday					

DEDUCE

There are a number of deductions you can make here by thinking about the most restricted elements. First, think about Z. Because of rules 1 and 3, the only thing that could be directly below a Z is M. Every Z (except the one on Sunday) will have an M below it.

Next, the same can be said for S. Because of rules 1 and 2, the only thing that could be below an S is a Z. Every S (except for the one on Sunday) will have a Z below it.

Now think about the relationship between Z and S. There's no way you could have more than one S on Friday or Saturday, since that would cause there to be more than one Z on the following day.

There's one final deduction. Every Z (except the one of Friday) must have an S above it. That's because if the S on the previous day were somewhere else, it would cause there to be a second Z on the next day.

All this can be put together to form the master diagram:

Master Diagram

		1	2	3	4	5
G M S[1] Z[1]	Friday					
G M S[1] Z[1]	Saturday					
G M S Z[1]	Sunday					

There is a [1] next to the S's on Friday and Saturday to remind you that there can be only one on each of those days. The conditional symbols mean that every S has a Z and an M below it, and every Z has an S above it and an M below it. (This obviously doesn't apply when it would cause the block to run off the edge of the diagram.)

Like most Pattern games, this one doesn't allow you to definitively place any element on the master diagram. You have to wait and see what happens in the questions.

The Rules

No movie is shown on the same screen on consecutive evenings.

Neither Gravity nor Monolith is shown on any screen on which Sleepwalking was shown the previous evening.

Neither Gravity nor Sleepwalking is shown on any screen on which Zanzibar was shown the previous evening.

On any evening, Zanzibar is shown on only one screen.

Question 11

11. Which one of the following could be the movies shown on screens 1 and 2 on Friday and Saturday?

(A) Friday: Gravity on screen 1, Zanzibar on screen 2
Saturday: Sleepwalking on screen 1, Monolith on screen 2

(B) Friday: Monolith on screen 1, Sleepwalking on screen 2
Saturday: Monolith on screen 1, Zanzibar on screen 2

(C) Friday: Sleepwalking on screen 1, Gravity on screen 2
Saturday: Zanzibar on screen 1, Zanzibar on screen 2

(D) Friday: Sleepwalking on screen 1, Sleepwalking on screen 2
Saturday: Monolith on screen 1, Zanzibar on screen 2

(E) Friday: Zanzibar on screen 1, Monolith on screen 2
Saturday: Gravity on screen 1, Gravity on screen 2

Even though it doesn't give you a complete grid in every answer choice, this is a Rule Tester question. Rule 1 is broken in choice (B), which has **M** on the same screen on consecutive evenings. Rule 2 is broken in choice (D), which has **M** below **S**. Rule 3 is broken in choice (E), which has **G** below **Z**. Rule 4 is broken in choice (C), which has two **Z**'s on the same evening.

Choice (A) is the correct answer.

Question 12

12. If on Friday, Gravity and Monolith are shown on screens 1 and 2, respectively, the movies that are shown on Saturday on screens 1 and 2, respectively, could be

(A) Gravity and Monolith
(B) Monolith and Gravity
(C) Monolith and Zanzibar
(D) Zanzibar and Monolith
(E) Zanzibar and Zanzibar

This is a Local Spot question. Put the new rule on the diagram and see what happens.

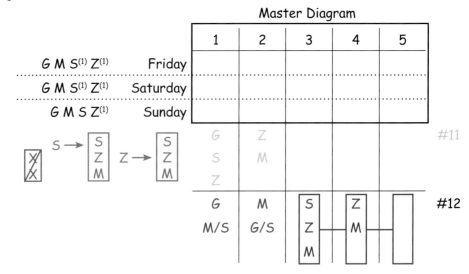

Screens 3, 4, and 5 are interchangeable, but you know that there must be an **S** and a **Z** somewhere on Friday. These trigger the conditionals and tell you what must be on the same screens later in the weekend. Now you can see that there is a **Z** somewhere on screens 3–5 on Saturday, so there can't be a **Z** on screen 1 or 2. You also can't repeat a movie on the same screen, so screen 1 must have an **M** or **S**, and screen 2 must have a **G** or **S**. Choice (B) matches the diagram.

Choice (B) is the correct answer.

Question 13

13. Which one of the following must be true?

   (A)   Sleepwalking is shown on exactly two of the screens on Friday.
   (B)   Sleepwalking is shown on exactly one of the screens on Saturday.
   (C)   Sleepwalking is shown on exactly two of the screens on Saturday.
   (D)   Sleepwalking is shown on exactly one of the screens on Sunday.
   (E)   Sleepwalking is shown on exactly two of the screens on Sunday.

This is a Universal Truth question, and it asks about the number of **S**'s permissible on certain days. In the initial deductions you saw that choice (B) must be true.

Choice (B) is the correct answer.

Question 14

14. If on Saturday, Zanzibar is shown on screen 1, which one of the following must be true?

   (A)   Gravity is shown on exactly one of the screens on Sunday.
   (B)   Monolith is shown on exactly one of the screens on Sunday.
   (C)   Gravity is shown on screen 1 on Friday.
   (D)   Monolith is shown on screen 1 on Friday.
   (E)   Sleepwalking is shown on screen 1 on Friday.

This is a Local Truth question. Put the new rule on the diagram and see what happens.

Master Diagram

The conditional involving **Z** is triggered, so you know what's on screen 1 on the other days. You can't figure out anything else, but this is enough to allow you to pick choice (E).

Choice (E) is the correct answer.

Question 15

15. If on Saturday, Gravity and Monolith are shown on screens 1 and 2, respectively, the movies that are shown on Friday on screens 1 and 2, respectively, could be

    (A) Monolith and Gravity
    (B) Monolith and Sleepwalking
    (C) Sleepwalking and Gravity
    (D) Sleepwalking and Zanzibar
    (E) Zanzibar and Gravity

This is a Local Truth question. Put the new rule on the diagram and deduce as much as you can.

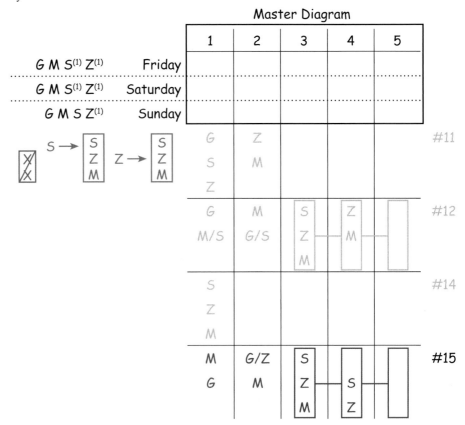

Again, screens 3, 4, and 5 are interchangeable. As on question 12, you can fill in an S and a Z somewhere on Saturday, which triggers both conditionals. Now look at Friday. On screen 1, you can't have a G because there's a G on Saturday. You can't have an S because you already have one on another screen, and you can't have a Z because you'd then need an M on Saturday's screen 1. Thus, there must be an M there. On Friday's screen 2, you can't have an M or S for the same reasons, but you could have a G or Z. This matches choice (A).

Choice (A) is the correct answer.

EXPLANATIONS

QUESTIONS 1–5

IDENTIFY

This is a Grouping game. You can tell because there is no mention of any order, and there are three groups—the display window, the lower shelf, and the upper shelf. Although the situation mentions some other considerations, such as the type of item and the metal, these are not factors you have to *figure out*. The situation tells you the type and metal for every element before you get started.

SET UP

Since this is a Grouping game, use the normal grouping diagram. The situation and the first rule give you some information about how many elements can fit into each group—a maximum of four in each—and how the elements must match up in the display window. You can symbolize these rules with shorthand notes above each group.

gold/silver pairs of same type
max 4 | max 4 | max 4
Display | Lower | Upper

One of the biggest challenges in this game is deciding how to deal with the stock. There are ten elements, and they each fit into two different *sets* of categories—each element has a type *and* a metal. When this happens, you have to create a two-dimensional grid to show how the categories overlap. Remember, this is not the main diagram on which you'll do your work. It's just the stock!

	Gold	Silver
Necklace	H I J	K M
Ring	P	Q
Watch	X	Y Z

Here's how to deal with the remaining rules:

Rule 2: You can create some antiblocks that apply to the shelves:

Shelves:

(any two)

Rule 3: This is a conditional rule. Since it is the only one, it's easiest to consider the display window as a *yes* and the shelves as a *no*. This eliminates the need for subscripts.

Display:

$$Y \text{ or } M \longrightarrow {\sim}J$$
$$J \longrightarrow {\sim}Y \text{ and } {\sim}M$$

DEDUCE

There's one important deduction to make. Since there are three gold necklaces, and since neither of the two shelves can hold more than one of them, then at least one gold necklace absolutely must be displayed. Since items are displayed in pairs, you also need a silver necklace to be displayed. You can reserve two spots in the display window for the pair of necklaces. Here's the master diagram:

	Gold	Silver
Necklace	H I J	K M
Ring	P	Q
Watch	X	Y Z

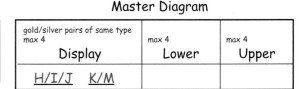

Master Diagram

Shelves:

(any two)

Display:

$$Y \text{ or } M \longrightarrow {\sim}J$$
$$J \longrightarrow {\sim}Y \text{ and } {\sim}M$$

The Rules

Neither shelf can contain more than four items.

Any two items that are both of the same metal and of the same type as each other cannot be on a shelf together.

Whenever either Y or M is in the display window, J cannot be in the display window.

Question 1

1. Which one of the following is a possible arrangement of the items?

	Display Window	Lower Shelf	Upper Shelf
(A)	H, I, K, M	J, Y, Z	P, Q, X
(B)	J, K, X, Y	I, M, Q	H, P, Z
(C)	P, Q, X, Y	I, K, M	H, J, Z
(D)	H, K	J, M, Q, Z	I, P, X, Y
(E)	H, K, M	J, Q, Z	I, M, P, X, Y

This is a Rule Tester question. Rule 1 is broken in choice (E), which has five items on the upper shelf. Rule 2 is broken in choice (C), which has two gold necklaces on the upper shelf, and in choice (A), which has two silver watches on the lower shelf. Rule 3 is broken in choice (B), which has both **J** and **Y** in the display window.

Choice (D) is the correct answer.

Question 2

2. Which one of the following lists two pairs of items that the jeweler can place in the display window at the same time?

    (A)   I and M; X and Z
    (B)   J and K; X and Y
    (C)   J and M; P and Q
    (D)   P and Q; X and Y
    (E)   P and Q; X and Z

This is a partial Rule Tester question because it only provides the elements in the display window, but you're still looking for the one choice that doesn't break any rules. Use the rules and deductions that apply to the display window. For example, rule 3 is broken in choices (B) and (C), which have both J and either Y or M. You also deduced that there must always be a pair of necklaces on display, and choices (D) and (E) lack necklaces. Choice (A) must be correct.

Choice (A) is the correct answer.

Question 3

3. If H and I are among the items that are placed on the shelves, then it must be true that

    (A)   Q is in the display window.
    (B)   X is in the display window.
    (C)   Z is in the display window.
    (D)   K is on one of the shelves.
    (E)   Y is on one of the shelves.

This is a Local Truth question. Put H and I on the shelves. As long as they aren't together, they could be on either shelf.

	Gold	Silver
Necklace	H I J	K M
Ring	P	Q
Watch	X	Y Z

Master Diagram

gold/silver pairs of same type max 4		max 4	max 4
Display		**Lower**	**Upper**
H/I/J	K/M		
H	K	J M Q Z	I P X Y	#1
I M	X Z			#2
J K		H I Y M	(either shelf)	#3

Shelves:

[H̶I̶J] [Y̶Z̶] [K̶M̶]
(any two)

Display:

Y OR M ⟶ ~J
J ⟶ ~Y AND ~M

Since you need to have at least one gold necklace, J must be displayed. That triggers the conditional and puts Y and M on the shelves (again, either one is fine). Finally, with M out, the only silver necklace left to pair with J is K. According to the diagram, choice (E) must be true.

Choice (E) is the correct answer.

Question 4

4. If H and K are among the items placed on the shelves, which one of the following is a pair of items that must be in the display window?

(A) I and M
(B) J and M
(C) P and Q
(D) X and Y
(E) X and Z

This is a Local Spot question. Put **H** and **K** on the shelves. Again it appears that there isn't any difference between the two.

Since you need at least one silver necklace there, **M** must be in the display window. That triggers the conditional and puts **J** on one of the shelves. Now there is only one gold necklace left for the display window: **I**. Choice (A) matches the diagram.

Choice (A) is the correct answer.

Question 5

5. Which one of the following CANNOT be true?

(A) One pair of necklaces are the only items in the display window together.
(B) One pair of watches and one pair of necklaces are in the display window together.
(C) One pair of watches and one pair of rings are in the display window together.
(D) One pair of rings and one pair of necklaces are in the display window together.
(E) Two pairs of necklaces are in the display window together.

This is a Universal Truth question. Use your master diagram and previous work to examine each answer choice.

Choice (A): You saw that this could be true in question 1. *Eliminate it.*

Choice (B): You saw that this could be true in question 2. *Eliminate it.*

Choice (C): You deduced that you always need at least one pair of necklaces, so this choice is impossible. That's what you're looking for.

Choice (C) is the correct answer.

QUESTIONS 6–10

IDENTIFY

This is an Ordering game. You can tell because the elements must be placed consecutively, and all the elements fit into a single order.

SET UP

Use the normal Ordering diagram. The numbers 1–7 form the backbone of the diagram.

The stock is made up of the initials of the seven people, written to the left of the diagram. Next, symbolize the rules.

Rule 1: Use a soft block:

Rule 2: Another soft block:

Rule 3: This is a relative order rule. Y—W

Rule 4: Another relative order rule. P—K

Rule 5: Put this on the diagram as a forbidden spot for **R**.

DEDUCE

You can combine rules 1–4 into a large chain, which is very helpful. Notice that **L** is a free agent, so underline it in your stock. **R** is almost a free agent, with the one restriction that it can't be first. You could take the time to determine all the forbidden spots in the order that result from the large chain, but it's not really worth it. With only two elements having much freedom, this game is not that complicated, so just move on to the questions.

Here's the master diagram:

Master Diagram

1	2	3	4	5	6	7
~R						

Question 6

6. If Rivera is interviewed third, which one of the following could be true?

(A) Franklin is interviewed fourth.
(B) Kratzer is interviewed fifth.
(C) Kratzer is interviewed sixth.
(D) Lippay is interviewed fifth.
(E) Wiechecki is interviewed second.

This is a Local Truth question. Put **R** third and see what else happens.

Master Diagram

1	2	3	4	5	6	7
~R						
F—Y	R		~L	K—O		#6

Lecture 7 Explanations

F and Y can only fit in spots 1–2, and K must be sixth or seventh. W and P will fit somewhere in spots 4–6, and L's only restriction is that it can't separate W and P by being fifth. Choice (C) matches the diagram.

Choice (C) is the correct answer.

Question 7

7. The earliest that Kratzer could be interviewed is

(A) third
(B) fourth
(C) fifth
(D) sixth
(E) seventh

This is a Minimum/Maximum question. The general approach for all Minimum/Maximum questions is to consider the extreme and work backwards. In this case, look at the *earliest* spots first. From your combined chain, you can see that at least four elements must precede K, so K can't be third or fourth. Eliminate choices (A) and (B). What about choice (C)—can K be fifth? Yes, as shown here:

Master Diagram

F K L̲ P R W Y

(FY) — (WP) — K

1	2	3	4	5	6	7
~R						

| Ⓕ—Ⓨ | R | | ~L | Ⓚ—○ | | | #6 |
| F | Y | W | P | K | L | R | #7 |

Since choice (C) is the earliest one that works, it must be correct.

Choice (C) is the correct answer.

Question 8

8. If Ying is interviewed fourth, which one of the following must be true?

(A) Franklin is interviewed fifth.
(B) Kratzer is interviewed sixth.
(C) Lippay is interviewed first.
(D) Rivera is interviewed third.
(E) Wiechecki is interviewed fifth.

This is a Local Truth question. Put Y fourth and deduce as much as you can.

Master Diagram

F K L̲ P R W Y

(FY) — (WP) — K

1	2	3	4	5	6	7
~R						

Ⓕ—Ⓨ	R		~L	Ⓚ—○			#6
F	Y	W	P	K	L	R	#7
L	R	F	Y	Ⓦ—Ⓟ		K	#8

The only way to fit the chain in is to put F third, K seventh, and W and P, in either order, in 5–6. The only two elements left are L and R, and since R can't be first, it must be second, making L first. This matches choice (C).

Choice (C) is the correct answer.

Question 9

9. If Kratzer is interviewed at some time before Lippay is interviewed, which one of the following must be false?

   (A) Lippay is interviewed immediately before Rivera is interviewed.
   (B) Rivera is interviewed immediately before Franklin is interviewed.
   (C) Rivera is interviewed immediately before Kratzer is interviewed.
   (D) Wiechecki is interviewed immediately before Kratzer is interviewed.
   (E) Ying is interviewed immediately before Putnam is interviewed.

This is a Local Truth question, but the new rule is too vague to allow you to immediately put anything on the diagram. You can, however, symbolize the new rule to the right of the diagram:

$$(FY) - (WP) - K - L$$

Now the only element not part of this chain is R. Since R can't be first, F and Y must be 1–2, but after that R could be inserted at any point in the order (except fourth, which would separate W and P.)

Master Diagram

F K L P R W Y

$(FY) - (WP) - K$

	1	2	3	4	5	6	7	
~R	~R							
	F—Y		R		~L	K—O		#6
	F	Y	W	P	K	L	R	#7
	L	R	F	Y	W—P		K	#8
	F—Y			~R				#9

Because of the F and Y in spots 1–2, choice (B) is impossible.

Choice (B) is the correct answer.

Question 10

10. The order in which the candidates are interviewed is completely determined if which one of the following is true?

    (A) Franklin is interviewed immediately before Rivera is interviewed, and Wiechecki is interviewed immediately before Putnam is interviewed.
    (B) Franklin is interviewed immediately before Ying is interviewed, and Ying is interviewed immediately before Wiechecki is interviewed.
    (C) Franklin is interviewed immediately before Putnam is interviewed, and Wiechecki is interviewed immediately before Kratzer is interviewed.
    (D) Rivera is interviewed immediately before Franklin is interviewed, and Putnam is interviewed immediately before Kratzer is interviewed.
    (E) Rivera is interviewed immediately before Wiechecki is interviewed, and Ying is interviewed immediately before Franklin is interviewed.

This is a Complete Determination question. Each answer choice gives you a new rule, and you have to figure out which one results in a completely known order from 1–7. Unfortunately, the only way to approach a question like this is to start grinding through each answer choice.

The Choices:

(A)   Franklin is interviewed immediately before Rivera is interviewed, and Wiechecki is interviewed immediately before Putnam is interviewed.

(B)   Franklin is interviewed immediately before Ying is interviewed, and Ying is interviewed immediately before Wiechecki is interviewed.

(C)   Franklin is interviewed immediately before Putnam is interviewed, and Wiechecki is interviewed immediately before Kratzer is interviewed.

(D)   Rivera is interviewed immediately before Franklin is interviewed, and Putnam is interviewed immediately before Kratzer is interviewed.

(E)   Rivera is interviewed immediately before Wiechecki is interviewed, and Ying is interviewed immediately before Franklin is interviewed.

Choice (A): The new rule can be incorporated into the existing chain and symbolized like this:

$$\boxed{\text{YFR}} - \boxed{\text{WP}} - \text{K}$$

This doesn't nail down the order because L could be inserted into several different places in the order.

Choice (B): The new rule can be incorporated into the existing chain and symbolized like this:

$$\boxed{\text{FYWP}} - \text{K}$$

This doesn't nail down the order because L and R could be inserted into several different places.

Choice (C): The new rule can be incorporated into the existing chain and symbolized like this:

$$\boxed{\text{YFPWK}}$$

This doesn't nail down the order because L and R could come either before or after the big block.

Choice (D): The new rule can be incorporated into the existing chain and symbolized like this:

$$\boxed{\text{RFY}} - \boxed{\text{WPK}}$$

If you tried to put L between the blocks or after the second one, then R would be first, which is forbidden. Thus, to prevent that, L must be first, and all the other elements have to be in spots 2–7 in the order shown. Choice (D) completely determines the order, so it's correct.

Choice (D) is the correct answer.

QUESTIONS 11–15

IDENTIFY

You can identify this as a Grid game because there are three factors to deal with: 1) the day, 2) the shift, and 3) the person.

SET UP

Put the days across the top of the diagram and give yourself one row for each shift.

The workers are the elements. Ordinarily, you would symbolize the stock by writing the initials of each worker to the left of the diagram. That's not incorrect here, but before you got started with the set up, you should have noticed that the third through sixth rules specify which employees can work on which days. Because the rules are so specific, a better way to write the stock is to put a miniature stock on each day. Then, as you think about what element to place in a certain spot, you can look at the "menu" of elements for each day and choose from only those that are available for that day. The result looks like this:

	Mon HJL	Tue HLPR	Wed LP	Thur HLPR
Morning				
Evening				

Now you can symbolize the remaining rules.

Rule 1: You can use a generic vertical antiblock:

Rule 2: You can use another generic antiblock. A little note may be helpful to remind you that the rule applies across the entire row—no element may appear twice in a shift, even if the two occurrences are not consecutive:

whole row

Rule 7: Put L directly on the diagram on Tuesday morning.

DEDUCE

You can make a number of deductions here, all stemming from the L on Tuesday morning. Since L can't work any more morning shifts, P is the only element left to work Wednesday morning, and since P can't work again on the same day, L is the only element left to work Wednesday evening. Now you have two L's on the diagram, so you can't have any more.

That means H and J will have to be the two workers on Monday, although you don't know which one works which shift. Symbolize this with a barbell.

Finally, since both L and P are already signed up for morning shifts, the only two options for Thursday morning are H and R. Symbolize this with an either/or spot.

The master diagram now looks like this:

Master Diagram

	Mon HJL	Tue HLPR	Wed LP	Thur HLPR
Morning	Ⓗ	L	P	H/R
Evening	Ⓙ		L	

whole row

Question 11

11. Petra must work which one of the following shifts?

    (A)   Tuesday evening
    (B)   Wednesday morning
    (C)   Wednesday evening
    (D)   Thursday morning
    (E)   Thursday evening

To answer this Universal Element question, check your master diagram first. You deduced that P must be on Wednesday morning, and that matches choice (B).

Choice (B) is the correct answer.

Question 12

12. Which one of the following employees must work in the evening?

(A) Petra
(B) Heather
(C) Robbie
(D) Luke
(E) Julia

To answer this Universal Spot question, again check your master diagram. You deduced that L must work Wednesday evening, so you don't need to bother figuring out whether the others are required to work in the evening. You can confidently pick choice (D).

Choice (D) is the correct answer.

Question 13

13. If Robbie works twice in the week, then which one of the following statements could be true?

(A) Heather works Monday morning.
(B) Heather works Tuesday evening.
(C) Heather works Thursday morning.
(D) Petra works Tuesday evening.
(E) Robbie works Thursday evening.

This is a Local Truth question. You need to put R on the diagram twice, but where? You know R can only work Tuesday and Thursday, so R's two shifts must be on these two days. Tuesday morning is already taken, so R works Tuesday evening and Thursday morning. The options for Thursday evening are now limited to H and P.

Master Diagram

	Mon HJL	Tue HLPR	Wed LP	Thur HLPR
Morning	(H)	L	P	H/R
Evening	(J)		L	

		Mon	Tue	Wed	Thur	
✗/✗	✗✗ whole row	(H)	L	P	R	#13
		(J)	R	L	H/P	

According to the diagram, only choice (A) is possible.

Choice (A) is the correct answer.

Question 14

14. If Robbie does not work in the morning, then which one of the following statements could be true?

(A) Heather works Monday morning.
(B) Heather works Tuesday evening.
(C) Julia works Monday evening.
(D) Petra works Tuesday evening.
(E) Petra works Thursday morning.

This is another Local Truth question. If R doesn't work any mornings, then H must work Thursday morning. That in turn determines where H and J go on Monday, and leaves P and R (in either order) as the two remaining elements available for Tuesday and Thursday evening.

Master Diagram

	Mon HJL	Tue HLPR	Wed LP	Thur HLPR	
Morning	Ⓗ	L	P	H/R	
Evening	Ⓙ		L		
	Ⓗ	L	P	R	#13
	Ⓙ	R	L	H/P	
	J	L	P	H	#14
	H	Ⓟ	L	Ⓡ	

Only choice (D) is possible, according to the diagram.

Choice (D) is the correct answer.

Question 15

15. If Julia works Monday morning, then which one of the following statements CANNOT be true?

(A) Heather works Tuesday evening.
(B) Heather works Thursday morning.
(C) Petra works Tuesday evening.
(D) Robbie works Thursday morning.
(E) Robbie works Thursday evening.

This is a final Local Truth question. Having J on Monday morning puts H on Monday evening.

Master Diagram

	Mon HJL	Tue HLPR	Wed LP	Thur HLPR	
Morning	Ⓗ	L	P	H/R	
Evening	Ⓙ		L		
	Ⓗ	L	P	R	#13
	Ⓙ	R	L	H/P	
	J	L	P	H	#14
	H	Ⓟ	L	Ⓡ	
	J	L	P	H/R	#15
	H	Ⓟ	L	Ⓡ	

Again, P and R must take the two remaining evening shifts, and (as long as there aren't two R's on Thursday) Thursday morning is still open to either H or R. Choice (A) is the only one that's impossible.

Choice (A) is the correct answer.

Lecture 7 Explanations

EXPLANATIONS

QUESTIONS 1–5

IDENTIFY

This is a Grouping game. You can tell because there is no mention of any order, and there are three groups—the red, blue, and yellow teams.

SET UP

Your diagram needs three columns, one for each group. Since the situation tells you how many people are in each group, put the appropriate number of blank underlined spaces in each group.

Put the stock (the initials of the eight people) to the left of the diagram.

Now symbolize the rules.

> **Rule 1:** Symbolize this with an antiblock:

> **Rule 2:** Use a conditional symbol. Since there are three groups, you need to use subscripts:

$$N_B \longrightarrow H_B$$
$$\sim H_B \longrightarrow \sim N_B$$

> **Rule 3:** Use two more antiblocks for this rule:

> **Rules 4 and 5:** Put the elements directly on the diagram in the correct groups.

DEDUCE

You can deduce that **J** cannot be on the red team, because of rules 3 and 4. Otherwise, the antiblocks and conditionals, which are typically stingy types of rules, yield their characteristic few deductions. Move on to the questions.

Master Diagram

HJLMNOP

$H\llap{/}M$ $L\llap{/}J$ $O\llap{/}J$

Red	Blue	Yellow
O __ ~J	P __ __	__ __ __

$N_B \rightarrow H_B$

$\sim H_B \rightarrow \sim N_B$

The Rules

H cannot be on the same team as M.
If N is on the blue team, H must
  also be on the blue team.
Neither O nor L is on the same team
  as J.
O is on the red team.
P is on the blue team.

Question 1

1. Which one of the following is an acceptable assignment
    of contestants to the three teams?

    (A) Red team: H, O; blue team: J, N, P; yellow team: K,
         L, M
    (B) Red team: K, L; blue team: H, N, P; yellow team: J,
         M, O
    (C) Red team: N, O; blue team: K, L, P; yellow team: H,
         J, M
    (D) Red team: L, O; blue team: H, K, P; yellow team: J,
         M, N
    (E) Red team: N, O; blue team: H, K, P; yellow team: J,
         L, M

This is a Rule Tester question. Rule 1 is broken in choice (C), which has **H** and **M** on the same team. Rule 2 is broken in choice (A), which has **N** but lacks **H** on the blue team. Rule 3 is broken in choice (B), which puts **J** and **O** together, and in choice (E), which puts **J** and **L** together.

Choice (D) is the correct answer.

Question 2

This List question is best left until you have more work to look back on.

Question 3

3. If K is on the blue team, which one of the following is a
    contestant who must be on the yellow team?

    (A) H
    (B) J
    (C) L
    (D) M
    (E) N

This is a Local Spot question. Put **K** on the blue team and see what happens.

Master Diagram

HJLMNOP

$H\llap{/}M$ $L\llap{/}J$ $O\llap{/}J$

Red	Blue	Yellow	
O __ ~J	P __ __	__ __ __	
O L	P K H	N M J	#1
O __	P K __	__ __ __	#3

$N_B \rightarrow H_B$

$\sim H_B \rightarrow \sim N_B$

Unfortunately, you may not see much else that's immediately obvious. One strategy you have at this point is to check out the answer choices, and you should think about a smart way to do so. For example, look at your previous work. You can see that in question 1, **K** was on the blue team, and neither **H** nor **L** was on the yellow team. Thus, you can eliminate choices (A) and (C).

Now you can try out the other choices in your diagram. As the question stem asks what *must be true*, try to prove the answer choices *false* by putting the element in question somewhere *other* than the yellow team. For example, try out choice (B). This possible configuration proves that **J** is not required to be on the yellow team:

Master Diagram

H J L M N O P

~H̶M̶~ ~L̶J̶~ ~O̶J̶~

$N_B \rightarrow H_B$

$\sim H_B \rightarrow \sim N_B$

	Red	Blue	Yellow	
	O __ ~J	P __ __	__ __ __	
	O L	P K H	N M J	#1
	O M	P K J	H L N	#3

It also proves that **M** doesn't have to be on the yellow team—it's smart to try to rule out more than one answer choice at the same time. You can now eliminate choices (B) and (D); only choice (E) remains.

Choice (E) is the correct answer.

Question 4

4. If K is on the red team, each of the following is a pair of contestants who could be on the blue team EXCEPT:

(A) J and H
(B) L and H
(C) M and J
(D) M and L
(E) N and H

This is another Local Spot question. Put **K** on the red team and see what happens.

Master Diagram

H J L M N O P

~H̶M̶~ ~L̶J̶~ ~O̶J̶~

$N_B \rightarrow H_B$

$\sim H_B \rightarrow \sim N_B$

	Red	Blue	Yellow	
	O __ ~J	P __ __	__ __ __	
	O L	P K H	N M J	#1
	O M	P K J	H L N	#3
	O K	P (H)(J)——(L)(M) N		#4

Now the red team is full. What happens next? Take a look at the antiblocks. **H** and **M** have to be separated, so those two elements will each take up one spot on the blue and yellow teams. The same can be said for **J** and **L**. You can symbolize this with a couple of barbells. Now the blue group is full, so **N** has to be in the yellow group. Only choice (E) is impossible.

Choice (E) is the correct answer.

Question 5

5. Which one of the following must be true?

(A) If H and J are on the yellow team, K is on the yellow team.

(B) If L and M are on the blue team, N is on the red team.

(C) If L and M are on the blue team, H is on the red team.

(D) If K and M are on the blue team, L is on the red team.

(E) If K and N are on the yellow team, M is on the red team.

This is a nasty Universal Truth question because each of the answer choices is a conditional! The only way to approach questions like this is to plug in each answer choice and try it out. Since the stem is asking you what *must be true*, try to disprove each answer choice. For example, for choice (A), put H and J on the yellow team but try to put K somewhere *other* than the yellow team.

Here are some possible configurations proving choices (A)–(C) are not required.

Master Diagram

H J L M N O P

HM̸ LJ̸ OJ̸

$N_B \rightarrow H_B$

$\sim\!H_B \rightarrow \sim\!N_B$

	Red	Blue	Yellow	
	O __ ~J	P __ __	__ __ __	
	O L	P K H	N M J	#1
	O M	P K J	H L N	#3
	O K	P (H)(J)——(L)(M) N		#4
#5 (A)	O M	P K L	H J N	#5
(B) & (C)	O K	P L M	J N H	
(D)	O̶ __	P K M	L̶ __ __	

Trouble starts when you get to choice (D). With K and M filling up blue, if you try to disprove the choice by putting L somewhere other than red, you have to put L in yellow. But then you have nowhere to put J without violating one of the antiblocks. It's impossible to disprove choice (D), so it must be true.

Choice (D) is the correct answer.

Question 2

2. Which one of the following is a complete and accurate list of teams any one of which could be the team on which M competes?

(A) the red team
(B) the blue team
(C) the red team, the blue team
(D) the red team, the yellow team
(E) the red team, the blue team, the yellow team

Look back on your previous work, and you'll see that M has appeared on every team. Pick choice (E).

Choice (E) is the correct answer.

QUESTIONS 6–10

IDENTIFY

This is a Grid game. You can tell because the situation gives you a grid, and the game is about cars that have a spatial arrangement of both rows and columns.

SET UP

Use the grid you're given. Number the spots as shown in the setup.

The stock here is a little different. You don't find out what the elements are until you read **rules 1 and 2.** Then, you find out that each spot contains two elements: the car's manufacturer and the car's type. That's a little unusual, but you can easily deal with it by leaving room for two elements in each spot. For your stock, write the two choices for manufacturer on one line and the two choices for type on another, just so you don't get them confused.

Man.: V W
Type: H S

| 1 __ __ | 3 __ __ | 5 __ __ |
| 2 __ __ | 4 __ __ | 6 __ __ |

Now take a look at the remaining rules.

Rules 3 and 4: These rules may look somewhat complicated, but try to think about the simplest way to express them. The rules are basically saying that you're forbidden to surround a car from a certain manufacturer with cars from a different manufacturer, and likewise for the car types. For example, if you had a **V** in spot 1, you couldn't have **W**'s in both 2 and 3, because then the **V** would not be adjacent to another car of the same type.

You could try to symbolize this with some complicated blocks or antiblocks, but when you encounter such an idiosyncratic rule, often the best approach is to just understand it, internalize it, and write yourself a brief note to remind yourself to follow the rule. In this case, a note such as "**no loners**" next to the diagram can remind you that no element can be completely surrounded by its opposites.

Rules 5, 6, and 7: Put these exact spot rules directly on the diagram.

DEDUCE

There are some deductions to be made. For example, since the **S** in spot 3 must be adjacent to at least one more **S**, there has to be at least one **S** in spots 1 and 5. Similar deductions can be made for the **H** in 4 and the **W** in 5. You could symbolize these with barbells, or you could leave them off the diagram since they are fairly obvious and would lead to a somewhat cluttered master diagram.

Master Diagram

Man.: V W
Type: H S

| 1 __ __ | 3 __ S | 5 W __ |
| 2 __ __ | 4 __ H | 6 __ __ |

*no loners

Lecture 8 Explanations

Question 6

6. If all of the sedans are Vigorides, which one of the following must be true?

(A) Car 1 is a Welmayde.
(B) Car 2 is a Vigoride.
(C) Car 4 is a Welmayde.
(D) Car 5 is a sedan.
(E) Car 6 is a hatchback.

This is a Local Truth question, and it helps to symbolize the new rule as a conditional with its contrapositive:

$$S \longrightarrow V$$

$$W \longrightarrow H$$

Instead of ~V, you can write W since that's the only other choice for manufacturer. Similarly, ~S is the same as H. This contrapositive shows that all W's must also be H's. Now you can fill in a lot in your diagram.

Master Diagram

Man.: V W
Type: H S

*no loners

1 __ __	3 __ S	5 W __
2 __ __	4 __ H	6 __ __
V S	V S	W H #6
__ __	__ H	W H

First, put a V in 3 and an H in 5, per the new conditional rule. Next, notice that the W in 5 must be next to another W, but spot 3 is already taken up by a V. That means there must be a W in 6, along with an H, according to the new rule. Finally, the S in spot 3 must be next to another S, but spots 4 and 5 are already taken up by H's. Thus, there must be an S in spot 1, which means there is a V there as well. According to the diagram, only choice (E) must be true.

Choice (E) is the correct answer.

Question 7

7. It is possible that the only two Vigorides among the six cars are

(A) cars 1 and 4
(B) cars 1 and 6
(C) cars 2 and 3
(D) cars 2 and 4
(E) cars 2 and 6

This is a Universal question. If there are to be only two V's, they must be adjacent to each other. Look at the choices and your master diagram. Only choice (D) names two spots that are adjacent.

Choice (D) is the correct answer.

Question 8

8. If there are exactly three Welmaydes and three Vigorides, which one of the following cars must be a Vigoride?

(A) car 1
(B) car 2
(C) car 3
(D) car 4
(E) car 6

This is a Local Element question. If there are to be exactly three **W**'s, they must all be adjacent, since you wouldn't be allowed to have two adjacent and one loner. There is already one **W** on the diagram, in spot 5. Think about where you could put the other two in order to have all the **W**'s adjacent to each other.

You could put the three **W**'s across the top in spots 1, 3, and 5. You could put them clustered in the upper right corner in spots, 3, 5, and 6. Or you could put them clustered in the lower right corner in spots 4, 5, and 6. These are the only three possibilities, and the only spot that could never contain a **W** is spot 2. It's too far away from the **W** in spot 5. Thus, spot 2 must hold a **V**.

Choice (B) is the correct answer.

Question 9

9. If exactly two cars are Welmaydes and exactly two cars are sedans, which one of the following must be false?

(A) Car 1 is a sedan, and car 6 is a Welmayde.
(B) Cars 1 and 3 are both sedans.
(C) Car 2 is a sedan, and car 3 is a Welmayde.
(D) Car 3 is both a sedan and a Welmayde.
(E) Car 5 is a sedan.

This is a Local Truth question. The new rule is a little vague, but you can certainly figure some things out on your diagram. The second **W** must be adjacent to the one in spot 5, so it must be in either 3 or 6. That means spots 1, 2, and 4 must have **V**'s.

Master Diagram

Man.: V W	1 __ __	3 __ S	5 W __		
Type: H S	2 __ __	4 __ H	6 __ __		
*no loners	V S	V S	W H	#6	
	__ __	__ H	W H		
	__ __	__ S	W __	#8	
	V __	__ H	__ __		
	V __	__ S	W __	#9	
	V H	V H	__ H		

Similarly, the second **S** must be adjacent to the first, in either 1 or 5. Thus, spots 2, 4, and 6 must have **H**'s. Choice (C) is the one that contradicts the diagram since spot 2 must have an **H**.

Choice (C) is the correct answer.

Question 10

10.   Which one of the following could be true?

(A)   Cars 1 and 2 are two of exactly three hatchbacks.
(B)   Cars 1 and 6 are two of exactly three hatchbacks.
(C)   Cars 1 and 6 are two of exactly three sedans.
(D)   Cars 2 and 6 are two of exactly three sedans.
(E)   Cars 2 and 5 are two of exactly three sedans.

This is a Universal Truth question. Check the answer choices in light of your master diagram and your previous choices. Choice (A) looks possible since all three H's would be adjacent. See if you can make a complete configuration, just to be sure. Here's one that works:

Master Diagram

Man.: V W
Type: H S

*no loners

1 ___ ___	3 ___ S	5 W ___
2 ___ ___	4 ___ H	6 ___ ___
V S	V S	W H	#6
___ ___	___ H	W H	
___ ___	___ S	W ___	#8
V ___	___ H	___ ___	
V ___	___ S	W ___	#9
V H	V H	___ H	
V H	W S	W S	#10
V H	V H	W S	

Choice (A) is possible, so pick it.

Choice (A) is the correct answer.

QUESTIONS 11–15

IDENTIFY

This is an Ordering game as you have to put all the elements into a single order, with no elements left out.

SET UP

Use the normal Ordering diagram, with columns labeled 1–8.

The elements fall into three different categories. When you symbolize the stock, use uppercase, lowercase, and script to differentiate between musicals, plays, and workshops.

MUSICAL: J K L	1	2	3	4	5	6	7	8
play: q r								
workshop: x y z								

Now symbolize the rules.

Rule 1: You can put three forbidden spot symbols in the first spot, one for each of the three workshops.

Rule 2: Symbolize this with a block:

q	x

Rule 3: There are two things happening in this rule. Symbolize them with a relative order symbol and an antiblock:

$$z-y \qquad \boxed{z\,y}$$

Rule 4: Use a relative order symbol:

$$K-J$$

Rule 5: This is an idiosyncratic rule. Just jot a note next to the two relative order symbols to remind you that they must be the same distance apart.

DEDUCE

L and r are not constrained by any rules, so you can underline them as free agents. You can use the block to deduce that q cannot be eighth. You can also combine rules 3 and 5: if z can't immediately precede y, and if the two pairs must be the same distance apart, then K can't immediately precede J. Symbolize that with an antiblock. Finally, you can make some endpoint deductions from rule 3: z can't be last *nor can it be seventh* since y must follow z by at least *two* spots. You can make similar deductions about y, K, and J in the first and last two spots.

Master Diagram

MUSICAL: J K L
play: q r
workshop: x y z

$$\boxed{q\,x} \quad \boxed{z\,y} \quad \boxed{K\,J}$$

$$\left.\begin{array}{c} z-y \\ K-J \end{array}\right\} \text{same distance apart}$$

1	2	3	4	5	6	7	8
~x ~y ~z ~J	~y ~J					~K ~z	~q ~K ~z

Question 11

The Rules

The first event cannot be a workshop.
X must immediately follow Q.
Z must be scheduled for some time before Y, but Z cannot immediately precede Y.
J must be scheduled for some time after K.
J and K must be separated by the same number of events as separate Y and Z.

11. Which one of the following is an acceptable ordering of the events from first to eighth?

(A) Z, K, Y, J, Q, X, L, R
(B) L, X, Q, Z, K, Y, J, R
(C) L, Q, X, Z, Y, R, K, J
(D) K, Q, X, J, Z, R, L, Y
(E) Q, X, Z, L, Y, K, J, R

This is a Rule Tester question. Rule 1 is broken in choice (A), which has a workshop first. Rule 2 is broken in choice (B), where q follows x. Rule 3 is broken in choice (C) since z immediately precedes y. Rule 4 is not broken in any choice. Rule 5 is broken in choice (E) because the two pairs are not the same distance apart.

Choice (D) is the correct answer.

Question 12

12. The largest possible number of events that can separate Q from Z is

(A) two
(B) three
(C) four
(D) five
(E) six

This is a Minimum/Maximum question. Any time you encounter one of these, start with the most extreme number (in this case, the maximum) and work backwards. Can you have six events separating q and z? No. That would mean putting them first and eighth, and z can't go in either of those spots. Eliminate choice (E).

How about five events separating them? That would mean putting q and z in 1–7 or 2–8. But the forbidden spots on your master diagram show this is impossible as well. Eliminate choice (D).

Now try four. The closest you can get z to the edge of the diagram is in spot 2, and you can then put q in spot 7. Four spots separating them works, so pick choice (C).

Master Diagram

MUSICAL: J K L
play: q r
workshop: x y z

1	2	3	4	5	6	7	8
~x ~y ~z ~J	~y ~J					~K ~z	~q ~K ~z

q x	z y	K J

	1	2	3	4	5	6	7	8	
	K	q	x	J	z	r	L	y	#11
	L	z	K	y	J	r	q	x	#12

z—y
K—J } same distance apart

Choice (C) is the correct answer.

Question 13

13. If each of the three workshops is immediately followed by a musical, which one of the following events must be a play?

   (A) the first
   (B) the second
   (C) the third
   (D) the fourth
   (E) the fifth

This is a Local Element question. The new rule is hard to symbolize directly on the diagram, but if you think about it, it means that there are three blocks or "couples," each composed of a workshop followed by a musical. Because of rule 1, you won't be able to place any of those blocks in spots 1–2. Thus, spot 1 must be a play.

If you hadn't seen that deduction, you would have had to work through the answer choices by trying to disprove each one—try putting something *other than* a play first, second, third, etc. The spot in which it's impossible to do that would be the correct answer.

Choice (A) is the correct answer.

Question 14

14. The largest possible number of events that can separate K from J is

   (A) three
   (B) four
   (C) five
   (D) six
   (E) seven

This is another Minimum/Maximum question. Again, start with the most extreme number and work backwards. Can you have seven events separating J and K? No. That's nonsense—you would need nine spots on the diagram. Get rid of choice (E).

How about six? That would mean putting J and K first and eighth, but that's also impossible because you wouldn't be able to have y and z the same distance apart. Eliminate choice (D).

Now try five by trying to put K and J in 1–7 or 2–8. First and seventh seems to work, but try to fill in the rest of the diagram just to make sure.

Master Diagram

MUSICAL: J K L
play: q r
workshop: x y z

q x | x y | K J

z—y ⎫ same
    ⎬ distance
K—J ⎭ apart

	1	2	3	4	5	6	7	8	
	~x ~y ~z ~J	~y ~J					~K ~z	~q ~K ~z	
	K	q	x	J	z	r	L	y	#11
	L	z	K	y	J	r	q	x	#12
	K	z	r	L	q	x	J	y	#14

Indeed, it does work. The trick is to realize that the two pairs can overlap each other in order to be the same distance apart. Since five is the largest number that works, pick choice (C).

Choice (C) is the correct answer.

Question 15

15. If Q is scheduled as the fifth event, then which one of the following is a complete and accurate list of the positions in the schedule any one of which could be Z's position?

(A) first, third, fourth
(B) first, second, third
(C) second, third, fourth
(D) second, third, fourth, sixth
(E) third, fourth, sixth, seventh

This is a Local List question. Put the new rule on the diagram and see what happens.

Master Diagram

MUSICAL: J K L
play: q r
workshop: x y z

q x | x y | K J

z—y ⎫ same
    ⎬ distance
K—J ⎭ apart

	1	2	3	4	5	6	7	8	
	~x ~y ~z ~J	~y ~J					~K ~z	~q ~K ~z	
	K	q	x	J	z	r	L	y	#11
	L	z	K	y	J	r	q	x	#12
	K	z	r	L	q	x	J	y	#14
					q	x			#15

You can deduce that *x* must be sixth, but that's about it for the easy deductions. However, you can get started on eliminating some answer choices. Your master diagram shows that *z* can't be first, seventh, or eighth, so you can get rid of any choice that contains one of those spots. That eliminates choices (A), (B), and (E).

Now that only two choices remain, look at the difference between them. The only difference between choices (C) and (D) is the presence of *sixth* on the list. Can *z* be sixth? No, since *x* is already there. Eliminate choice (D) and pick the only remaining choice, (C).

Choice (C) is the correct answer.

Lecture 8 Explanations

About the Author

David Lynch has been teaching test preparation since 2001. He has scored in the 99th percentile on the LSAT, GMAT, SAT, and GRE, and enjoys turning his abilities into unique and powerful materials that can help others achieve their career goals. He has won several awards for his teaching and has authored all the books in the Examkrackers LSAT series. He currently resides in Philadelphia with his wife.